WELCOME!

to Lakeland E... ...ful during your stay in the Lake D...

D0776280

Whether you are here to walk... ...ul surroundings, have a restful time and thank... ...ide.

Best wishes
Mark Norton, Director, Norton Publishing Ltd.

Mark Norton

BIENVENUE!

à 'Lakeland Explored'. J'espère que ce livre vous sera utile durant votre sèjour dans le 'Lake District'.
Que vous soyez ici pour faire des randonnées, pour visiter des sites ou tout simplement pour vous détendre dans un cadre de toute beauté, je vous souhaite de bien vous reposer et vous remercie d'avoir choisi notre livre comme guide.

Cordialement.

WILKOMMEN!

in Lakeland Explored, ich hoffe dass Sie dieses Buch wahrend Ihres Aufenthalts in dem Lake District für nützlich halten. Ob Sie hier sind um zu wandern, um de Sehenswürdigkeiten zu besichtigen, oder einfach um in einer schönen Umgebung zu entspannen, geniess von einem ruhigen Aufenthalt und Danke dass Sie unseres Buch als Ihren Reisefuhrer ausgewählt haben.

Mit freundlichen Grussen

VÄLKOMMEN!

till Lakeland Explored. Jag hoppas att denna bok kommer att vara er till både nytta och nöje under er vistelse i the Lake District. Oavsett om ni är här för att vandra, titta på severdheterna eller bara för att vila i en vacker omgivning, så önskar vi er en skön semester och tack för att ni valde våran bok som er guide.

Bästa hälsningar

WELKOM!

in Lakeland Explored, ik hoop dat dit boek u van pas komt tijdens uw verblijf in het Lake District. Of u hier bent om te wandelen, om de bezienswaardigheden te bewonderen of gewoon om in een schitterende omgeving uit te rusten, geniet van een ontspannen verblijf en dank u dat u ons boek als uw gids heeft uitgekozen.

Met vriendelijke groet

BEN VENUTI!

per Esplorare (Lakeland). Spero che troverete questo libbro utile. A fare belle paseggiate o a gustare le belle vedute panoramiche o a riposarvi. Grazie per aver shelto questa guida.

Buone vacanze

JAPANESE

この度は"Lakeland Explored"をお選びいただきまして、誠にありがとう存じます。
湖水地方ご滞在中に旅の友としてお役立ていただけることを願っております。
山歩き、ご観光、美しい環境でのリラックス。目的は様々だと思いますが、どうぞ
ごゆっくり当地を満喫されてください。

楽しいご滞在を。

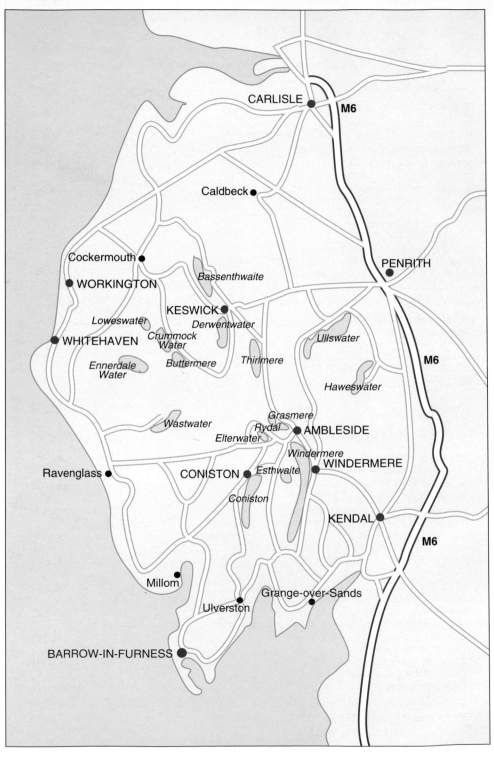

Contents

Introduction

Elterwater. Val Corbett.

Thank you for buying Lakeland Explored, the new guide to England's glorious Lake District. I hope you like the way the book has been divided into separate sections, allowing you to easily find a guided walk, an attraction or a piece of background information.

GUIDED WALKS

As the Lake District provides some of the finest walking in the country, we have created a special selection of 20 circular guided walks with detailed instructions ensuring all you have to worry about is which one to do first!

Each walk has been graded "easy", "moderate" or "tough" allowing the most suitable walk to be chosen. The walks are almost all low level in

nature (although for higher views, ascents of Haystacks and Red Pike have been included) and are suitable for family groups or for those who want to enjoy classic walking in attractive countryside without having to go too high. Indication of refreshment and toilet facilities as well as detailed maps are all included.

MINI WALKS, VIEWPOINTS & WATERFALLS

This is a section designed to allow visits to specific features such as tarns and waterfalls, viewpoints to take your breath away and shorter walks which can be done on the way back from a longer walk or if your 'weather window' is restricted. As with the guided walks, each one is graded, albeit subjective, to help guide you to the walk most appropriate to your requirements.

Spout Force, Whinlatter. Val Corbett.

GAZETTEER

No trip to the Lake District would be complete without some understanding of the history concerning key people and places. This, coupled with articles on Lakeland life will ensure a wider appreciation of all that the area has to offer. Included in the Gazetteer is a profile of each lake with full details of parking areas, shore access and principal viewpoints. The mountain section of the Gazetteer details the principal routes of ascent of summits such as Helvellyn, Great Gable and Skiddaw.

ATTRACTIONS

Lakeland is blessed with some of the finest attractions in the country with historic houses and gardens, fascinating museums and exhibitions as well as farm animal parks, steam railways and lake cruises. All the details have been gathered from the attractions themselves to ensure you can accurately plan your day out in advance. Details of admission charges have not been included as these can vary widely within the life of a book and are often subject to change depending on party size, time of year etc. If in doubt, ring beforehand. Also included are ideas for places to go and things to see that do not include an admission charge such as museums, prehistoric sites, churches, castles and much more.

USEFUL INFORMATION

SUPERSTORES

ASDA
Walney Rd, Barrow-in-Furness
(01229) 826011
Chandler Way, Parkhouse, Carlisle
(01228) 26550
Burton Road, Kendal   (01539) 741416

BOOTH E.H
45 Highgate, Kendal   (01539) 723731

FOOD GIANT
9 Globe Street, Carlisle   (01228) 31666

MORRISONS
Kingstown Road, Carlisle   (01228) 511771
Queen Katherine Street, Kendal
(01539) 734554

SAFEWAY
Lancashire Road, Millom   (01229) 773344
Brunswick Road, Penrith   (01768) 867631
Quay Street, Whitehaven   (01946) 66667
Derwent Drive, Workington
(01900) 64336

TESCO
Hindpool Road, Barrow-in-Furness
(01229) 871190
Victoria Viaduct, Carlisle   (01228) 20926
Warwick Road, Carlisle   (01228) 595572
Bransty Road, Whitehaven
(01946) 591101
New Bridge Road, Workington
(01900) 870100
St. John's Precinct, Workington
(01900) 605241

BANKS

Given the changing nature of the banking industry, it may be advisable to ring first to be certain of the branch's opening arrangements.

ABBEY NATIONAL
69 English Street, Carlisle   (01228) 24496
225 Dalton Road, Barrow-in-Furness
(01229) 827024
43 King Street, Whitehaven
(01946) 61241

BARCLAYS
Boroughgate, Appleby   (01768) 351412
The Promenade, Arnside   (01524) 761223
96 Duke Street, Barrow-in-Furness
(01229) 824383
18 Main Street, Bentham   (01524) 261325
1 Hornby Road, Caton   (01524) 770643
30 Main Street, Cockermouth
(01900) 823120

Bridge End, Coniston   (01539) 441249
26 Market Place, Egremont
(01946) 820360
Church Bridge, Grasmere (01539) 435241
The Square, Hawkshead   (01539) 436333
Appleby Road, Kendal   (01539) 722112
Market Square, Keswick   (01768) 772057
33 Market Street, Kirkby Stephen
(01768) 371379
1 Church Street, Milnthorpe
(01539) 562308
Market Square, Penrith   (01768) 864221
Strand Street, Whitehaven (01946) 64444

LLOYDS
121-135 Dalton Road, Barrow-in-Furness
(01229) 822077
21 Lowther Street, Carlisle   (01228) 22304
11 Finkle Street, Kendal   (01539) 724496
4 Main Street, Keswick   (01768) 772073
5-6 King Street, Penrith   (01768) 862218
27 King Street, Wigton   (01697) 342210

MIDLAND
30 King St, Abbeytown   (01697) 366500
King Street, Wigton, Abbeytown
(01697) 366300
Station Road, Silloth, Abbeytown
(01697) 366400
Market Place, Alston   (01434) 362500
1 Front Street, Brampton (01697) 753600
The Square, Broughton-in-Furness
(01229) 716205
Montogomery Way, Carlisle
(01228) 604091
29 English Street, Carlisle (01228) 604000
15 Main Street, Bentham, Calpham
(01524) 255300
29 Main Street, Kirkby Lonsdale
(01524) 255200
Market Street, Kirkby Stephen
(01768) 365100
7 High Street, Longtown (01228) 604200
50 Senhouse Street, Maryport
(01900) 323100

NATIONAL WESTMINSTER BANK
The Promenade, Arnside   (01524) 761373
Market Square, Aspatria (01697) 320203
Ramsden Square, Barrow-in-Furness
(01229) 835488
12 Station Road, Bentham (01524) 261209
92 English Street, Carlisle (01228) 34336
Rosehill Business Park, Carlisle
(01228) 515331
Hornby Road, Caton   (01524) 770401
23 Station Road, Cockermouth
(01900) 822831
Eskdale Green, Eskdale   (01946) 723332

Main Street, Grange-over-Sands
(01946) 732292
Sandylands Road, Kendal   (01539) 740303
28 Main Street, Keswick   (01768) 772091
55 Main Street, Kirkby Lonsdale
(01524) 271227
Main Street, Milnthorpe   (01539) 562227
24-25 Devonshire Street, Penrith
(01768) 864511
54 Main Street, Sedbergh (01539) 620214
Central Buildings, Shap   (01931) 716651
9 Eden Street, Silloth   (01697) 331336
2 Windermere Road, Staveley
(01539) 821448
North Lonsdale Road, Ulverston
(01229) 585746
59 High Street, Whitehaven
(01946) 67361
14 High Street, Wigton   (01697) 342444
2 High Street, Windermere
(01539) 446257
115 Senhouse Street, Workington
(01900) 65767

ROYAL BANK OF SCOTLAND
234-236 Dalton Road, Barrow-in-Furness
(01229) 830590
37 Castle Street, Carlisle   (01228) 39606
37 Lowther Street, Carlisle (01228) 23292
6 Market Place, Kendal   (01539) 727870

TSB
140-146 Dalton Road, Barrow-in-Furness
(01229) 870970
Market Place, Brampton, Cumbria
(01697) 72677
Lowther Street, Carlisle   (01228) 29326
50 Main Street, Cockermouth
(01900) 822129
1 Lowther Gardens, Grange-o-Sands
(01539) 532628
12 Finkle Street, Kendal   (01539) 720391
39 Main Street, Keswick   (01768) 772691
109 Senhouse Street, Maryport
(01900) 812880
41 King Street, Penrith   (01768) 892122
Union Street, Ulverston   (01229) 583134
59 Lowther Street, Whitehaven
(01946) 66442
20 High Street, Wigton   (01539) 442604

21-23 Murray Road, Workington
(01900) 602623

TOURIST INFORMATION OFFICES

CUMBRIA
M6 Service area, Forton.   (01524) 792181

ALSTON*
Alston Railway Station.   (01434) 381696

AMBLESIDE
The Old Courthouse, Church Street.
(01539) 432582

APPLEBY-IN-WESTMORLAND
Moot Hall, Boroughgate.   (01768) 351177

BARROW-IN-FURNESS
Forum 28, Duke Street.   (01229) 870156

BOWNESS-ON-WINDERMERE*
Glebe Road, Bowness Bay.
(01539) 442895

BRAMPTON*
The Moot Hall, Market Square.
(01697) 73433

CARLISLE
The Old Town Hall.   (01228) 512444

COCKERMOUTH
The Town Hall.   (01900) 822634

CONISTON*
Ruskin Avenue.   (01539) 441533

EGREMONT
Lowes Gallery, 12 Main Street.
(01946) 820693

GRANGE-OVER-SANDS
Victoria Hall, Main Street.   (01539) 534026

GRASMERE*
Red Bank Road.   (01539) 435245

HAWKSHEAD*
Main Car Park.   (01539) 436525

KENDAL
Town Hall, Highgate.   (01539) 725758

KESWICK
Moot Hall, Market Sq.   (01768) 772645

KILLINGTON LAKE*
Road Chef Service Area,
M6 (Southbound), nr Kendal.
(01539) 620138

KIRKBY LONSDALE
24 Main Street.   (01524) 271437

KIRKBY STEPHEN
Market Square.   (01768) 371199

LONGTOWN
Community Centre.   (01228) 791876

MARYPORT
Maritime Museum, 1 Senhouse St.
(01900) 813738

PENRITH
Penrith Museum, Middlegate.
(01768) 867466

POOLEY BRIDGE*
The Square.   (01768) 486530

SEATOLLER*
Seatoller Barn.   (01768) 777294

SEDBERGH
72 Main Streeet.   (01539) 620125

SELLAFIELD
Visitors Centre, Seascale.   (01946) 776510

SILLOTH-ON-SOLWAY
The Green.   (01697) 331944

SOUTHWAITE
M6 Service Area.   (01697) 473445/6

ULLSWATER*
Main Car Park, Glenridding.
(01768) 482414

ULVERSTON
Coronation Hall, County Square.
(01229) 587120

WATERHEAD*
Car Park, Ambleside.   (01539) 432729

WHITEHAVEN
Market Hall, Market Place.
(01946) 695678

WINDERMERE
Victoria Street.   (01539) 446499

Denotes Seasonal

CUMBRIA TOURIST BOARD
Ashleigh, Holly Road, Windermere,
LA23 2AQ.   (01539) 444444

PUBLIC TRANSPORT
Stagecoach Cumberland   (01946) 63222
(01946) 592000

CINEMAS
AMBLESIDE ZEFFERELLIS
Compston Road.   (01539) 431771

**BARROW-IN-FURNESS APOLLO 4
CINEMA,** Abbey Road.   (01229) 825354

BOWNESS ROYALTY CINEMA
Lake Road,   (01539) 443364

CARLISLE LONSDALE CINEMAS

Warwick Road.   (01228) 514654

CARLISLE CITY CINEMAS
Mary Street.   (01228) 594409

KENDAL BREWERY ARTS CENTRE
122a Highgate.   (01539) 725133

KESWICK ALHAMBRA CINEMA
St.John's Street.
(01768) 772195

PENRITH ALHAMBRA CINEMA
Middlegate.
(01768) 862400

ULVERSTON ROXY CINEMA
Brogden Street.   (01229) 582340

WHITEHAVEN GAIETY CINEMA
Tangier Street.   (01946) 693012
(01228) 25586

**WORKINGTON RENDEZVOUS TWIN
CINEMA** Oxford Street.   (01900) 602505

RADIO FREQUENCIES

BBC RADIO CUMBRIA

North	95.6 FM
West	95.6 FM
	& 104.1 FM
South	96.1 FM
Kendal	95.2 FM
Windermere	104.2 FM

THE BAY

Lancaster area	96.9 FM
South Cumbria	103.2 FM
Kendal area	102.3 FM

HOSPITALS

Casualty departments are available at:

FURNESS GENERAL HOSPITAL
Dalton Lane, Barrow-in-Furness
(01229) 870870

CUMBERLAND INFIRMARY
Newtown Road, Carlisle   (01228) 23444

PENRITH NEW HOSPITAL
Bridge Lane, Penrith —casualty for
minor injuries only—   (01768) 245300

WEST CUMBERLAND HOSPITAL
Whitehaven   (01946) 693181

WESTMORLAND GENERAL
Burton Road, Kendal   (01539) 732288

Gazetteer

The Gazetteer section is designed to introduce the reader to the key towns and villages within Lakeland as well as major geographical features such as passes, fells and lakes. To provide an overview of all that Cumbria has to offer, towns and villages some distance from the National Park, such as Carlisle, Kirkby Lonsdale and Barrow-in-Furness, have been included. Each one has much to offer the visitor, particularly if the weather prevents a planned walking or sightseeing trip. To find out further information on museums or exhibitions referred to in the text, find the page reference in the index for the relevant entry within the Attractions section.

All sixteen major lakes within the Lake District have been profiled giving full details on the best viewpoints and access by road, foot and boat. The accompanying maps are illustrative only, that is to say not to scale, and are based on surveys completed on the ground. All access details are based on known rights of way or permissive paths although it is imperative that walkers check the existence of these at first hand as rights of way can change within the lifetime of this book. Eleven key fells have been included with details of the most popular routes of ascent. If attempting to walk these fells, do ensure you have the relevant O.S. maps, strong boots and waterproof clothing and only attempt high fell walks in good weather with plenty of daylight to complete your route. Always ensure that someone knows where you are going and what time you will be returning, particularly if walking alone.

Ambleside

Although a settlement has been on this site since pre Roman times, present day Ambleside is largely Victorian. The Romans valued its location on the main routes north through central Lakeland and westward to their port at Ravenglass, reached via the Wrynose and Hardknott passes. As a consequence, a fort (named Galava) was built in Ambleside by the Romans, housing a garrison of some 500 soldiers. The fort was a stone structure, built by the Emperor Trajan in AD100 and replaced an earlier timber fortification built in AD79 (see Attractions section for further history and directions to the remains).

The opening of the Lake Windermere ferry terminus at Waterhead in 1845 generated further expansion of Ambleside, St. Mary's Church with its 180 foot high spire was constructed in 1854. The church holds an annual rushbearing ceremony here on the first Saturday of each July dating back to medieval times when rushes which were the principal floor covering were renewed.

William Wordsworth, having an office here as a result of his role as Distributor of Stamps for Westmorland, knew Ambleside well and was much concerned with the preservation of the Lake District, viewing the expansion of the railway network and its resultant tourism influx with great trepidation. He was instrumental in stopping the planned extension of the railway line to Ambleside from Windermere; his sonnet famously imploring "Is then no nook of English ground secure from rash assault?"

Nevertheless, Ambleside has become one of the major tourist resorts of Lakeland with shops, hotels and restaurants providing a draw for visitors. The Stock Ghyll Force waterfall, popular since the early days of Victorian tourism, can be reached after a short walk from the town centre (see index), with the much photographed Old Bridge House sitting astride the lower reaches of the same stream. Constructed originally as a summer house and apple store for the now demolished Ambleside Hall, the property is now in the care of the National Trust, providing a unique and interesting information centre.

Nearby Waterhead has a National Park Information Centre as well as being the northern terminus for steamer trips on Lake Windermere.

Ambleside. Val Corbett.

Appleby-in-Westmorland

Appleby's origins as a settlement date back to Norman times; the steep sided hill overlooking a river provides a naturally defensive location suitable for a castle. Following a turbulent history, Appleby Castle was rebuilt in the seventeenth century by Lady Anne Clifford, one of the area's most important and benevolent aristocrats who was also responsible for rebuilding work at Pendragon and Brougham Castles. Appleby Castle is now a conservation centre and open to the public (see Attractions).

A charter in 1179 ensured that the settlement would grow through trade and in fact during the Middle Ages, Appleby was one of the most important towns in the area with a population recorded as approaching 10,000 inhabitants. Despite the death and destruction associated with Scottish raids in the fourteenth century, the town continued to develop and remained the county town of the old county of Westmorland before its amalgamation within modern day Cumbria.

The town is also famous for the siting of the Appleby Horse Fair. Held in June each year, the fair is believed to be the biggest gathering of gypsy people in Britain with the buying, selling and racing of horses making for a colourful and lively event.

Bassenthwaite. Val Corbett.

Barrow-in-Furnace

Unfortunately overlooked by many visitors to the Lake District, Barrow has much to see and remains one of the most populous towns in Cumbria. Although the town's population numbered only a few hundred in 1840, the arrival of the railway and the discovery of large iron ore deposits over the next decade led to a rapid expansion of the settlement towards the centre it is today.

By 1876, the Barrow steelworks were the largest in the world, leading in turn to the development of a great iron shipbuilding industry.

This is echoed today in that the work provided by the town's submarine building industry remains a crucial part of Barrow's economic activity.

Before the dissolution of the monasteries in the sixteenth century, Furness Abbey, just to the north of Barrow, the ruins of which most visitors head for, was the second richest Cistercian house in the country, owning large parts of Lakeland as far north as Derwentwater. The red sandstone remains date from 1147 and are one of England's great Abbey remains, now in the care of English Heritage.

A more modern attraction is the recently opened Dock Museum (see Attractions).

Bassenthwaite Lake

The Lake District's most northerly lake, owned by the National Park Authority since 1979. Bassenthwaite is the fourth largest stretch of water in the Lake District and the only one referred to as a lake (the others being waters or meres). It is just under three miles long and half a mile wide with a maximum depth of nearly 60 feet.

Bassenthwaite was once part of a larger lake incorporating Derwentwater before division by glacial debris after the ending of the Ice Age. The two are now joined by the River Derwent. The Lake was

Gazetteer

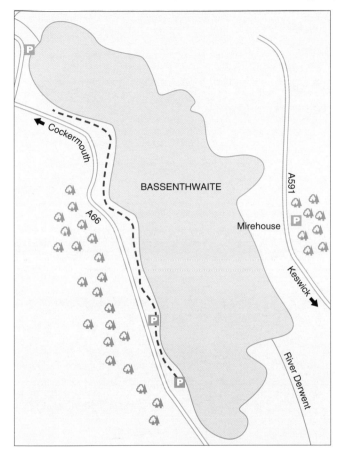

ACCESS

BY ROAD

From the A66 at Keswick, head north on the A591 (signed Carlisle and Mirehouse) to follow the course of the eastern shoreline which offers only occasional glimpses of the lake. The B5291 tops its northern shore and joins the A66 which hugs the western shore of the lake, similarly offering only partial views.

BY FOOT

There are two parking areas which provide access to a section of lakeshore footpath on the western side. At Ouse Bridge, there is a National Park parking area with access to the shoreline in addition to one at Blackstock Point near the southern end of the lake. The latter provides access to a bird hide with views over the nature reserve.

BY BOAT

Boating is fairly restricted on the lake with the northern section limited to Bassenthwaite Sailing Club only. Powerboats are forbidden across the length of the lake. In the south boating is not permitted, due to its use as a wildlife sanctuary.

PRINCIPAL VIEWPOINTS

A small parking area at the eastern end of the B5292 Whinlatter Pass provides an extensive view of the lake. Lord's Seat (1811 feet) in the west and popular Skiddaw (3054 feet) to the east are two of the main summits in the proximity overlooking Bassenthwaite.

declared a National Nature Reserve by English Nature in 1993 with the southern end a haven for birds, where over 70 species have been recorded during the summer period. Tufted Ducks and Greylag Geese are two of many Scandinavian species that winter here whilst their homelands are frozen.

Bassenthwaite is also home to the Vendace, a rare and endangered fish species in Britain found only here and in Derwentwater.

The importance of the lake as a nature reserve restricts man's use of it, it is hence rarely busy. Unfortunately, the rather busy A66 which hugs its western shore ensures Bassenthwaite is not sought out by those looking for peace and quiet.

Mirehouse, a large Georgian house owned by the Spedding family and open to the public (see Attractions) is found on the south eastern edge of the lake. Alfred Tennyson was a frequent visitor here and it is believed the lake inspired him in his description of King Arthur's final hours regarding the sword in the lake legend within his "*Idylls of the Kings*".

Black Combe

Located in the far south western corner of the National Park, Black Combe is one of the oldest hills in the world. The broad dome of Black Combe is a gigantic slate outcrop, similar to the northern hills of Skiddaw and Blencathra. Black Combe was the site of intense Neolithic activity, the whole area is littered with burial cairns although of the four known stone circles, only Swinside remains. This circle of 55 stones is comparable to the more famous example at Castlerigg near Keswick. Though on private land, Swinside Stone Circle can be seen from a nearby path (see Mini Walks).

Black Combe is in many ways a forgotten fell, a result of its location away from central Lakeland and the rather bland two mile ascent to the summit. Although only 1970 feet high, the ascent is well worthwhile given the fell's reputation as the most extensive viewpoint in Britain. Fourteen counties, the Irish Mountains of Mourne and the Isle of Man are said to be visible on a clear day. Wordsworth no less, was a devotee, praising in particular the view across his beloved Duddon Valley. His *'View from the top of Black Combe'* was published in 1813.

Blencathra

Also known as Saddleback, Blencathra is derived from a Celtic word meaning summit, though at 2847 feet, a little short of the four Lake District summits above the 3,000 foot mark. Less popular than its eastern sister Skiddaw, Blencathra arguably offers more for the walker, with a deep blue tarn and dramatic narrow arretes. Sharp Edge, overlooking Scales Tarn, is held by many to be superior even to Helvellyn's Striding Edge and is not for the fainthearted.

Perhaps the best route to the summit is east to west availing excellent views across south western Lakeland. From Scales, a route climbs via Mousthwaite Comb and Scales Fell to Sharp Edge before heading south to the summit. An alternative route via the southern face of Blencathra leaves Gategill and climbs via Hall's Fell Ridge, a shorter but far steeper ascent and not one marked as a Public Right of Way on O.S. maps. Descent can be made via Knowe Crags to the east or Doddick Fell to the west.

Blencathra. Val Corbett.

Borrowdale. Val Corbett.

Borrowdale

A classic Lake District valley, stretching from Seathwaite high in the central fells, down to the head of Derwentwater, an area much loved by painters, photographers and visitors alike.

Home to the well known Lodore Falls (see Mini Walks), Borrowdale is also the location of the much visited Bowder stone, a 2,000 ton rock boulder deposited by a retreating glacier 10,000 years ago (see Attractions).

The famous 'Jaws of Borrowdale' provide a spectacular backdrop when looking south across Derwentwater. This is where the River Derwent flows between two upland areas and is the principal access to Borrowdale. The most westerly of the two 'Jaws' is Castle Crag, a National Trust owned summit responsible for the Borrowdale name itself. Borrowdale, meaning *'Valley of the Fort'* refers to ancient hill fortifications at the summit of Castle Crag, used by the British tribes at the time of the Roman invasion in the first century. The Guided Walks section includes a 3 mile ascent of the 980 foot summit and viewpoint.

Before being cleared in part for farming by Norse settlers, Borrowdale was once thickly wooded and in more recent times the valley supplied much of the wood needed for smelting the copper and lead ores extracted from nearby mines. Areas settled by Norse farmers can be identified throughout the Lake District, particularly where place names end in *-thwaite*, meaning literally 'a clearing'. In Borrowdale, this name ending is evident at the settlements of Seathwaite and Rosthwaite, the latter providing the starting point for a further Guided Walk from Borrowdale to the scenic National Trust hamlet of Watendlath.

Gazetteer

Bowness

Bowness, with a bustling somewhat cosmopolitan feel to it, is like no other town in the Lakes. Its charm lies in its lakeside location which has led to a multitude of shops and restaurants helping to make it one of the premier resorts of southern Lakeland.

The development of the town was as a result of two not unconnected factors; proximity to Lake Windermere and the railway expansion of the mid nineteenth century. Bowness' position next to a narrow part of the lake made it inevitable that a ferry service would be introduced here, saving a 10 mile detour to the important medieval market town of Hawkshead. A modern car ferry operates throughout the year and is a far cry from the original rowing boat service of the fifteenth century.

The arrival of the railway at nearby Windermere in 1847 led to rapid expansion of both settlements, so much so that it is difficult to divide them. The railway facilitated the growth of mass tourism in the Lake District and allowed workers to escape their northern factories and enjoy day trips to the town. Even today, Bowness is the most popular destination in Lakeland for day trippers. Wealthy Manchester businessmen built large lakeside villas (now mostly hotels) in perhaps one of the earliest examples of commuting in England. The most famous was perhaps H. W. Schneider, who lived at Belsfield and had a special pier constructed to allow him each morning to catch a steam launch to Lakeside, at the southern end of Lake Windermere. From here he caught a special train to his office at Barrow, its practice of waiting for him was no doubt aided by his ownership of the railway company!

Bowness boasts a large National Park Information Centre as well as the Windermere Steamboat Museum and World of Beatrix Potter Exhibition. It is of course also the principal departure point for trips on Lake Windermere (see Attractions).

Brampton

Situated in the far north east of Cumbria, Brampton is a small market town dating back to 1250 when it first received its charter. Like many settlements in the border area, Brampton was not a safe place to live in the thirteenth and fourteenth centuries with Scottish raids a frequent occurrence. As a result, the substantial fortress of Naworth Castle was constructed in the early fourteenth century and renovated by the Howard family in the seventeenth century. Its present owner, the Earl of Carlisle, is a direct descendant of Sir Charles Howard who received the earldom from Charles II in 1661.

The church at Brampton dates back to the twelfth century and is renowned for its colourful Burne-Jones windows. Nearby are the ruins of Lanercost Priory, founded by Augustinian monks in 1169 and rated second only in interest to the ruins of Furness Abbey.

Lanercost Priory is now in the care of English Heritage and, like Brampton Church, was partially constructed using stone taken from Hadrian's Wall, some three miles to the north.

The Tourist Information Centre in the market place at the centre of the town occupies the nineteenth century Moot Hall, the original having been constructed in 1648.

Buttermere

Buttermere village lies just to the north of the lake of the same name and is at the heart of the high fell country of north west Lakeland.

The classic combination of lakes and mountains guaranteed that Buttermere would become a must for visitors from the very earliest beginnings of tourism in the Lake District. The 'Buttermere Round', popular from the early nineteenth century until the 1930's, involved day long trips by coach and horses to the valley, passing through the Borrowdale Valley and onto Buttermere via the Honister Pass, returning to Keswick via the Newlands Valley. This route was as popular as a car tour is today, although the modern traveller thankfully does not have to descend through the Honister Pass on foot as was once required due to the steepness of the gradient for horse drawn carriages.

In the centre of Buttermere village is the Fish Inn, made famous in the nineteenth century as the home of the 'Beauty of Buttermere'. Mary

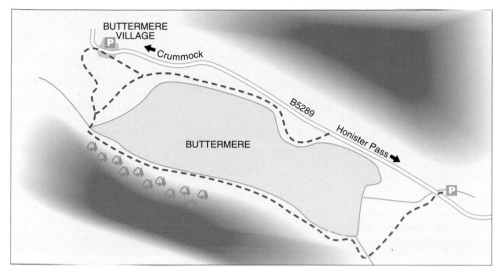

Robinson, the landlord's daughter, was 'discovered' in the 1790's by an early guide book writer, her beauty so acclaimed that people travelled for miles to see her. One such visitor was a Colonel Alexander Hope MP who courted her and married her. Unfortunately he turned out to be a liar, bigamist and forger and was eventually hanged for fraud in Carlisle. Mary later remarried and had 7 children; her grave can be found in the churchyard at Caldbeck.

Nowadays a visit to Buttermere is principally for its natural attractions, as the area offers some of the best walking country in Lakeland. Three of the walks in the Guided Walks section start from Buttermere; Walk 17 a circuit of Buttermere Lake; Walk 18 the climb to the 1960 feet summit of Haystacks and Walk 19 a 5 mile circuit of Red Pike which includes Scale Force, Lakeland's highest waterfall.

Buttermere Water

Located in the north west of the Lake District, Buttermere is the first in a chain of three lakes (the others being Crummock and Loweswater) which was once a single lake before it was divided by debris from the surrounding fells. The high wall of fells encircling much of the lake (High Crag, High Stile and Red Pike are all over 2400 feet) has led many to describe Buttermere as the most picturesque of all the lakes.

It has a maximum depth of just over 90 feet, suited to the charr fish, a relative of the salmon and trout and a popular delicacy in this part of the Northwest. In England, the distinctive red bellied fish is found only in the Lake District and rarely grows larger than 12 inches (30cm) in length. Elsewhere in the world, the charr is a migratory species, feeding in the sea but returning to fresh water to spawn, rather like the salmon. The lake populations are thought to have originated in the Ice Age 8-10,000 years ago, with changes in sea level relative to the land resulting in populations being trapped within individual lakes and water basins.

The whole of the 230 acre lake and much of the surrounding fell is in the care of the National Trust, consequently there is good public access around the whole of the shoreline (see Guided Walk 17 for an enjoyable 4.5 mile ramble that circuits the lake).

The name Buttermere is translated as "lake of the dairy pastures" although like many of the names in the Lake District may have actually derived from a previous Norse owner, in this case *Buthar*, hence *"Buthar's mere"*.

ACCESS
BY ROAD

From Keswick via Borrowdale and the Honister Pass, the

Gazetteer
Caldbeck

Buttermere. Val Corbett.

B5289 passes close to the northern shore and offers excellent views over the length of the lake.

BY FOOT

A circular route around Buttermere provides one of the most enjoyable lakeside walks in the district and is described in Guided Walk 17. Parking is available at either Gatesgarth Farm or in Buttermere village.

BY BOAT

Power boating is banned although rowing boats can be hired from Gatesgarth Farm.

PRINCIPAL VIEWPOINTS

Though the lakeside path provides excellent panoramas across Buttermere, to really appreciate its overall setting it is worth climbing the surrounding fells (see Guided Walk 18 (Haystacks) and 19 (Red Pike).

The most northerly village of the National Park, Caldbeck is located in an area referred to locally as 'Back (north) O' Skiddaw' and is consequently often overlooked by visitors to the Lakes.

The settlement grew up as a result of the mineral resources found in the surrounding Caldbeck Fells, mainly copper and lead although over 20 different types of mineral have been identified. The second factor responsible for the growth of the village is explained in the Caldbeck name, meaning perhaps unsurprisingly 'cold stream'. The availability of an excellent source of water power ensured Caldbeck would flourish as a milling centre. The nineteenth century bobbin mill powered by a 42 foot diameter water wheel which was once the second largest in the world, employed 60 men in its heyday before ceasing operation in 1908 and later in 1959 destroyed by fire. The ruins of the mill are passed en route to the Howk, a miniature limestone chasm with a stunning waterfall described in the Mini Walks section. Caldbeck is also renowned as the burial place of John Peel, famed huntsman and father of 13, immortalised in the ballad "*D'ye ken John Peel*". His grave, carved with hunting motifs, can be found in the churchyard together with the final resting place of Mary Robinson, the 'Beauty of Buttermere' (see index).

Caldbeck. Val Corbett.

Carlisle

There are few places in the country that have had a more troubled history than the cathedral city of Carlisle, Cumbria's capital. Its location on England's border with Scotland ensured the development of a frontier town as a bulwark against northern invaders, in turn making it the prime target of the Scots.

Carlisle's long history began as Luguvalium, a Roman military garrison with a small civilian settlement at the end of Hadrian's Wall. It was linked to Northumbria by a fortified road with a further link westwards to Maryport where a supply port and fort had been constructed. The garrison at

Carlisle included a 1,000 strong cavalry unit which could be moved quickly to quell rebellion in the surrounding areas.

Although Norse raiders devastated the town in the tenth century, the following 400 years saw the town burnt or besieged primarily by its northern neighbours. Established as a frontier stronghold against the Scots by Norman barons, Carlisle and its castle was attacked in 1173, 1174 and 1215 with perhaps the most intense conflict for much of the fourteenth century. This was in no small part a result of Edward I, the 'Hammer of the Scots', ruthlessly persecuting the Scots in a series of military campaigns. His sacking of

Berwick-on-Tweed for example, involved the slaughter of the town's 17,000 inhabitants. Even in the seventeenth century, Carlisle's troubles continued, this time at the hands of the Parliamentarians, the Royalist stronghold surrendering after an eight month siege which had seen horses, dogs and cats consumed once other food supplies were depleted.

Nowadays, Carlisle is the principal commercial centre of Cumbria with a wide selection of shops and restaurants as well as the castle and cathedral which are open to visitors. Near to the cathedral is Tullie House, an impressive exhibition and museum recounting the turbulent history of the city (see Attractions).

Carlisle. Val Corbett.

Cartmel

Located just south of the National Park boundary on a small peninsula jutting out into Morecambe Bay is the village of Cartmel, famed for its priory, established by Augustinian monks in 1190. Surviving the dissolution of the monasteries, the church of St. Mary and St. Michael has a presence and grandeur likened to that of a cathedral.

A more modern attraction on the edge of the village, is the smallest National Hunt race course in the country, holding four meetings per year. Nearby Holker Hall is a fine stately home incorporating splendid gardens as well as the Lakeland Motor Museum (see Attractions).

Cockermouth

Located just outside the National Park's northern boundary, Cockermouth grew up at the junction of the two most important rivers in the area. Here the River Derwent, draining Bassenthwaite and Derwentwater meets the River Cocker, flowing from the lakes of Buttermere, Crummock and Loweswater.

A castle, constructed in the twelfth century, was the inevitable result of this strategic position. As a consequence of ravages by Robert the Bruce, most of the existing structure was rebuilt in the fourteenth century though with some more modern additions.

The granting of a market charter in 1221 ensured the growth of the town ideally situated at a natural meeting place for many of the roads from the surrounding farming country. In time, Cockermouth became the premier commercial centre for Cumberland, one of the three original counties that were combined to form modern Cumbria. Even today, the town is the main district centre for the north west quadrant of the Lake District, with busy markets held every Monday.

Today's visitors are attracted by the town's otherwise Georgian calm and the fact that William and Dorothy Wordsworth were born here. Their large Georgian house in Main Street is now in the care of the National Trust (see Attractions).

Cartmel. Val Corbett.

Coniston

Coniston village, located close to the head of the lake of the same name is dominated by the high fells to its east, in particular the Old Man summit of 2635 feet. The large quantities of copper and slate located in these fells and the availability of the lake for transport ensured the growth of a settlement here.

It is believed that the Romans were the first to mine for copper, though the peak of prosperity was in the early nineteenth century when hundreds of men and boys were employed, many working at depths of over a thousand feet. Mining activity centred on the Church Beck area above the village, now known as Coppermines Valley. Levers Water, high in the fells, was once a reservoir for the mines.

The slate grey village is now a tourist centre with the Old Man range a magnet for walkers. The National Trust steam yacht 'Gondola', built in 1859, has been restored and put back into service by the Trust and can often be seen as she circuits the lake, with its distinctive plume of smoke. A further draw is the home of Coniston's most famous resident, John Ruskin, the critic, author, artist and social philanthropist who lived at Brantwood on the eastern side of the lake until his death in 1900. It is open to the public and contains many of his personal possessions. Ruskin is buried beneath an elaborately carved cross in the village churchyard, spurning an opportunity to be buried at

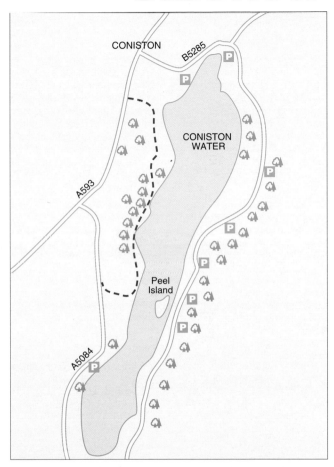

Westminster Abbey in favour of his much loved Lakeland.

Coniston Water

Previously known as Thurston's Mere after a tenth century Norse settler, Coniston's five mile length is the third largest of the lakes. It provided an important fish source for the monks of Furness Abbey who owned the lake and much of the

surrounding land in the thirteenth and fourteenth centuries. More recently, Coniston was used to transport slate and ore from the many mines worked in the Coppermines Valley above Coniston village. Small iron ore furnaces (bloomeries) were also developed on the lakeshore, using the surrounding woodland to produce the charcoal required for smelting.

This industrial heritage now seems a far cry from the peaceful scenery enjoyed today. Like Windermere,

Coniston has more than one basin, the northerly with a depth of 150 feet and a southerly basin with a maximum depth of 184 feet near Peel Island. It is this depth that goes some way in explaining why Sir Donald Campbell's body was not recovered after his boat Bluebird disintegrated during an attempt to reach 300mph and break the world speed record in January 1967. It was little consolation that Campbell was believed to be travelling at over 320 mph when he died.

Overlooking the lake is John Ruskin's home, Brantwood, open to the public and detailed further in the Attractions section. Although somewhat forgotten, Ruskin had enormous talents, and, as a writer, artist, social critic and philanthropist, was enormously influential in the latter part of the nineteenth century. He lived at Brantwood for the last 28 years of his life having purchased the house for £1,500 to help a friend, without having previously seen it, reasoning that any

house on the shores of Coniston would be worth living in.

The steam yacht 'Gondola' was originally built in 1859 before its acquisition by the National Trust who returned it to lake service in 1980. One of a pair, built for the Furness Rail Company, the sister yacht 'Lady of the Lake', was broken up in the 1950's.

ACCESS

BY ROAD

The minor road running along the eastern shore provides excellent views across the lake and towards the Old Man range. There are numerous parking areas set in light woodland, many with picnic tables.

BY FOOT

West   Guided Walk 3 provides a 3.5 mile circular walk across Torver Common, returning to the parking area via the lakeshore. Alternatively, from an access just south of the guided walk parking area, a two mile lakeshore path winds

its way north to Coniston Hall. The National Trust Brown Howe parking area at the southern end of the lake also provides access to the shore as well as toilets and a disabled path to a viewpoint.

East   There are numerous opportunities to visit the lakeshore from the picnic areas dotted along the minor road.

BY BOAT

The launching of motorboats is forbidden. A far grander and more sedate method is to take the one hour round trip aboard the National Trust steam yacht 'Gondola'. Accessed via the National Park Monk Coniston car park at the northern end of the lake (see Attractions for details of services etc.).

PRINCIPAL VIEWPOINTS

Low level views can be obtained from the parking areas detailed above. Obviously, routes in the Old Man range will also provide panoramic views across the lake.

Coniston. Val Corbett.

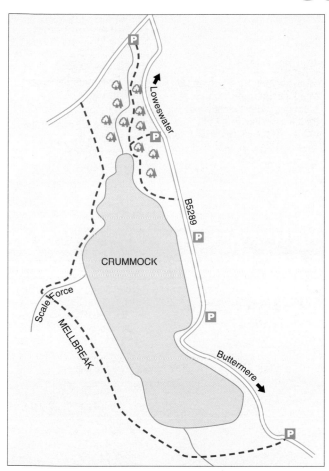

Crummock Water

Crummock Water is the largest of the three lakes that run from Buttermere to Loweswater in the north western quadrant of the Lake District. The three were once part of a single lake before deposit from the surrounding hillsides gradually created low lying fields between them. Crummock Water is sometimes overlooked given the startling beauty of neighbouring Buttermere.

The great whaleback of a fell, Mellbreak, watches over the eastern shoreline whilst to the west, the mighty but rarely frequented Grasmoor dominates the skyline. Crummock, owned by the National Trust, has an overall length of 2.5 miles and a maximum depth of 144 feet. Late nineteenth century tourists frequented the lake, hiring rowing boats to visit the waterfall of Scale Force rather than undertaking the two mile walk from Buttermere village. The 170 foot waterfall is Lakeland's tallest and is

encountered on Guided Walk 19.

ACCESS

BY ROAD

From Buttermere, the B5289 to Cockermouth hugs Crummock's eastern shoreline offering excellent views across the lake to Mellbreak.

BY FOOT

Lakeshore paths exist on both sides of the lake. One access is from Lanthwaite Wood at the lake's northern end.

BY BOAT

None.

VIEWPOINTS

A good view is from the northern end of the lake, looking up the valley as described above from Lanthwaite Wood. Alternatively, Rannerdale Knotts and Low Bank provide views from the southern end of the lake (see Mini Walks).

Dacre

Dacre is a small village rich in history, situated between the A66 Keswick/Penrith road and the north eastern end of Ullswater. The Norman church is built on the site of an Anglo Saxon monastery and contains an eighth century Anglian Cross as well as a tenth century Viking Cross, the latter carved with the figures of Adam and Eve. More intriguing however, are the four stone bears found within the churchyard. Their origin and purpose is unclear though they are believed to show a bear, on awakening, being attacked by a wild cat before it finally kills and eats the cat.

The churchyard also provides the opportunity to view Dacre Castle (not open to the public),

Dacre. Val Corbett.

an excellent example of a fourteenth century Pele Tower. These are found throughout the Lake District and are substantial buildings which were constructed for protection against Scottish raids. Once hillside beacons had been lit to raise the alarm, livestock were driven into the ground floor, with protection provided for its human occupants in the upper storeys. Provisions were kept to allow resistance during periods of siege by the bloodthirsty northern raiders.

Open to the public is nearby Dalemain House, a Georgian fronted stately home of medieval origin (see Attractions).

Derwentwater

Often regarded as the 'Queen of the Lakes', Derwentwater, situated close to the resort town of Keswick, is the most popular lake in northern Lakeland. Roughly oval in shape, it is three miles long and fairly shallow with a maximum depth of only 72 feet. In hard winters, the northern part of the lake can freeze giving access for ice skating. Two submarine ridges run north south along the length of the lake resulting in four islands, all large enough to support trees. A fifth 'island', in fact a mass of vegetation brought to the surface by methane, can sometimes be seen in the south of the lake. Derwentwater was a favourite of Beatrix Potter, first introduced to the lake whilst enjoying family holidays at Lingholm on its north western shore. It was at this time that

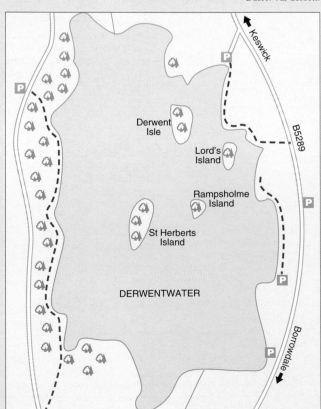

Potter met Canon Rawnsley, a local clergyman who went on to found the National Trust. Brandelhow Park on Derwent's south western shore was the Trust's first acquisition in the Lake District (1902).

ACCESS

BY ROAD

East   The Borrowdale road (B5289) runs south from Keswick offering views across the lake.

West   More impressive views can be obtained from the minor road running parallel with the western shoreline. From the A66 west of Keswick, turn off signed to Portinscale. Pass Lingholm following signs for Grange whereupon the road climbs out of the trees to offer views from beneath the Cat Bells summit.

BY FOOT

East   The National Trust Great Wood and Kettlewell car parks can be used to access the adjacent shoreline. Immediate access also from the National Trust owned Crow Park and Friars Crag (see Mini Walks) after parking in the main lakeside Keswick car park

adjacent to the Century Theatre. Friars Crag is accessible for pushchairs and by the disabled due to its level terrain. The stunning view across Derwentwater to Borrowdale was thought by Ruskin to be one of the top three views in the world.

West   Southern half of shoreline accessible through Manesty Woods and Brandelhow Park via numerous, though busy small parking areas.

BY BOAT

Derwentwater is an out and out boating lake with rowing boats for hire from the landing stages adjacent to the lakeside car park. A boat trip service operates on the lake stopping off at 6 landing stages.

DERWENT ISLE

The largest and most northerly of the lake's four islands. In the fifteenth century, it was home to German miners, brought in for their mining expertise in the nearby copper mines of the Newlands Valley. In the eighteenth century, the island was home to Joseph Pocklington, an eccentric, responsible for building a stone

circle and fort in addition to organising mock sea battles as part of the Keswick regatta.

ST HERBERT'S ISLAND

Named after the saint whose hermitage existed here in the seventh century. Monks would come from Friars Crag to be blessed by him. St Herbert is believed to have died on the same day in 687 as his great friend St Cuthbert, Bishop of Lindisfarne.

LORD'S ISLAND

Once owned by the monks of Furness Abbey and now in the care of the National Trust. The Earl of Derwent had a manor house here at one time.

RAMPSHOLME ISLAND

Owned by the National Trust and named after the ramp or wild garlic that once grew here.

PRINCIPAL VIEWPOINTS

Guided Walks 14 and 15 to Cat Bells and Castle Crag offer excellent panoramas. Castle Head, Ashness Bridge and Surprise View (see Mini Walks for details) also offer superb opportunities for viewing the lake.

Derwentwater. Val Corbett.

Duddon Valley

Known also as Dunnerdale, this river valley runs from the Wrynose Pass in central Lakeland, winding through fairly isolated fell country to its river estuary near Broughton-in-Furness.

The lack of a lake and its relative inaccessibility ensures Dunnerdale is often quiet, although William Wordsworth celebrated the area in his '*Duddon Sonnets*' and thought it to be one of the most beautiful valleys in Lakeland. A road follows the course of the river past a car park at Birks Bridge from where there are Forestry Commission paths within Dunnerdale Forest.

Further to the southwest is Ulpha, a small hamlet and the only settlement of any size, located where the valley is joined by the Eskdale road. A pool at the foot of a waterfall in nearby Holehouse Gill is known as 'Lady's Dub' after a local folklore relating to a woman drowned here whilst fleeing from a wolf. This is used by some as the derivation of Ulpha's name, given the Norse 'ulfr' for wolf, although a more likely reason is that the settlement was founded by an 'Ulf' shortly after the Norman Conquest.

At Duddon Bridge in the far south west of the valley, are the remains of an important iron furnace, established in 1736.

Duddon Valley. Val Corbett.

Egremont. Val Corbett.

Gazetteer

Egremont

Situated outside the National Park boundary on the western coastal plain, Egremont, with a market charter since 1267, has a long history. Dating from the same time is the town's Crab Fair, an annual event held on the third Saturday of September. It is a celebration of the crab apple, some of which are thrown to the public from the Apple Cart during the festivities. The carnival atmosphere continues with attempts to climb the 30 foot greasy pole, which in medieval times had the prize of a sheep attached to the top. In the evening, the World Gurning Championships take place, an unusual competition where the winner is the person who can pull the most grotesque face whilst a horse collar is placed around the neck!

The Norman castle here was largely destroyed in the sixteenth century; the sandstone remains of the gatehouse are situated in a public park which has free access (see Attractions).

Elterwater

Elterwater, to the west of Ambleside, was once a much larger lake than it is today. Its decrease in size is as a result of it draining both the valleys of Great and Little Langdale. The resultant alluvial deposits have helped over thousands of years to create an increasingly reed fringed and rather marshy lake which will eventually cease to exist. The lake is consequently rather undefined in shape and

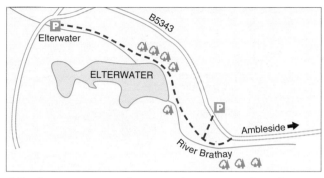

difficult to view compared to other lakes within the district.

The name Elterwater is derived from the Norse word for swan; fittingly Whooper Swans often winter here when their Scandinavian homelands are frozen over. The lake is one of the few in Lakeland to be privately owned.

ACCESS

BY ROAD

The B5343 provides glimpses over the lake when driving east from Chapel Stile.

BY FOOT

A right of way exists along

Elterwater's northern shore from the village to the impressive waterfall at Skelwith Bridge. Guided Walk 6 utilises the route on the return from Loughrigg Tarn.

BY BOAT

None.

PRINCIPAL VIEWPOINTS

It is difficult to gain an overall view of Elterwater other than the lakeside path on the northern shore. However, the distinctive hump of the Langdale Pikes provides a stunning backdrop to the area.

Elterwater. Val Corbett.

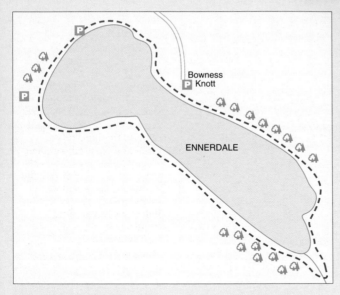

Ennerdale Water

Ennerdale, the most westerly of the lakes and the most remote, offers, even in high season a place to escape ones fellow human beings. It is 2.5 miles long with a maximum depth of 148 feet and serves as a reservoir for the coastal towns to the west.

The acquisition of land by the Forestry Commission in the 1920's and 1930's has led to large scale conifer planting in the area. This is particularly the case in the River Liza valley, a name derived from the Icelandic word *'lysa'* meaning bright water.

ACCESS
BY ROAD

Ennerdale is served by only two roads, one ending at Bowness Knott halfway along its northern shore, the other reaching only as far as the western end of the lake (see Mini Walks for directions to Bowness Knott).

BY FOOT

It is possible to walk around the whole of the lake, mainly on land owned by either the National Trust or Forestry Commission. At Bowness Knott, a Forestry Commission parking area with toilets marks the start of three waymarked trails ranging from three to ten miles.

BY BOAT

No private craft allowed on the lake.

PRINCIPAL VIEWPOINTS

Best views are from the lakeshore paths and approach road to Bowness Knott parking area. Pillar mountain provides backdrop to eastern end of the lake. Guided Walk 19 also provides extensive valley views from the summit of Red Pike.

Eskdale

An attractive, fertile valley running from the high central fells at Hardknott down to the sea at Ravenglass. The valley was the main supply route of the Romans, with their fort at Hardknott (Mediobogdum to the Romans) guarding the route to Ambleside from the Roman port of Glannoventa at modern day Ravenglass.

Eskdale. Val Corbett.

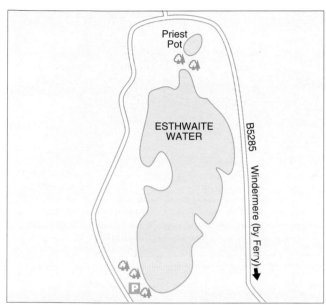

Eskdale was also an important packhorse route for the Lakeland woollen industry; two attractive seventeenth century packhorse bridges cross the Whillan Beck at Boot. A restored corn mill dating from one hundred years before is a further draw for visitors to the valley.

Though Eskdale has no lake, it is a popular destination, with many visitors seeking out 'L'aal Ratty', the Eskdale and Ravenglass Miniature Railway. The seven mile long line was opened in 1875 to help exploit iron ore deposits, supplementing an existing granite quarrying industry dating from the previous century. Closed in 1913 and converted to 15 inch gauge, the railway continued to transport granite until the 1950's. In 1961, the railway was purchased by a preservation society which now provides year round services for visitors (see Attractions).

The attractively wooded waterfall of Stanley Force (also known as Dalegarth Falls) is a short walk from the railway terminus at Dalegarth and is described in the Mini Walks section.

Esthwaite Water

Centrally situated between Windermere and Coniston, Esthwaite has much in common with Elterwater, both in size and form. With a length of just 1.5 miles and fairly shallow (the deepest part is only sixty feet), the lake is rich in nutrients and vegetation. The low lying nature of the lake to the surrounding farmland and light woodland ensures the support of fish species such as trout, perch, pike and roach. Like Elterwater, Esthwaite was once larger than it is today. Priest Pot, a small nature reserve just to the north of the lake, was originally part of

Esthwaite although it is now separated by silt.

Whilst attending nearby Hawkshead Grammar School, William Wordsworth witnessed the gruesome recovery from the lake of the body of James Jackson, a local schoolmaster. Aged only nine, Wordsworth reported finding a pile of clothes on the northern shore. The dragging of the lake with grappling irons resulted in the recovery of the unfortunate teacher's body, later buried in Hawkshead churchyard. Wordsworth recalls in *The Prelude;*

"Went there a company, and, in their boat,

Sounded with grappling irons and long poles.

At length, the dead man, 'mid that beauteous scene

Of trees, and hills and water, bolt upright

Rose with his ghastly face"

ACCESS
BY ROAD
Roads run either side of the lake although the views are probably best from the B5285 when heading south from Hawkshead to the Sawreys and the Windermere ferry.

BY FOOT
The lake is privately owned.

BY BOAT
Esthwaite is popular with fishermen; boats can be hired from the trout farm at the southern end of the lake. No powercraft are allowed.

PRINCIPAL VIEWPOINTS
Guided Walk 2 allows views across Esthwaite from above Hawkshead.

Gazetteer

Fairfield

Situated to the north of Ambleside and Rydal, Fairfield (2863 feet) is famed as offering one of the finest ridge walks in the Lake District. The 'Fairfield Horseshoe', so called due to the shape of the ridges approaching its summit, is a long and fairly gruelling walk, although the panoramic views across to Windermere and Coniston as well as northwards across Grisedale Tarn to the Helvellyn range, are the reward.

From Scandale Bridge, north of Ambleside, a public footpath passes through Rydal Park to climb Heron Pike via Lord Crag. Continue via Great Rigg to the flat summit plateau of Fairfield. Return is via Hart and Dove Crags, descending via High and Low Pikes to Low Sweden Bridge and on to Ambleside. An alternative is to ascend from Patterdale via Hartsop above How. The ascent to Fairfield is then via Hart Crag, the return by the curiously named St Sunday Crag.

Glenridding

Situated on the western bank of southern Ullswater, Glenridding is a small village now entirely devoted to tourism. Many people use Glenridding as the starting point for an ascent of Helvellyn, at 3113 feet Lakeland's third highest and easily most popular mountain. The ascent is via the rocky arretes of Swirral and Striding Edge, knife edge routes around Red Tarn created as a result of glacial action. The village is also the main southern landing stage of the Ullswater Navigation Company steamers (see Attractions) for boat trips across beautiful Ullswater.

The history of the area, detailed within the National Park Information Centre located here, states that Glenridding was formerly an important lead mining centre with the very successful Greenside Lead Mine, dating back to the sixteenth century, reaching its peak in the 1870's. Traces of the industry can still be seen in the valley above the village where in 1929, a reservoir used by the mines, burst, flooding the village below although miraculously with no casualties.

Gosforth

Located in the far west of Lakeland, Gosforth is most famous for the content of its churchyard, situated in the east of the village. A slender, fragile looking 15 foot high sandstone cross was erected here by Viking settlers to the area, early in the tenth century. It is carved with Norse figures and dragons representing a story of good prevailing over evil. What makes it intriguing to scholars is that it also depicts Christ's crucifixion, reflecting the beliefs of the settlers who increasingly embraced Christian values but were unwilling to totally reject their pagan history.

Glenridding. Val Corbett.

Grange-over-Sands

A quiet rather charming village, Grange-over-Sands lies just outside the southern boundary of the National Park on the bank of the Kent Estuary. The over-Sands part of the name refers to its importance as the northern terminus of a 7.5 mile route across the treacherous sands of Morecambe Bay to Bolton-le-Sands in Lancashire. Used since medieval times, the route saves a substantial detour, but with the constantly changing nature of the sands, quicksand and fast incoming tides, the crossing nowadays should only be attempted with a guide.

The town itself has been dubbed the 'Torquay of the north', being something of a natural geographical suntrap and reputed as having the mildest climate in Cumbria. The arrival of the railway in 1857 facilitated the growth of a Victorian seaside resort complete with mile long esplanade, the whole effect quite unlike any other part of the Lake District.

Grasmere

Like many of the settlements in the Lake District, Grasmere was founded by Norse settlers who cleared the woodlands for farming. In Grasmere's case this was only a partial clearance, the remaining woodland being used to graze pigs ('*Gris*' being the old Norse word for swine).

Grange-over-Sands. Val Corbett.

Today, Grasmere can be one of the busiest villages in Lakeland, its attraction a combination of beautiful location, peaceful lakeside walks and the strong association with William Wordsworth.

Wordsworth regarded Grasmere as the "*loveliest spot that man hath ever found*" and went on to live in four houses in the area, the most famous of which, Dove Cottage, is open to the public and found in nearby Townend. The house was originally the 'Dove and Olive Bough' Inn and the nine years Wordsworth lived here were certainly his happiest and arguably his most creative. His last home, Rydal Mount, at the nearby hamlet of Rydal is also open to the public (see Attractions section for further details of both houses).

At St. Oswalds Church, in the centre of Grasmere, is the churchyard containing the Wordsworth family graves, a site chosen by William and close to yew trees that he planted. The church, like St. Marys in Ambleside, holds a colourful rushbearing ceremony each year, on the Saturday nearest to August 5th, St. Oswalds Day. The ceremony celebrates the medieval use of rushes as the principal floor covering of the church, scattered over the bare earth floor and replaced annually.

Another important annual event in the village's calendar is the Grasmere Sports, held each August and the Lakeland equivalent of a Highland Games where massive crowds come to watch Cumberland Wrestling, Hound Trailing and races up the fells. The event's popularity increases every year and it is worth getting there early to secure a parking space. The car park next to the National Park Information Centre is the starting point for two guided walks celebrating the life and landscape of the poet Wordsworth (see Guided Walks 9 and 10).

Gazetteer

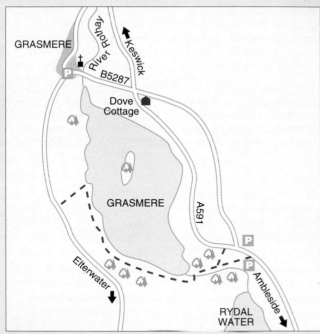

GRASMERE · River Rothay · Keswick · B5287 · Dove Cottage · GRASMERE · A591 · GRASMERE · Elterwater · Ambleside · RYDAL WATER

Grasmere Water

'The loveliest spot that man hath found' was Wordsworth's famous quote describing the area he most loved in Lakeland. The small island at the centre of the lake was a favourite destination for the Wordsworths whilst living at nearby Dove Cottage, often rowing across to picnic and compose letters and poems. Grasmere, a gentle lake only a mile long, now owned by the National Trust, derives its name from the Norse word 'gris' meaning pig, when the surrounding woodlands were used by the early Norse settlers to provide pannage for their swine.

ACCESS

BY ROAD

The A591 from Ambleside and Rydal hugs the eastern shoreline. A minor road from the village heads south alongside the western shore towards Elterwater.

BY FOOT

Primarily the lakeshore path on the western shoreline, encountered on Guided Walk 10. Alternatively, park in the White Moss Common car park on the A591 between Rydal and Grasmere and cross the footbridge at the foot of the lake next to a weir (see Mini Walks).

BY BOAT

The lake is open for canoeing and sailing with boats for hire in front of a refreshment kiosk on the south western shore.

PRINCIPAL VIEWPOINTS

Views of Grasmere are encountered on the following Guided Walks: Walk 9 to Alcock Tarn, Walk 8 to Rydal and Walk 10 from Grasmere itself. Loughrigg Terrace (see Mini Walks) offers views across the length of Grasmere as does Helm Crag at the northern end of the village.

Great Gable

Now the symbol of the National Park, Great Gable's superb location at the head of

Grasmere. Val Corbett.

Wasdale, flanked by Kirk Fell and Lingmell, cannot fail to inspire. Short of the magical 3000 feet by only 50 feet, Great Gable provides some of the finest views in the Lake District. The view from the Westmorland Cairn (erected in 1876) across Wasdale and Wastwater is held by many to be unsurpassed.

The Great Napes crag formations on the southern side of the mountain were in former times central to the development of rock climbing in this country. A particular challenge to the early pioneers was the detached 100 foot Napes Needle, conquered first by Walter Parry Haskett Smith in 1886. Graves in the tiny

Wasdale Head Church record for posterity the dangers associated with rock climbing in this area. Suitably, the Fell and Rock Climbing Club were responsible for purchasing over 1000 acres of Great Gable for the National Trust in 1923 as a memorial to colleagues lost in the war. A memorial plaque on the summit cairn is the site of an annual service on Rememberance Day.

There are several well used routes to the summit, all of which can be hard going. The first, from Wasdale Head, ascends via the Gavel Neese ridge to Beck Head from where there is an obvious route to the summit. The descent is via Windy Gap and Aaron Slack,

passing through the Sty Head Pass and back to Wasdale alongside Lingmell Beck. From Borrowdale, Great Gable is reached via the Sty Head Pass, returning via Green Gable and Sourmilk Gill. A third route, from Honister Pass, is popular given the starting elevation of 1000 feet. This traverses Brandreth to Green Gable and Windy Gap before the final push to the summit.

Grizedale Forest

Grizedale Forest Park has been under the control of the Forestry Commission since 1936 and is now the largest forestry plantation in the Lake District. Strategically sited between Lakes Coniston and Windermere, the original mixed woodland provided a rich source of fuel for the charcoal burners which supplied the smelting furnaces in the area.

As well as being a working forest, Grizedale Forest is a fully fledged leisure area with a visitor and wildlife centre, picnic sites and over 10 miles of cycle trails. Most people however, come for the splendid walks in the forest, with series of waymarked trails of between 1 and 9 miles (see Mini Walks) often rewarding the walker with glimpses of red and roe deer. In addition, intricate wood sculptures have also been strategically sited on the routes. A further attraction is the Theatre in the Forest which has a varied programme each year and capable of seating over 200 people (see Attractions).

Great Gable. Val Corbett.

Hardknott Pass

As the only major route west from central Lakeland, the Hardknott Pass is as important today for motorists heading towards Eskdale and Wasdale as it was for the Romans. What remains of the Roman fort of Mediobogdum at Hardknott is in the care of English Heritage and boasts a stunningly impressive location some 800 feet above sea level overlooking the Eskdale Valley (see Attractions section for directions to the remains).

The need for a fort in such a relatively inhospitable location was an inevitable consequence of protecting the supply route from the large Roman port of Glannoventa (modern day Ravenglass) to the Roman fort at Ambleside (Galava), itself guardian of north south communications in central Lakeland. Built between AD117 and AD138, the Hardknott Fort housed a garrison of 500 men; an inscribed tablet found nearby indicates that the construction was undertaken by a cohort of Dalmatians, originating from what used to be known as Yugoslavia.

The fort was built to a standard Roman plan and contained barrack blocks, granaries, store rooms and a commandant's house. The soldiers' bath house, just to the south of the main structure, can clearly be seen with separate rooms used for the cold, warm and hot stages of their bath. A levelled area to the north east of the fort is believed to have been the parade ground.

The Hardknott Pass reaches a maximum height of 1291 feet and is surpassed only in Lakeland by the Kirkstone Pass, which has an easy wide road by comparison. Reached via the Wrynose Pass which in itself is a thrilling route, the Hardknott Pass is justifiably known as the most difficult road in England. The twisting, dramatic route follows the course of the original Roman road and is mainly single car width with passing places throughout its length. At the height of the season the pass should only be attempted by confident drivers in well maintained vehicles!

Haweswater

Perhaps the loneliest stretch of water in the Lake District, Haweswater's relative inaccessibility ensures it has a lovely, remote atmosphere unlike any other in Lakeland. It is in fact a reservoir; a 120 feet dam at its eastern end has enlarged the lake from two to four miles in length making it the largest reservoir in the

Hardknott Pass. Val Corbett.

Gazetteer

North West. Since 1940 it has been a principal source of water for Manchester; its location 600 feet above sea level allowing relatively easy transportation of water to towns over 50 miles away.

The flooding of the valley included the loss of Mardale Green village although subsequent periods of severe drought have revealed parts of the drowned settlement once again.

ACCESS

BY ROAD

Given its remoteness, Haweswater is relatively traffic free although a minor road runs along its southern shore offering views across the whole of the reservoir.

BY FOOT

From the small car park at the end of the minor road alongside the southern shore, footpaths allow access to the shoreline.

BY BOAT

None

PRINCIPAL VIEWPOINTS

The best views are from the fells at the reservoir's south western tip. These include the summits of High Street and Mardale Ill Bell overlooking Blea Water, Lakeland's deepest tarn.

Haweswater. Val Corbett.

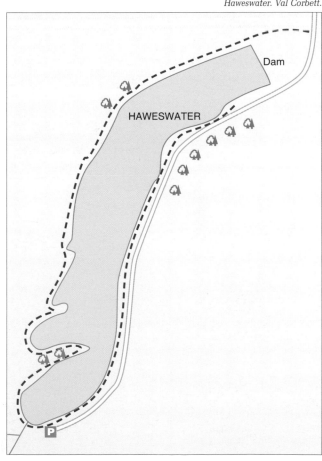

Hawkshead

Situated between Lakes Coniston and Windermere, Hawkshead's name is derived from that of its Norse founder, *'Haukr'*.

Hawkshead has a long history, once owned by the monks of Furness Abbey at the heart of a substantial estate which included the whole of the Grizedale Forest and extending as far north as Borrowdale and the shores of Lake Derwent. The 500 year old Court House to the north of the village is all that remains of Hawkshead Hall, the Abbey's manorial building.

As a market town, Hawkshead was at its height in the latter part of the eighteenth century, although the bulk of the architecture is largely seventeenth century, dating from the village's importance as a centre of the woollen industry, supplying the Kendal mills, makers of the famous 'Kendal Green' cloth.

Wordsworth attended the Old Grammar School here from 1779 to 1787, lodging with Ann Tyson, whose house is passed on the Hawkshead Guided Walk. A further literary connection is the one time solicitors office of William Heelis, husband of Beatrix Potter, which is now in the care of the National Trust and houses an annually changing exhibition of Beatrix Potter's original illustrations from her children's books (see Attractions section for opening times).

Hawkshead, with its narrow streets and whitewashed cottages, complemented by a modern National Park

Hawkshead. Val Corbett.

information centre as well as shops and cafes, consequently gets very busy at peak periods. The sheer charm of the village and its proximity to other tourist 'honeypots' such as Tarn Hows and the Grizedale Forest, ensures the village is usually on the itinary of most visitors to central Lakeland.

Helvellyn

At 3113 feet, Helvellyn is the third highest peak in the Lake District and without doubt the most popular. Easily accessible from the main settlements of central Lakeland, you are unlikely to be alone when reaching the summit. Helvellyn lies at the centre of a broad 6 mile long ridge of peaks stretching from Great Dodd in the north to Dollywagon Pike in the south. The length of the ridge is perhaps best appreciated when in 1926, the summit plateau was able to accommodate an aeroplane landing and taking off again!

The summit has a memorial to a faithful dog which stayed by its master's side for 3 months after he fell to his death below Red Tarn in 1805. A further memorial to a huntsman who died in Nethermost Cove, dates from 1858.

The two sides of Helvellyn are very different, with the west being steep and relatively smooth and the east pockmarked as a result of glacial action in the Ice Age. The western approach can be made from Wythburn Church in the Thirlmere Valley or alternatively from the North West Water Swirls car park further to the north. More popular nowadays is the eastern approach from either Glenridding or Patterdale. Although longer, the ascent is more gradual and more dramatic; the narrow arrete of Striding Edge providing a spectacular final part of the Helvellyn ascent. Descent is usually via Swirral Edge just to the north of Red Tarn, noted as the only mountain tarn to contain the rare schelly fish.

High Street

The highest point (2718 feet) of the most easterly of the main Lake District ridges, High Street also refers to the name of the Roman road that was built across its summit. The ten mile long range of fells, many of which are above 2000 feet, had long been used by Neolithic Man as a communication route providing protection from surprise attack. This route was developed by the Romans as a means of communication between their forts at Brougham, near Penrith, and Ambleside. The southern part of the route which descends into the Troutbeck Valley is known as the Scot's Rake, a reference no doubt to the activities of Scottish raiders in the Middle Ages.

The summit plateau is broad and grassy; its alternative name of Racecourse Hill dating back to the regular meetings of the Mardale shepherds. These were often boisterous events which included wrestling, horse racing and beer drinking although the original purpose of the meetings, to exchange stray sheep, also took place right through to the last meeting in 1835.

The area is seldom crowded with walkers although an increasingly popular route can be traced from Mardale Head at the southern end of Haweswater. This climbs to Small Water and onto the Nan Bield Pass before bearing north to Mardale Ill Bell and across the High Street summit. The descent is via Long Stile and Riggindale with Blea Water below on the right. The latter's depth of water at 207 feet makes it the deepest Lakeland tarn, only the lakes of Windermere and Wastwater are deeper.

Honister Pass

The Honister Pass links Borrowdale with Buttermere in the north west quadrant of the Lake District and rises to a height of 1176 feet, at times in gradients of 1 in 4 with a National Trust car park near to the slate works at the top.

Most traverse the pass east to west on a circular route from Keswick via Borrowdale to Buttermere, returning via the Newlands Valley, and it is this route, known as the 'Buttermere Round' that was popular with nineteenth century tourists when coach

High Street. Val Corbett.

and horses left Keswick at regular intervals for the day long trip. Upon reaching the top of Honister, travellers would be asked to alight and walk down the incline towards Buttermere, the gradient being too much for the horses to cope with fully laden.

Contemporary travellers recorded the extraordinary endeavours of the slate workers who transported the slate down hill at speed on wooden and steel sleds that could carry a quarter of a ton each. Each man would be responsible for 7 or 8 loads per day, the descent of a few minutes followed by a half hour return climb to the quarry face. The slate was highly regarded due to its excellent quality, taking first prize in the Victorian Great Exhibition of 1851.

Slate is still quarried here today; the Buttermere and Westmorland Slate Company near the summit of the pass a continuation of an industry that was first recorded in 1643.

Kendal

The 'Auld Grey Town' of Kendal is an important regional centre sited just outside the south eastern corner of the National Park and within Cumbria second only in size to Carlisle and Barrow.

In 1189, Kendal was the first Lakeland town to receive a market charter. It was here, earlier, that the Romans had established their fort of Aluana in a strategic crook of the River Kent, just south of the town. This guarded supply routes to Ambleside and across the High Street mountain range to a further fort at Brocavum near Penrith. The Normans in turn recognised the opportunity for an important centre and the remains of an eleventh century fort can be seen at Castle Howe on the west side of the town. A second castle, this time of stone, was built in the thirteenth century on the eastern side of the River Kent and it was here that Henry VIII's last wife Katherine Parr was born. Her marriage gift to the king was a coat made of 'Kendal Green' cloth, symbolic of the industry that led to Kendal's prosperity. Flemish weavers had settled in Kendal from about the thirteenth century and had stimulated the growth of an important woollen industry. The 'Kendal Green' cloth was the mainstay of their exports; reference is made to the fabric in Henry IV (Part1) in addition to it being the traditional garb of Robin Hood.

A further product for which

Kendal. Val Corbett.

Gazetteer

Kentmere. Val Corbett.

the town is well known is Kendal Mint Cake, a hard mint flavoured sweet, favoured by mountaineers for its energy giving qualities, found on sale throughout the area.

Held every year in late August is the Kendal 'gathering'; a festival of music, exhibitions and entertainment that ends with a torchlight procession.

Modern attractions include the National Trust property of Sizergh Castle and a Museum of Natural History and Archeology. The Abbot Hall Art Gallery and Museum of Lakeland Life and Industry provide a further draw for the visitor (see Attractions).

Kentmere

A long quiet valley, stretching north from Staveley near Windermere to the small hamlet that gives the valley its name, the area is principally the destination of walkers seeking to escape the busier central fells. A popular destination is the High Street mountain range lying to the north of Kentmere Reservoir, built to regulate water supplies to the mills in the valley below. Walkers also cross to the Troutbeck Valley in the west and the Longsleddale Valley in the east.

Kentmere can seem remote and isolated, its lack of a lake deterring the large number of visitors who are attracted to nearby Windermere for example. It is surprising however that such a place in the nineteenth century, could have achieved notoriety for the reputation of its public house. Now a private residence, the pub was the first in England to lose its licence as a result of drunkenness and immorality!

Keswick

Keswick's outstanding position between the huge bulk of Skiddaw and the gentle beauty of Derwentwater, acts as a magnet for visitors to the area. Now the major centre of tourism in the northern lakes, the town's growth as a tourist resort began in the late nineteenth century. The extension of the rail network to Keswick in 1865 saw to it that the town's future lay in serving the needs of an increasingly mobile population who came to wonder at the surrounding landscape. Much of the original interest in the area had been aroused by the writings of the Romantic poets such as Coleridge and Southey, who made the town their home. This coupled with the Wordsworth influence throughout Lakeland resulted in Keswick providing a natural base from which to see the attractions of Borrowdale, Buttermere and Derwentwater.

With hindsight, the surge of tourism could not have come at a better time as the two industries upon which Keswick had previously been based, mining and wool, were in serious decline. Important deposits of lead and copper and to a lesser extent gold and silver had been mined from the fifteenth century in the nearby Newlands Valley. The founding of the Company of Mines Royal by Elizabeth I in 1565 led to increasing prosperity in the area with Bavarian mining experts brought in to supervise mineral extraction. Graphite

Keswick. Val Corbett.

found in the area had led to the formation of the Cumberland Pencil Company, the first pencil factory in the world and now a museum open to the public (see Attractions). Similarly, as with the once important woollen industry in the sixteenth and seventeenth centuries, mining activity gradually declined, leaving today, the attractive market town that visitors to Keswick enjoy.

Consequently, there is a wealth of activity for visitors in the Keswick area, with few able to resist the charms of Derwentwater itself, generally regarded as the 'Queen of the Lakes'. Launches circuit the

lake from the piers adjacent to the lakeside car park, the location also of Keswick's Century Theatre. Originally a travelling theatre, the 'Blue Box' is now permanently based in Keswick. Sited just outside of the town, is the Neolithic Stone Circle of Castlerigg, smaller in size and scope than Stonehenge though its mountain setting arguably giving the antiquity a more dramatic experience.

For the visitor, the town has a wealth of shops and restaurants as well as a National Park information centre in the Moot Hall, one of Keswick's oldest buildings, dating from 1813.

Kirkby Lonsdale. Val Corbett.

Kirkby Lonsdale

Lying some 15 miles to the south east of Kendal, Kirkby (pronounced Kirby) Lonsdale is situated amidst gloriously scenic countryside with impressive views over the River Lune Valley. Indeed, in the north of the town is Ruskin's View, the nineteenth century artist and philanthropist considering it *'...one of the loveliest scenes in England'*.

Kirkby Lonsdale is one of Cumbria's oldest towns with a settlement here since Roman times, a parish church recorded as early as the Domesday Book and a market charter dating from 1227. The Queen Elizabeth School was founded as a free Grammer School in 1591.

Present day visitors are drawn to the beauty of the fifteenth century Devil's Bridge, a three arched crossing of the River Lune. The bridge is so named because of the legend that it was constructed by Satan himself. Nearby, at Cowan Bridge, Charlotte Bronte attended the school.

Kirkby Stephen

Lying at the head of the fertile Eden Valley, Kirkby Stephen is a small market town, formerly at the centre of a knitted stocking industry. The ancient and attractive church of St Stephen, built in the thirteenth century, contains the unusual 'Bound Devil', a figure of Satan chained and horned as well as an effigy to Sir Richard de Musgrave who is reputed to have killed the last wild boar in the district during the fifteenth century.

Nearby is Pendragon Castle, connected in local legend with Uther, father of King Arthur. The castle in fact dates much later, from Norman times, was burnt by the Scots and subsequently restored in both the fourteenth and sixteenth centuries.

Kirkstone Pass. Val Corbett.

Kirkstone Pass

At 1481 feet, the Kirkstone Pass is the highest road pass in the Lake District (though much less of a driving challenge than the passes of Hardknott, Wrynose or even Honister) and usually the first to get snow. To the uninitiated, especially in winter, it may seem that the top of the pass is continually covered in 'fog'. This in fact is not the case, instead you are now driving at such a height above sea level that you are actually passing through low cloud! On clear days however, the height of the pass ensures excellent panoramic views across the Troutbeck and Patterdale valleys .

The southern end of the Kirkstone Pass is joined by roads from Ambleside and Windermere, the former known as the 'struggle'. This dates from a time when horse drawn carriages could not traverse the pass without passengers alighting and proceeding on foot. Luckily, just below the summit of the pass is the Kirkstone Inn, the third highest inn in England and over the years a welcome refreshment stop for visitors. The derivation of the Kirkstone name is attributed to a rock formation resembling a church ('*Kirk*'), found on a fell near here.

The pass descends in the north to the Patterdale Valley and Ullswater, passing the picturesque tarn of Brotherswater and nearby hamlet of Hartsop, famous for its seventeenth century spinning galleries built onto several of the cottages here. A guided walk circling Brotherswater and visiting Hartsop can be found in the Guided Walks section.

Langdale Pikes

The central location of the Langdale Pikes, within easy reach from Grasmere and Ambleside, ensures that this is not a place for those seeking solitude. Indeed, the sheer pressure of hundreds of thousands of feet each year seriously threatens the landscape which has attracted visitors for so long. Only the footpath restoration work carried out by the National Park Authority and the National Trust prevents more serious damage. The combination of large visitor numbers and the dramatic mountain landscape, results in the Langdale Mountain Rescue Team being one of the busiest in Britain. What attracts the visitor is superb fell walking, breathtaking

Langdale Pikes. Val Corbett.

views and some of the best rock climbing crags in Lakeland. Gimmer Crag and Raven Crag on the southern face are almost as impressive as Pavey Ark, a towering wall of rock overlooking Stickle Tarn.

The Langdale Pikes refer specifically to two summits, Harrison Stickle (2403 feet) and Pike of Stickle (2323 feet). These provide the distinctive humps that can be seen from across south eastern Lakeland. Three other summits are also generally regarded as within the Langdale range; Bow Fell (2960 feet), Crinkle Crags (2876 feet) and Pike of Blisco (2304 feet). They are to the west and south of the Pikes and make up the remainder of the mountain ridge dominating the head of the Great Langdale Valley.

The Pike of Stickle summit is well known as the site of one of Britain's earliest industries. A vein of hard volcanic rock was used by Neolithic Man to make stone axes which were traded throughout the country. The level of activity here has led archaeologists to dub the area 'axe factories', part of the scree is undoubtedly waste from their activities.

The Langdales most popular route is in an anticlockwise direction from New Dungeon Ghyll Hotel past Dungeon Ghyll Force and on across Stickle Ghyll. From Stickle Tarn with the cliffs of Pavey Ark above, a path ascends to Harrison Stickle before descending via Loft Crag.

Loweswater

Tucked away in a wooded valley in the far west, the National Trust owned Loweswater is a quiet gentle lake that is rarely busy. Due to its location on the edge of the National Park, Loweswater is often forgotten although its one mile length allows an excellent lake circuit, described in Guided Walk 20. The "leafy lake" is unique within the Lake District in that it is the only lake which

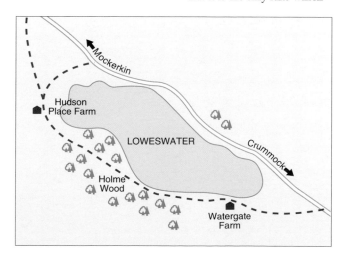

Maryport

drains towards the centre of Lakeland; to Crummock Water with which it was once joined.

National Trust signs warn against bathing or drinking water from the lake due to the presence of blue/green algae.

ACCESS

BY ROAD

A minor road from Mockerkin off the A5086 south of Cockermouth follows the northern shore with views across the vale to Crummock and its distinctive fell of Mellbreak.

BY FOOT

Guided Walk 20 offers a four mile circuit of the lake

passing through Holme Wood on its southern shoreline.

BY BOAT

Boat hire is available from the National Trust Watergate Farm at the south eastern end of the lake.

PRINCIPAL VIEWPOINTS

Largely low level viewing from around the lake.

Situated on the north western coastal plain of Cumbria, Maryport was the site of a Roman port built to complement the more important Roman harbour at Ravenglass, far to the south. A nearby fort, dating from the fifth century, guarded the supply route and was one of a series of fortifications constructed by the Romans in the Solway Firth area, then the furthest northern outpost of their known world.

Today's small industrial town owes its development to Humphrey Senhouse, Lord of the Manor, who decided to develop the small fishing village of Ellenfoot into a coal

Loweswater. Val Corbett.

Sculpture, Maryport. Val Corbett.

port during the 1750's. With its name taken from the wife of the founder, the settlement of Maryport, like Whitehaven, was a planned town with terraces of cottages built on a gridiron concept and employment centring on coal mining and ship building. Planned as a rival to the prosperous port of Whitehaven, Maryport enjoyed moderate success although the harbour was eventually closed to shipping in 1961.

Following the growth of tourism, Maryport harbour has been developed into an interesting place to visit with three steam powered tugs open to the public, including the *Flying Buzzard*, built in 1951. Nearby is a maritime museum housing a wealth of objects, pictures, models and paintings illustrating the proud maritime tradition of the area.

Old Man of Coniston

The most southerly of the major Lakeland peaks, the Old Man of Coniston overlooks the village and lake of the same name. At 2631 feet, it is only 1 foot higher than its northern neighbour, Swirl How.

The summit provides excellent views across Coniston Water and towards Morecambe Bay, consequently the mountain is popular with walkers throughout the year.

This is classic fellwalking country with attractive tarns (Low Water and Goat's Water) as well as impressive ridge walks and towering crags. Of the latter, Dow Crag is the most famous; its 600 foot wall providing a draw for rock climbers since its first ascent in 1886.

Man's impact on the surrounding landscape is clearly visible in the form of disused mine buildings and spoil heaps from the copper mining industry in the valley above Church Beck (Coppermines Valley). German miners brought down from Keswick were instrumental in establishing an industry that was to last 350 years. At its height in the nineteenth century, several hundred miners were employed at

Old Man Coniston. Val Corbett.

depths of over a thousand feet.

Even earlier evidence of man's activity in the area provides one of the main routes used to climb the Old Man. The Walna Scar Road on its south western flank follows the route of a prehistoric track, later used as a packhorse route. The track passes the tiny Boo Tarn and across Little Arrow Moor before turning right to pass alongside Goat's Water. Keen ridgewalkers can alternatively continue ahead on a thrilling route along Brown Pike and the top of Dow Crag. Descent from the Old Man summit can be via the track heading east past Low Water and via Church Beck. However, many prefer to continue the ridge walk to Levers Hawse and onto Swirl How, descending from Swirl Hawse past Levers Water. An option from Swirl

How is to ascend the final summit of Wetherlam (2502 feet).

As a word of warning, it is advisable to remember that the previous mining activity here can present dangers for the unwary. Keep to the obvious tracks and be confident of good weather before climbing.

Penrith

Penrith, a large town acting as a regional centre for the north eastern Lake District, lies just outside the National Park boundary. Its position on the strategic route to and from Scotland resulted in its development since Roman times as a military centre. The Roman fort of Brocavum was built a mile downstream on

the River Eamont and housed a thousand soldiers. In turn, the stone from the ruins of the fort was used by the Normans to build Brougham Castle and to this day substantial parts of the castle remain with maintenance carried out by English Heritage. A further castle was built in Penrith itself in 1399, the red sandstone remains of which can be visited at Castle Park (see Attractions).

The need for all this military fortification resulted from the border warfare that troubled the town for many centuries when it was attacked and burned by the Scots on at least three occasions, in 1314, 1345 and 1382. A hill to the north of the town was the site of a beacon, much used to warn of approaching danger.

Today, Penrith is a pleasant market town with many shops and fortunately much quieter

Pillar

since the M6 replaced the A6 as the major communication north.

South of the town at Eamont Bridge are two prehistoric sites of note. King Arthur's Round Table believed to have been constructed around 3,000 years ago, is a sizeable earthwork, the purpose of which is unknown but was possibly used as a meeting place. Nearby Mayburgh Henge, dating from the same period, consists of a huge circular embankment nearly 400 feet in diameter with a nine foot standing stone at its centre, probably the remainder of what was once a stone circle (both antiquities are detailed in the Attractions section).

Deep in the heart of the western fells near Ennerdale lies Pillar, at 2927 feet Lakeland's seventh highest peak and famed home to Pillar Rock, a stunning 500 foot buttress protruding vertically from the fellside. The first recorded ascent of the outcrop

Pillar. Val Corbett.

Pooley Bridge. Val Corbett.

was by a local shepherd, John Atkinson, in 1826, only a few years before guide books had declared Pillar Rock as 'unclimbable'. The buttress sits on the northern (Ennerdale) side of Pillar though probably the best place to see the daring climbers at work is from Robinson's Cairn on the western approach path to the summit. This is part of the most popular route to Pillar, starting behind the Wasdale Head Inn near Wastwater and passing along the western flank of Kirk Fell before climbing to the Black Sail Pass. From here it is a case of bearing west to the summit, the deep glacial trough of Mosedale below to your left and the afforested slopes of Ennerdale below on the right. A longer and more tiring route

is from Ennerdale, starting at the Bowness Knott parking area and passing through Ennerdale Forest to the Black Sail Youth Hostel, England's remotest, before climbing to Looking Stead and then on to Pillar. A circular walk using this route is attained by returning via Scoat Fell and bearing right from Haycock to descend via Tewit How.

Pooley Bridge

Pooley Bridge, a quiet hamlet, which derives its name from an attractive stone bridge over the River Eamont which drains north from Ullswater, is served with several pubs and cafes, together with a

National Park Information Centre. Adjacent to the bridge is a small car park which can be used as the starting point for a walk alongside the river or to the small hillock of Dunmallard Hill (see Mini Walks). Archeologists have discovered the remains of an Iron Age hill fort here and recovered a number of stone axes. Pooley Bridge is the third and most northerly calling point of the Ullswater Lake Steamers which also stop at Glenridding and Howton. A superb seven mile walk along the southern shores of Ullswater from Howton leads back to the steamer departure point at Glenridding.

Two miles away is Dalemain, a Georgian country house with medieval origins and landscaped gardens.

Ravenglass

Ravenglass is the only true coastal town within the National Park, with the gullery on nearby Drigg Dunes being an important maritime nature reserve and home to Europe's largest colony of Black Headed Gulls.

A settlement was originally established here as a result of Roman activity, for it was here that the important Roman supply port of Glannoventa was set up. Ravenglass was therefore a regional supply point for much of the north west with a Roman road created through the Hardknott Pass to the Roman fort at Ambleside. The Hardknott Fort, the remains of which are now in the care of English Heritage was built to guard the supply route from the port

through to Eskdale.

Ravenglass itself was occupied by the Romans for over 300 years and had a garrison of a thousand soldiers. Although the remains of the fort here were obliterated by the development of a railway in the nineteenth century, the bath house known as Walls Castle (see Attractions) which has the tallest surviving walls of any Roman building in northern Britain, can be visited. The extent of the remains found in the area has led some scholars to believe that Ravenglass might have been developed as a supply base for an invasion of Ireland which subsequently did not take place.

Ravenglass is also home to 'L'aal Ratty', the Ravenglass and Eskdale Miniature Railway which follows a

seven mile route from Ravenglass to Dalegarth Station in Eskdale. Originally constructed to transport granite and copper ore from the Eskdale mines, the line is now a major tourist attraction with services operating throughout the year (see Attractions). The train stops at 7 stations en route, the first from Ravenglass is at Muncaster Mill, a restored working water mill. From here it is a short walk to Muncaster Castle, an owl conservation centre and home to the Pennington family since the thirteenth century. Within the Guided Walks section is a five mile walk across nearby Muncaster Fell using the train on the return journey. This walk offers the chance to visit both the castle and the mill if a full day is at hand.

Ravenglass. Val Corbett.

Dora's Field near Rydal Church. Val Corbett.

Rydal

The small hamlet of Rydal, south of Grasmere, does not receive as many visitors as its larger neighbour, although its attractions in the form of a lake and a Wordsworth residence are similar.

Wordsworth spent the last 37 years of his life at Rydal Mount (see Attractions), moving here from Grasmere in 1813. By this time he was already famous and fairly wealthy, using the house to receive many visitors. His time here was marred by some sadness though; his beloved sister Dorothy had a long mental illness and his daughter Dora died. Dora's Field, behind Rydal Church, was bought by Wordsworth and planted with daffodils in her memory, the National Trust being its current guardian. Wordsworth's period here lacked the productivity of earlier years with his best work generally felt to be whilst at Dove Cottage in Grasmere. He

almost seems to have tired of writing, preferring instead to tend the substantial gardens at the house. Indeed during the seven years as Poet Laureate before his death in 1850, Wordsworth produced no poetry.

Guided Walk 8 circuits Rydal Water and passes Rydal Mount and church.

Rydal Water

A popular lake in central Lakeland given its attractive location and Wordsworth connections. It is one of the district's smallest lakes, only half a mile long and with a maximum depth of just sixty feet. Steps lead up to

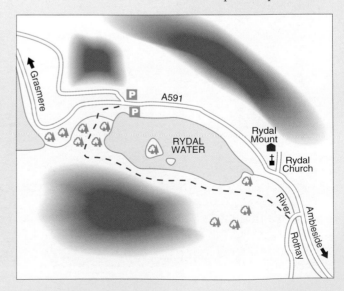

'Wordsworth's Seat', a rocky knoll at the western end of the lake, reportedly the favourite viewpoint of the poet.

At its eastern end the River Rothay flows under the attractive stone architecture of Pelter Bridge draining both Grasmere and Rydal into Windermere.

Overlooking the lake is Nab Cottage, now a guest house but once familiar to the Wordworths as the one time home of Hartley Coleridge, Samuel Taylor's son. Hartley was a favourite of the Wordsworths and is buried close to them in the graveyard at Grasmere. Nab Cottage was also home to Thomas De Quincey, author of the notorious 'Confessions of an English Opium Eater'. His marriage to a farmer's daughter, Margaret Simpson, was thought to be ill-judged by the increasingly snobbish Wordsworths and their close circle. Dorothy had never forgiven De Quincey for the garden alterations at Dove Cottage after he took over the tenancy following the Wordsworth's move to Allan Bank.

ACCESS

BY ROAD

The A591 from Ambleside to Grasmere skirts the northern shoreline though a far better way to view the lake is to follow the old Ambleside road south from Dove Cottage, rejoining the A591 at White Moss Quarry car park.

BY FOOT

See Guided Walk 8. Alternatively, the southern shore can easily be accessed from the White Moss Quarry car park on the A591 between Rydal and Grasmere (see Mini Walks).

BY BOAT

None

PRINCIPAL VIEWPOINTS

Loughrigg Terrace and White Moss Common provide the most popular viewpoints; both are described in the Mini Walks Section.

Rydal from White Moss Common. Val Corbett.

Sawreys
(Near & Far)

Made up of two hamlets, Near and Far, referring to their distance from Esthwaite Water, not as one might expect from the nearby Windermere ferry by which most visitors would reach them. Nevertheless Near Sawrey is the larger and more famous of the two, it being the one time home of Beatrix Potter.

Beatrix lived in London with her parents for much of her life, holidaying with them each summer in the Lake District overlooking Lake Windermere at Wray Castle. Later, the family started to holiday near Esthwaite Water, an area which captured Beatrix's imagination. The royalties from her first book,

Peter Rabbit, allowed her to buy Hill Top, now in the care of the National Trust and open to the public. She was at her most productive here, until her eventual marriage to a local solicitor William Heelis led to a move to Castle farm in the same village. Here she assumed the role of a landowning farmer developing a special interest in the native Cumbrian Herdwick sheep. The Herdwick is a hardy breed which has some genetic similarities with Scandinavian species suggesting they may have been imported at the time of the Viking settler invasions of the tenth century. Following her death in 1943, Beatrix Potter's flocks were bequeathed to the National Trust along with substantial land holdings.

Scafell Pike and Sca Fell

The Scafell (pronounced Scawfell) Pike summit of 3210 feet is the highest point in England and consequently a magnet for serious hill walkers. It stands only 48 feet above the neighbouring summit of Sca Fell, although the broken crags of Broad Stand prevent any direct route between the two. The summit can be crowded in high season, unlike the famous ascent by Samuel Taylor Coleridge on August 5th 1802. The essayist was so impressed by the view that he wrote to his friend Wordsworth from the summit, the first ever to do so.

The Scafell Group lie in the heart of Lakeland, an area

Far Sawrey. Val Corbett.

where the geology belongs to the Borrowdale Volcanics, a hard rock characterised by chasms and crags. The boulder strewn surfaces are in direct comparison to the smooth, rounded form of summits such as Cat Bells and Skiddaw in the north of the Lake District where the underlying geology is of slate. For this reason, the Scafell range, the very top of England, became a centre for British rock climbing. The Fell and Rock Climbing Club was founded at Wasdale Head in 1886, since when climbers have headed for the challenges of Scafell Crag and Broad Stand.

Over 2,500 acres of the main range including the Scafell Pike Summit is owned by the National Trust. Much of this land was donated during the early 1920's in tribute to the fallen of the First World War. A plaque has been positioned on the summit as a memorial.

There are many routes to the summit of Scafell Pike, all of which must be treated with respect. The geography of the mountains here can be very confusing and treacherous in poor visibility or bad weather. The shortest and steepest route is from Wasdale Head via Lingmell Gill, Brown Tongue and Hollow Stones. Alternative, longer routes commence from Seathwaite in Borrowdale and Brotherilkeld in Eskdale. From Seathwaite, the route is via Sty Head Gill and the Sty Head Pass before following the corridor route on the western flanks of Scafell Pike. From Brotherilkeld ascend via a long and demanding route on the eastern side of the River Esk, crossing the Great Moss basin and on to the summit via either Mickledore or Little Narrowcove.

Seathwaite

More famous than its namesake in the Duddon Valley, Seathwaite in Borrowdale has the reputation as the wettest place in England, with a current average rainfall of around 125 inches per year. Rainguage Cottage, the site of the original measuring instrument, is owned by the National Trust along with large parts of the valley.

Seathwaite Fell to the south was the site of an important graphite mine which was instrumental in prompting the establishment of Keswick's famous pencil industry.

Today, Seathwaite is primarily the destination of walkers who come to explore the high surrounding fells of Great Gable and Glaramara and of course the long haul via the Styhead Pass to the Scafell range and England's highest mountain, Scafell Pike.

Nearby is the tiny hamlet of Seatoller, nestling at the eastern foot of the 1 in 4 Honister Pass which links the Borrowdale and Buttermere valleys. The pretty collection of cottages originally grew up to house workers employed in the slate quarries near the top of the Honister Pass. The main packhorse route for the transportation of the slate led west from Seatoller via Seathwaite and the Styhead Pass to Wasdale and the coast.

A National Park information centre is found in a converted barn in the centre of the hamlet.

Scafell. Val Corbett.

Sedbergh

Situated some 10 miles east of Kendal in the Lune Valley, Sedbergh is an attractive market town with a Yorkshire Dales feel about it though it has been part of modern day Cumbria for over 20 years. Much of the present town dates from the late eighteenth and early nineteenth centuries; the cobbled streets and laid back atmosphere adding to the overall ambiance.

Sedbergh School, founded in 1525, is a well known seat of learning: famous pupils include William Wordsworth's son and more recently, Will Carling, former captain of the England Rugby team.

Sedbergh also makes an excellent place from which to explore the Howgill Fells, that favourite destination of the redoubtable Wainwright.

Shap

The small village of Shap lies on the A6 below the barren and lonely Shap Fells which mark the eastern boundary of the National Park. The settlement grew up to house workers from the nearby granite quarries, the stone from which was used in the building of St. Pancras Station and the Albert Memorial.

The remains of Shap Abbey, dating from 1180, are situated beside the River Lowther to the west of the village. The Abbey was the last to be dissolved, probably as a result of its use as a shelter point on the major communications route north. The west tower survives fairly intact with the whole site in the care of English Heritage (see Attractions).

Shap Abbey. Val Corbett.

Skiddaw

At 3054 feet, Skiddaw is the smallest of the four peaks in the Lake District over the important 3,000 feet mark and the easiest to climb. As a consequence, family parties can often be seen ascending the broad track to the top throughout much of the year. Skiddaw's towering bulk combines with the neighbouring summit of Blencathra to act as an obvious northern boundary to the Lake District. Their northern slopes are unpopulated and lonely, referred to by locals as 'Back o' Skiddaw'. The mountain is a gigantic lump of slate, the oldest rocks in Lakeland and some of the oldest in the world. Consequently, Skiddaw's landscape is rounded and smooth, its lack of drama accounting for some people dismissing the mountain as dull or boring. However, although the ascent is not dramatic, it is undertaken in order to enjoy the tremendous views across Derwentwater, Bassenthwaite, Borrowdale and central Lakeland. On clear days Scotland, the Pennines and the Isle of Man are also visible.

The ascent of Skiddaw is recorded as popular as far back as the seventeenth century. Wordsworth and Southey, the Poet Laureate, held a famous picnic and bonfire on its summit in 1815, celebrating Wellington's victory at the battle of Waterloo. The arrival of the railway at Keswick in the 1860's saw the growth of 'mass tourism' for the first time with Skiddaw the most frequented target of visitors to the area.

Present day visitors generally ascend from the Underscar car park, located to the east of Applethwaite, the route via Jenkin Hill, Little Man and on to the Skiddaw summit plateau. An alternative route, shorter and steeper, is from Millbeck (west of Applethwaite) and ascending via White Stones and Carl Side.

Skiddaw. Val Corbett.

St. Bees Head

Cumbria's most westerly point, St. Bees Head is a 300 foot high headland just to the south of Whitehaven. It was here that St. Bega, an Irish nun, was shipwrecked in the seventh century. Befriended by Lady Egremont, the legend goes that St. Bega and the other surviving nuns decided to build a priory here and duly asked Lord Egremont for some land on which to build. His response given in mid summer, decreed that they could have any land covered by snow the following day. Not surprisingly, some land between the castle and the sea was duly covered in snow the following day allowing the building of St. Bees priory to commence.

A nature reserve on the headland harbours England's only colony of Black Guillemots.

Thirlmere

Thirlmere is located to the west of the Helvellyn range and just north of Dunmail Raise, the traditional north/south dividing line of the Lake District. Thirlmere has a controversial place in Lakeland history for it was the first reservoir to be flooded by the Manchester Waterworks Corporation. Previously, the vale had contained a small lake, Leatheswater, crossed by a bridge with the settlements of Armboth in the north and Wythburn in the south. All

St Bees. Val Corbett.

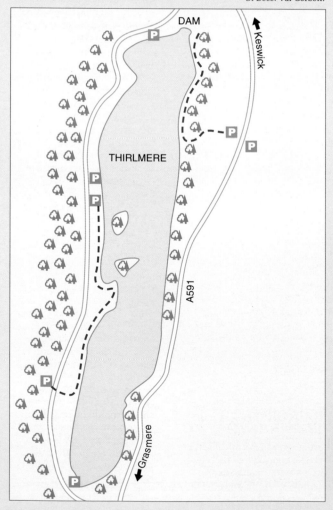

DAM

Keswick

THIRLMERE

A591

Grasmere

Thirlmere. Val Corbett.

this was submerged at the end of the nineteenth century when the construction of a dam raised the water level by fifty feet. Only Wythburn church, situated on slightly higher ground, escaped.

This took place against a background of considerable opposition, both on a local and national basis. Although the protesters lost the Thirlmere battle, the campaign was something of a catalyst for the setting up of the National Trust, formed in 1895.

The conifers planted throughout the valley from 1908 have lost some of their austere appearance with broadleaf tree species increasingly planted nowadays.

ACCESS
BY ROAD

East   The A591 runs the length of the eastern shore, with good views particularly from the Station Coppice car park situated midway along the lake's length.

West   A minor road can be accessed at both ends of the lake offering only occasional glimpses of Thirlmere because of it being fairly well wooded. Lakeside views are therefore somewhat restricted.

BY FOOT

East   See Guided Walk 12 from Swirls or Station Coppice car parks.

West   A 2 mile lakeside path runs from Armboth car park to Dobgill. Similar access can be obtained from the Steel End car park at the south of the lake.

BY BOAT
None

PRINCIPAL VIEWPOINTS

From the Helvellyn range in the east and Watendlath Fells in the west, especially the summit of High Tove (1665 feet) accessed from Armboth

car park. The return from Harrop Tarn (see Mini Walks) also provides a good view up the length of Thirlmere.

Troutbeck

Both a village and a valley, located north of Windermere on the approach to the Kirkstone pass. The village is a conservation area and stretches the mile between Townend and Town Head on the northern side of the valley. The seventeenth and eighteenth century 'statesman' or yeoman farms and cottages for which the area is well known were built around a series of wells, the most famous example being at Townend itself. Acquired by the National Trust in 1944, the house was the Browne family's residence right from its construction in 1626. Carved woodwork as well as books and furniture from the family's period of occupation, can be seen (see Attractions section for opening availability).

The famous sheep farm of Beatrix Potter, Troutbeck Park Farm, occupies nearly 2,000 acres of the north eastern part of the valley. After Potter's marriage she became an accomplished sheep farmer, leaving strict instructions in her bequest to the National Trust that only the native breed of Cumbria, Herdwick sheep, should be raised on her properties. The Roman road traversing the High Street mountain range enters the property near Thornthwaite Crag.

Gazetteer

Ullswater

At 7.5 miles in length, Ullswater is the second largest lake in Lakeland, with only Windermere longer. Ullswater's rather sinuous shape ensures that the visitor needs to gain height before much of the entirety of the lake can be seen. It is still however generally regarded as one of the most beautiful of Lakeland's waters, its head firmly in the mountains of Patterdale before curving around Place Fell and stretching to Pooley Bridge. Ullswater has several basins, the deepest of which is found between Aira Point and Birk Fell at just over 200 feet. Its name derives from a previous Norse owner *'Ulf'* and is the only lake to contain the rare schelly fish.

The Wordsworths were familiar with the valley; William describing Ullswater as the "happiest combination of beauty and grandeur, which any of the Lakes affords". Gowbarrow Park on Ullswater's northern shore near Aira Force is where

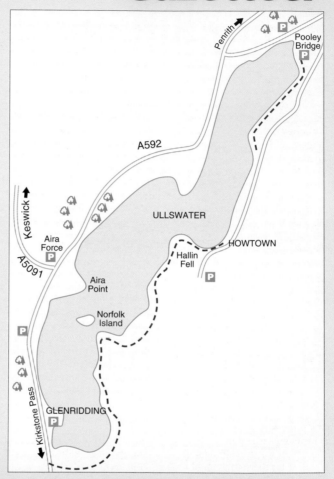

Ullswater. Val Corbett.

William and Dorothy famously encountered the 'golden host' of daffodils that was to become the subject of William's most famous poem.

ACCESS

BY ROAD

There are a number of lakeshore parking areas offering views across the lake on its northern shore between Glenridding and Pooley Bridge (A592). A minor road runs halfway along the southern shore from Pooley Bridge but with only an occasional sight of the lake.

BY FOOT

Possibly the best lakeshore walk in Lakeland is found on Ullswater's south eastern shore. The seven mile non circular route from Howtown to Glenridding provides striking views across Ullswater's most attractive section (this walk starts by taking a steamer trip from Glenridding - see Attractions). Alternatively, Hallin Fell (see Mini Walks) provides a short but fairly steep ascent with excellent views. Gowbarrow Fell and Yew Crag are similarly worthwhile and are included in Guided Walk 13.

BY BOAT

Courtesy of the Ullswater Navigation Company who run a steamer service from Pooley Bridge to Glenridding calling in at Howtown (see Attractions)

PRINCIPAL VIEWPOINTS

Namely Hallin Fell, Gowbarrow Fell and Yew Crag.

Ulverston

Situated on the Furness Peninsula south of the National Park, Ulverston, named after its Saxon founder *'Ulph'*, grew steadily following the granting of a market charter in the thirteenth century. In the eighteenth century a population explosion occurred, following the construction of a mile long canal linking the town with the Leven Estuary and Morecambe Bay. Ulverston became a busy port and shipbuilding centre exporting iron ore, slate, timber and gunpowder. However, it was not to last. Unlike other towns which benefited massively from the railways, the arrival of the railway at Ulverston in 1856 led to a *decline* in the town's fortunes as it provided an alternative, cheaper method of transporting goods. Parts of the canal fell into disuse and the population declined by 70% from its peak of 50,000.

As well as being a pleasant country market town, Ulverston is noted as the birthplace of Stan Laurel, where a small museum commemorates the actor and comedian's life (see Attractions).

Ulverston. Val Corbett.

Wasdale. Val Corbett.

Wasdale

A remote valley in the far west, Wasdale is surrounded by some of the highest peaks in the Lake District. The name of the valley derives from its lake Wast Water, at 258 feet the deepest in England. The lake is bordered by The Screes, a high ridge of tumbled rock giving a real sense of darkness and foreboding. This coupled with the peaks of Great Gable and the Scafell Pike range draws visitors to sample a rawness and isolation unlike any other in the Lake District.

The late nineteenth century saw Wasdale at the height of its fame, for it is generally regarded as the birthplace of British rock climbing. Climbers came to tackle the challenging rock formations of Great Gable, the most famous of which, Napes Needle, was first climbed by Walter Parry Haskett-Smith in 1886. The tiny St. Olafs Church contains several graves of climbers lost in the surrounding mountains, although it was over 100 years after the church was built before it was licensed for burials. Previously, coffins had to be transported on a 'corpse' route across Burn Moor to Boot in Eskdale.

Wasdale Head, a small hamlet near the head of the valley, boasts of holding four English records. The highest mountain (Scafell Pike at 3206 feet), the deepest lake (Wast Water) and the smallest church (St. Olafs). The fourth record, that of biggest liar, refers to a previous landlord of the Wasdale Head Inn, Will Ritson. Ritson was renowned in the area for his tall stories and has a nearby waterfall named after him. The Inn can be used as a refreshment stop on a guided walk around Wasdale which is listed in the Guided Walks section.

Wastwater

Adjectives such as foreboding, grim, austere and awesome are all justifiably used to describe England's deepest lake. A combination of dramatic mountain landscape at the head of the valley (home to Scafell Pike, England's highest mountain) and the menacing magnificence of The Screes ensures Wastwater leaves a lasting impression on all of its visitors. The Screes are a 2000 foot high mass of broken rock which plunge sharply into the lake and continue underwater for some distance at the same angle. This landscape provides few nutrients within the lake which has a dark, almost black appearance that even *looks* deep. The bed of the lake, some 258 feet below the surface is actually 58 feet below the level of the Irish Sea; its cold depths home to the charr. The lake is in the care of the National Trust and provides carefully managed water supplies to the nuclear power station at Sellafield.

ACCESS

BY ROAD

A narrow minor road runs the length of Wastwater's northern shore to the hamlet of Wasdale Head. The relatively treeless landscape ensures excellent views across the lake.

BY FOOT

Guided Walk 5 explores Wasdale Head and approaches the most northerly part of the lake. A lakeside path continues under The Screes although the nature of the landscape here provides a very unstable terrain.

BY BOAT

None

PRINCIPAL VIEWPOINTS

The treeless nature of the landscape allows unforgettable views from very low levels. If your desire is to go higher, Illgill Head above The Screes or Yewbarrow and Kirk Fell can be climbed.

Wastwater. Val Corbett.

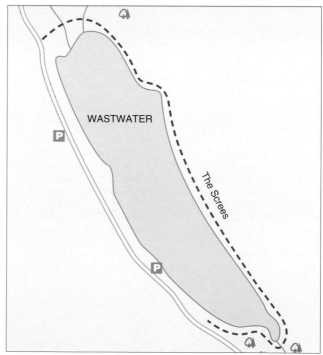

Gazetteer

Watendlath. Val Corbett.

Watendlath

The National Trust owned hamlet of Watendlath sits high between the Borrowdale and Thirlmere valleys. It is 847 feet above sea level with an attractive blue black tarn surrounded by fells in a classic 'hanging valley'. This occurs when glacial action has resulted in a valley being left behind by a more substantial valley, in this case the creation of Borrowdale. Consequently 'hanging valleys' usually have a waterfall where the two valleys meet and in this example Watendlath Beck sources the falls at Lodore.

The falls were a must for the Victorian tourist as much as they are today and directions to them are described in the Mini Walks section.

Watendlath has an attractive packhorse bridge, a National Trust tearoom and a cottage close to the car park which is marked as the fictional home of the heroine of Hugh Walpole's novel, *Judith Paris*. All of this ensures a steady stream of visitors to the hamlet. However, it can be quite an ordeal for the driver in high season as Watendlath is reached via a very narrow road with passing places. A better alternative is to park in Rosthwaite in Borrowdale and follow the well marked path

across Grange Fell. Watendlath Tarn is revealed to the walker in all its glory with the National Trust tearoom a welcome refreshment point before the return journey. The 4.5 mile route is well within the reach of most walkers and is detailed within the Guided Walks section (walk 16).

Whinlatter Pass

The most northerly of the major road passes in the Lake District and certainly the easiest to traverse. From Braithwaite, west of Keswick, the pass climbs to a height of 1040 feet, heading for Lorton from where the road continues to Cockermouth. At the eastern end of the pass, a large lay-by provides excellent views across Bassenthwaite Lake and the lower reaches of the Skiddaw mountain range.

Most visitors to the pass head for the Whinlatter Forestry Commission Visitor Centre which houses an exhibition, and in the surrounding plantations, forest trails. Trees planted here in 1919 were the first by the Forestry Commission anywhere in England (see the Mini Walks section for details on some of the routes available in the northern forests). Details of a circular walk to the attractive 30 foot waterfall at Spout Force can be found in the same section.

Whitehaven/ Workington

Outside the National Park on the western coastal plain of Cumbria, Whitehaven and Workington are two of the county's most populous towns. The industrial nature of the towns reflects a history based largely on the mining of coal which dates from 1272 although it was not until the discovery of large deposits in the seventeenth century that the industry really boomed. Mining was carried out under the auspices of rich landowning families such as the Curwens and Lowthers with some pits extending out under the sea for over a mile. The Candlestick Chimney on the south side of the harbour

at Whitehaven marks the Wellington Pit, scene in 1910 of a mining disaster which claimed 136 lives.

An unusual episode in the area's history was the surfacing of a German submarine in 1915 off the coast at Whitehaven; the town receiving several shells before the submarine vanished beneath the waves!

Both Whitehaven and Workington boast some fine museums with Whitehaven Museum, the Helena Thompson Museum and Carnegie Theatre and Arts Centre are detailed in the Attractions section.

Whinlatter Pass. Val Corbett.

Gazetteer

Windermere

Windermere's expansion into the town it is today is due largely as a result of the expansion of the rail network here in 1847. Previously known as Birthwaite, Windermere was little more than a couple of houses with a few grand lakeside villas constructed by rich northern businessmen. The railway company's original intention had been for the railway line to continue through Windermere to Keswick via Ambleside and Grasmere. The public outcry raised by Wordsworth, Ruskin and other conservationists ensured the plan was abandoned and Windermere became the line's northern terminus, resulting in a rapid growth of the settlement.

Like adjoining Bowness, Windermere now functions largely as a centre for tourism with hotels and guest houses in abundance. Just to the north of the town is the Brockhole National Park Visitor Centre offering a wide selection of exhibitions and slide shows as well as landscaped gardens and a lakeside walk (see Attractions).

Windermere

Windermere has the longest history of human colonisation in Lakeland with evidence of Roman settlement at Galava Roman Fort at Ambleside as well as the remains of a Roman villa discovered on Belle Isle. This was followed by Viking

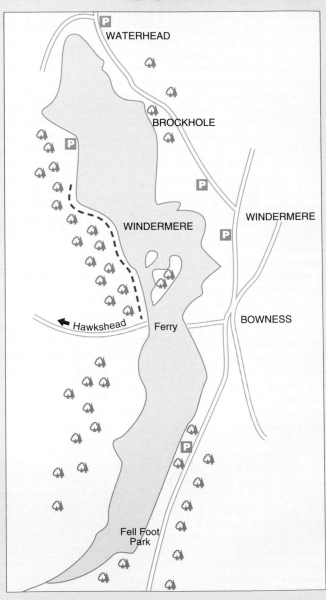

occupation in the tenth century; the name Windermere deriving from an original Norse owner 'Vinand'. In the late nineteenth century, wealthy businessmen from the Lancashire cotton towns built large residences overlooking

the lake, many, over a period of time were converted to hotels. Nowadays, Windermere is a mecca for watersports enthusiasts with over 10,000 boats registered here. Sailing, canoeing, windsurfing and water-skiing are all in evidence.

Gazetteer

Windermere. Val Corbett.

Windermere is the only lake at present without a speed limit.

It is of course England's largest lake; its 10.5 mile stretch made up of two basins with a shallow middle around Belle Isle. The northern basin is the deeper at a maximum of 219 feet. The first recorded swim of the length of Windermere was in 1911.

ACCESS

BY ROAD

Primarily via the A592 along its eastern shore although views are often fleeting and undramatic. To see the lake from your car, follow a minor road (signed Cartmel Fell) from the A592 just south of the entrance to Fell Foot Country Park. A Forestry Commission parking and picnic area is located on the right hand side.

BY FOOT

A parking area located immediately after the ferry crossing allows a public right of way to be explored northwards on the western shoreline. The National Trust owned Fell Foot Country Park (see Attractions) at the southern end of the lake has good views and lakeshore access.

BELLE ISLE

At 38 acres the largest lake island in the National Park and the location of the first circular house in Britain, built by Thomas English in 1774. Parts of a Roman pavement were uncovered at the time of its construction. The island is named after Isabella Curwen who purchased it in 1776.

WINDERMERE FERRY

Lakeland's only ferry crossing, originally dating from medieval times and still saving a considerable detour when heading for Grizedale Forest or Hawkshead. The modern chain link ferry is a far cry from the original rowing boats, one of which sank in 1635 drowning 47 wedding guests returning from Hawkshead.

PRINCIPAL VIEWPOINTS

Gummers How, Biskey Howe, Jenkin Crag, Latterbarrow and Orrest Head are all good viewpoints and are detailed in the Mini Walks section. Guided walks 1, 7 and 9 also contain views across Windermere.

Windermere Lake. Val Corbett.

Wrynose Pass

The Wrynose Pass is the eastern half of the only east west route from central Lakeland to the western coast and combining with the Hardknott Pass provides the most thrilling and challenging drive in the Lake District. The road is very narrow with gradients of 1 in 3 and with a summit height of 1281 feet the pass can often be closed in winter. It follows a route used by the Romans which connected a fort at Ambleside with their supply port at Ravenglass. Hardknott Fort in the adjacent pass was a Roman garrison fort housing 500 soldiers, the remains of which can be visited.

Close to the summit of the Wrynose Pass is the Three Shires Stone, the meeting point of the three old counties of Lancashire, Westmorland and Cumberland, parts of which were combined to form the modern county of Cumbria. The pass is also the source of two of Lakeland's most important rivers, the Duddon and the Brathay.

Wrynose Pass. Val Corbett.

I hope you enjoyed this brief overview of the history and geography of the Lake District. There are literally hundreds of books available on this subject, although from personal experience, the following few are well worth seeking for a indepth look at some of the topics covered in this section:

The Companion Guide to the Lake District, Frank Welsh, 1989

The Lake District, Michael Dunn, 1988

The Lake Counties, W G Collingwood, Revised edition 1988

Portrait of Windermere, Chris Taylor, 1983

A Literary Guide to the Lake District, Grevel Lindop, 1993

Towns and Villages of the Lake District and Cumbria, Alan Bryant 1997

The Lake District, Chris Barringer, 1984

Break new ground! go...

CD-walking

Access over 100 of the best weekend walks on your home computer.

I f you have access to an IBM compatible PC or an Apple Macintosh computer, you can now enjoy virtual reality walking on your own screen at home.

Over 100 routes suitable for one day, two day and multiday walks in the Lake District, the Peaks, Central Highlands, Snowdonia, Yorkshire Dales and North York Moors.

You can choose a route simply by selecting points on the maps which appear on your screen. Scroll through 360 degree breathtaking hill-top video panoramas in either direction, move in close to examine any area in greater detail, find information on accommodation, camp-sites and attractions or check out transport opportunities.

There is a safe walker feature from the British Mountaineering Council and features on the Duke of Edinburgh award scheme, the National Parks, The Ramblers' Association, the Forestry Commission plus data on many more information pages. This disk is highly visual and fun to use.

E ach selected walk is explained in day-by-day sections and is illustrated with a map and gradient chart. There is also a fact file relating to each walk. When you are ready to undertake your walk you can print-out the described route to take with you.

W ithin each area the proposed walks are graded by the degree of effort required to undertake them. A long walk is included within every area featured and the menu will allow you to access support information like where to stay, Tourist Information Centre locations and other data to help you plan your walk.

If you like walking in the British countryside, this CD will encourage you to obtain a CD-rom computer if you haven't done so already. It's the most comprehensive multimedia guide to walking in the UK ever produced.

Grasmere. Val Corbett.

send to:
**RELATIVE TECHNOLOGIES
PO BOX 3, SEDBERGH,
CUMBRIA LA10 5GB**

HOW TO ORDER
By post
Please return the coupon to the above address
By phone
Call **(01926) 854559** Quoting Reference LE

Ashness Bridge. Val Corbett.

Striding Edge in dawn light. Val Corbett.

WILLIAM WORDSWORTH

by Mark Norton

Few visitors spending any length of time in the Lake District can fail to be aware of Cumbria's most famous son, William Wordsworth. Along with his friends Samuel Taylor Coleridge and Robert Southey, the three were known as the 'Lake Poets', influencing the growth of the picturesque movement with its emphasis on mountains and lakes, clouds, skies and nature in general. Wordsworth in particular was a magnet for the literary circle of the time, with visitors such as Keats, Shelly, Tennyson and Ruskin, the latter eventually settling at Brantwood on the shores of Lake Coniston.

That so many people today should seek out a poet, dead for nearly 150 years, is testament to the man's great works and influence upon the

William Wordsworth, courtesy of the Wordsworth Trust, Dove Cottage.

development of English Verse. Dove Cottage, Rydal Mount and the Wordsworth family graves at Grasmere attract thousands of visitors each year, with Dove Cottage in particular being something of a shrine to the poet.

Wordsworth was born in 1770 at Cockermouth, one of five children brought up by their grandparents after the death of his father when William was only thirteen. He was sent to Hawkshead Grammar School for his education, where his initials are carved in one of the desktops and lodged with Anne Tyson in a nearby cottage. Having no children of her own, Ann Tyson had many boarders, each paying her the sum of five guineas for a twenty one week school term, although laundry was extra! Wordsworth's own mother had died when he was only eight and it is of some significance that her shows his deep appreciation of his landlady in the following lines from his autobiographical *The Prelude*:

*"The thoughts of gratitude shall fall like dew,
Upon thy grave, good creature: while my heart,
can beat I never will forget thy name"*

In 1799, after studying at Cambridge, he returned to Cumbria with enough money from a legacy to purchase his first property, Dove Cottage at Townend near Grasmere. The cottage dated from the early seventeenth century and was formally a pub called 'The Dove and Olive Bough'! Although damp and cold, it was just what he and his sister Dorothy had been looking for and it was to become their home for nine years. The Wordsworths had little money at this time and consequently lived in fairly impoverished circumstances. Indeed, Sir Walter Scott whilst staying with them, famously sneaked out of a window to take breakfast at the nearby Swan Hotel!

It was while living at Dove Cottage that Wordsworth was at his most prolific and arguably

Dove Cottage. MDN.

St Oswald's Church. MDN.

his best. His work naturally centred on the lakes and mountains around him, his deep appreciation of the natural landscape encouraged by his views of Dove Cottage as a suitably humble abode for a romantic such as he.

William married Mary Hutchinson in October 1802, the couple living with Dorothy at Dove Cottage for the first six years of their marriage. By 1808 however, a growing family (John born 1803, Dora 1804 and Thomas 1806) led to a move to Allan Bank at the northern end of Grasmere under Helm Crag. They lived here for three years where they had two further children, Catherine and William, before moving in 1811 to another property, the Old Parsonage opposite the church in central Grasmere. They stayed for only two years, the poor living conditions here blamed by

Wordsworth for the infant deaths of both Catherine and Thomas. The final move, to Rydal Mount in 1813, coincided with Wordsworth being given the position of Distributor of Stamps for Westmorland. This was a largely nominal position involving little work, although the £400 salary per annum kept them comfortable, allowing the poet to continue to write a little as well as spending time in his garden which was becoming an increasing passion. Dora's Field, adjacent to Rydal Church, now in the ownership of the National Trust, was bought at this time and planted with daffodils in remembrance of his oldest daughter. The poet's output gradually declined and though he succeeded Robert Southey as Poet Laureate in 1843, he was not to publish any new material before his death seven years later at the age of 80.

Although Wordsworth's contribution to English Literature cannot be understated, it is timely to note the role and influence of his sister Dorothy. Their time together at Dove Cottage and their walks in the surrounding hills during this time clearly inspired William to develop his talent. Dorothy kept a journal detailing her and William's life in their early years at Dove Cottage although her journal faded after his marriage to Sara Hutchinson in 1802. Her last entry in January 1803 records William having "*a fancy for some ginger bread*" with Dorothy walking to Grasmere to buy 6 pennyworth (Grasmere gingerbread is famous for its gingery shortcake taste and is still made to a secret recipe - Sara Nelson's Gingerbread Shop can still be found adjacent to the lychgate of St. Oswald's church).

Indeed her writings show an insight and eye for detail that could have made her more widely read but for the shadow of her brilliant brother. *Daffodils* for example, William's best known piece, was inspired by Dorothy's notes on a walk some two years earlier at Gowbarrow Park near Ullswater. Wordsworth acknowledged this importance in a poem entitled *The Sparrow's Nest:-*

"She gave me eyes, she gave me ears,
And humble cares, and delicate fears;
A heart, the fountain of sweet tears;
And love, and thought, and joy".

Dorothy survived her brother by five years and her grave can be seen alongside William and his wife Mary at St. Oswald's Church in Grasmere.

Gingerbread shop sign. MDN.

WORDSWORTHIAN ATTRACTIONS IN LAKELAND

Please refer to Index for page ref..

■ Wordsworth House, Cockermouth (his birthplace).

■ Hawkshead School (see Guided Walk 2)

■ Anne Tyson's house (not open to the public but passed on Guided Walk 2).

■ Dove Cottage (see Guided Walks 9 and 10).

■ Rydal Mount (see Guided Walk 8).

■ Family graves at St Oswalds Church, Grasmere (see Guided Walks 9 and 10).

River Duddon. Val Corbett.

LANGUAGE & PLACE NAMES

by Mark Norton

T he study of place names has always played an important part in allowing historians and geographers to understand the nature of life in centuries gone by. Our preference to refer to places and objects by name inadvertently provides the historian with the earliest and most basic form of written history. Unlike archeological evidence, place names do not have to be unearthed, they are all around us and can act quite literally as signposts to the past.

Within the Lake District, the distribution of certain types of place name gives a clear description of not only where people lived but also the nature of their lives. Place names deriving from the early Celtic tribes are largely on the lower lying fringes of Lakeland suggesting an agricultural system more at home here than in the central uplands. Names such as Penrith and Blencathra are two such examples in the far north. Similarly, the

predominance of churches dedicated to Celtic saints on the fringes of Lakeland supports the belief that permanent settlement was restricted to the outer peripheries of the Lake District. A more important legacy of these tribes was in the naming of Cumberland, one of the three original counties that later formed modern day Cumbria.

The gradual migration of Anglo-Saxon peoples is similarly recorded in the area. River names such as the Eden and Leven are Anglo-Saxon in origin as are place names ending *-ton* (e.g. Workington and Ulverston) again predominantly on the fringes of Lakeland indicating an influx of peoples who practised lowland farming as their primary agricultural method. This influx is corroborated by physical evidence of artefacts such as the Irton Cross in south west Lakeland, erected by migrants over a thousand years ago.

An altogether more profound influence followed

Loughrigg Tarn - the Norse "tjorn" means small lake. Val Corbett.

the influx of Norse invaders in the tenth century. Viking raiders from Scandinavia were gradually followed by more peaceable settlers who through place name evidence alone can be seen to have colonised much of central Lakeland. The landscape of mountains, forests and lakes was of course very similar to their homelands, allowing a straight forward continuation of their agricultural systems. Consequently, there are quite literally hundreds of modern day place names that originate from this period of Norse invasion. For a start, most of the generic names for features in the landscape are of Norse derivation. Dale, derives from *'Dals'* meaning valley, beck is from the Norse *'bekkr'* meaning stream, *'tjorn'* referring to a small lake has become tarn while *'gil'* meaning ravine is used today as gill or ghyll. Place names can also explain the activities of these early settlers, an example perhaps being the most common name ending *'-thwaite'* meaning clearing. This confirms the archeological evidence that the Lake District was once covered in trees which were gradually cleared for fuel and pasture. Applethwaite near Keswick, takes this one step further suggesting that the clearing was in an area occupied by apple trees. Similarly, Birthwaite, the settlement upon which modern day Windermere was founded, confirms that at one time the birch was the primary tree species which grew here.

An important practice in Norse agriculture was that of summer pasturing. Herds of sheep would be driven further up the fell sides to the summer pasture (*'saeter'*) to prevent overgrazing and take advantage of the higher vegetation available. Places such as Seatoller and Seathwaite in Borrowdale were clearly used for this purpose with Satterthwaite in the Grizedale forest revealing that the summer pasture involved the clearing of trees.

Names also provide other important lessons about the flora and fauna of centuries gone by.

Elterwater for example, takes its name from the Norse for swan, indicating that Whooper Swans were wintering on the lake a thousand years ago, as they often do today. The name of Rydal, near Ambleside, is evidence of the success of rye as a major crop in the area whilst the Norse for pigs - *'gris'* is found in place names such as Grizedale and Grasmere, indicating areas where woodland was being used to provide pannage for swine.

Proof of the early inhabitants of the Lake District and their activities can thus be gleaned from even the most everyday source. Some place names however, tell us little more than the individuals involved with Hawkshead being the summer pasture of a Norseman call *'Haukr'*, Ullswater remembering an *'Ulfr'* whilst Lake Windermere must have originally been the territory of *'Vinand'*, as the lake's historical name is Vinand's mere.

Colwith Force - the Norse 'foss' means waterfall. Val Corbett.

THE NATIONAL TRUST

by Mark Norton

By both ownership and leasing, the National Trust protects over 50,000 hectares in the Lake District, comprising of almost all the central fell area and major valley heads, six main lakes and much of their shoreline. This represents approximately 25% of the total Lake District National Park which in turn equates to about a quarter of the National Trust's entire holding within England and Wales. Along with its designation as a National Park, the work of the Trust is perhaps the most important force acting to preserve one of England's most beautiful and fragile landscapes for future generations.

Whilst both the National Park Authority and the National Trust are involved in the preservation of Lakeland, the two organisations are very different. The National Park Authority is a government sponsored organisation dating back to the creation of Britain's first National Parks in the 1950's (see separate article), whereas the National Trust is a charity that has its origins some 50 or so years before but is completely independent of the state and Government. The outcry against Manchester Corporation's plans in the late nineteenth century to create a reservoir at Thirlmere together with the planned expansion of

Little Langdale Tarn. The National Trust.

Dry stone walling. The National Trust.

the railway network across Cumbria acted as a catalyst for those seeking to protect an increasingly fragile landscape. This, coupled with a massive growth in population, increasing industrialisation and piecemeal planning control, seriously threatened England's and Cumbria's landscape. Accordingly, in 1895, three individuals,

Miss Octavia Hill, Sir Robert Hunter and Canon Hardwicke Rawnsley established the National Trust for places of Historic Interest or Natural Beauty.

Canon Rawnsley's involvement is worthy of particular note as he was vicar at Crosthwaite, near Keswick and in 1883 had previously founded the Lake District Defence Association, successfully opposing the construction of a railway in the Ennerdale Valley. His significance in the story of the Trust in Lakeland is also derived from his friendship with Beatrix Potter, where his encouragement of the fledgling authoress and her subsequent introduction to the conservationist cause resulted in Potter becoming a staunch supporter of the National Trust. After the eventual success of her children's books, she was able to use her royalties to purchase large tracts of farmland which she bequeathed to the trust on her death in 1943.

The Trust's first acquisition in the Lake District

Pitched footpath. The National Trust.

was Brandlehow Wood, purchased in 1902 to ensure public access to the south western shoreline of Derwent Water. By 1927 the total had risen to 24 properties, mainly small lakeshore areas amounting to less than 2,782 hectares. In 1928, G.M. Trevelyan's substantial gift in the Langdale Valley began the establishment of the Trust as a major landowner. Now, nearly 70 years later, the Trust owns 90 farms, 25,000 Herdwick sheep, 7000 hectares of woodland and over 2000 miles of boundary stone wall within the Lake District. As well as six of the major lakes, beauty spots such as Brotherswater, Tarn Hows and Aira Force are under its protection, in addition to the principal Derwentwater viewpoints of Friars Crag and Castle Head, acquired in 1922 and 1925 respectively, and it is particularly fitting that the Trust's holdings in the National Park includes the bed of England's deepest lake (Wastwater) and the summit of its highest mountain (Scafell Pike). One of the most significant aspects of Trust ownership is that since 1907, the Trust has the unique power to declare its land inalienable, meaning that it cannot be sold or mortgaged, thus ensuring that land acquired today, will forever be held in safe keeping for the nation.

In addition to previously mentioned acquisitions, the Trust also protects some fascinating properties; in certain cases whole hamlets such as Watendlath in Borrowdale. The tiny functional Bridge House information centre at Ambleside compares with the Georgian magnificence of Wordsworth's birthplace in Cockermouth, and likewise the sixteenth century 'statesman' farmhouse at Townend in Troutbeck compares with fourteenth century Sizergh Castle; very different properties but all equally important to preserve for future generations.

Another aspect of the Trust's activities is footpath maintenance. The passage of millions of pairs of feet each year can quickly turn a narrow grassy path into a deep and dangerous scar up to 30 metres wide. Through the use of the traditional method of 'pitching' stone paths, and drainage work, such ugly erosion scars have been repaired in many areas, including Helm Crag, Sour Milk Ghyll, Sty Head Pass and Great Gable (Note: in recognition of the importance of ensuring that Lake District footpaths are preserved for future generations, for every copy sold of this edition of Lakeland Explored, a small donation will be given to footpath restoration projects - see back cover).

The Trust's main sources of income include legacies, admission fees, donations, sponsorship, rent from properties and of course members' subscriptions. The National Trust Lake District Appeal has been set up to raise funds to help finance vital projects in the Lake District which include woodland management, dry stone wall repairs and footpath preservation. If you would like to help (£5 plants one oak tree, £50 repairs three metres of upland footpath) please send donations to the following address: The National Trust Lake District Appeal, The Hollens, Grasmere, Cumbria LA22 9QZ. Additionally, why not become a member of the National Trust:

Creating a drainage route. The National Trust.

HOW TO JOIN:

For immediate membership providing free access to National Trust properties, you can join at most all National Trust properties and shops during your visit.

Alternatively, telephone the membership Department on 0181 464 1111, Mon. to Fri., 9am to 5.30pm. Allow 28 days for receipt of your membership card.

National Trust Properties contained within the Attractions Section (see index for page ref.)

■ **Acorn Bank Garden and Watermill** ■ **Beatrix Potter Gallery**
■ **Fell Foot Park and Garden** ■ **Hill Top** ■ **Sizergh Castle**
■ **Stagshaw Garden** ■ **Steam Yacht Gondola**
■ **Townend** ■ **Wordsworth House**

MINI WALKS, VIEWPOINTS & WATERFALLS

WALK GRADE

EASY: Well within the reach of most families and largely on level terrain or with fairly gentle uphill sections on well made paths.

MODERATE: Requiring more exertion and likely to include uphill walking.

TOUGH: High Fell walks and strenuous routes involving sections of steep climb and/or rough terrain.

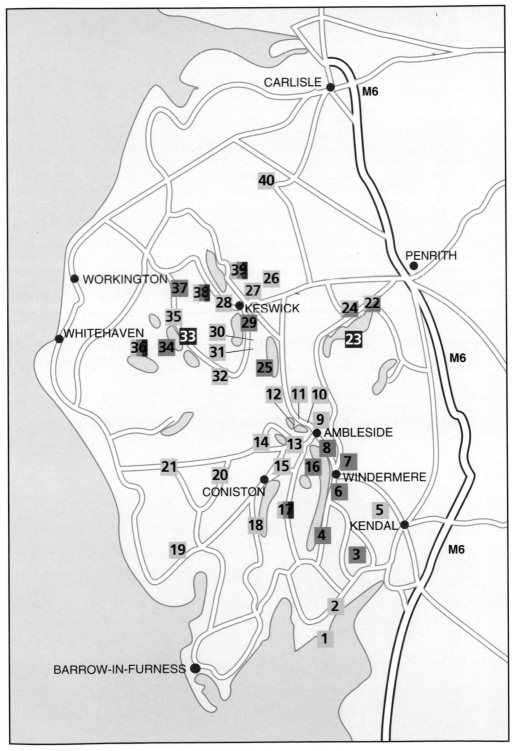

INTRODUCTION

As the name suggests, this section is designed to guide you to some of the key mini walks, waterfalls and viewpoints found in the Lake District. Mini walks are ideal if time is short, the 'weather window' restricted or to supplement a longer walk completed earlier in the day. The viewpoints chosen are of course just a small selection of that available and are generally low level in nature and easily reached. No trip to Lakeland would be complete without at least one visit to a waterfall or force as they are generally referred to in Cumbria; the added bonus of waterfalls are of course their suitability and visual impact in wet weather when other longer walks across more open ground may not appeal!

Each suggestion has been graded in the same way as the guided walks, allowing the most suitable option to be chosen when considering time and energy/fitness levels available. The maps have been included for illustration purposes and are not to scale; by following the instructions carefully you should have no problems at all. The opposite page has been included to allow you to record which of the mini walks, waterfalls and viewpoints you have visited.

All map references refer to the start point car park.

Whilst every care has been taken to ensure accurate, easy to follow walk directions, the publishers cannot accept responsibility for errors or changes to the details given. Fences, walls and stiles can all be removed, footpaths can be re-routed and permissive paths can be changed or closed. It is therefore essential that footpaths are always confirmed on the ground and any indicated diversions followed.

NB To check the weather forecast before setting out, why not ring the Lake District Weatherline (24 hours) on **017687 75757**

Derwentwater. Val Corbett.

YOUR WALKS RECORD

Use this page to record the dates on which you completed each walk/waterfall/viewpoint:

		Date completed			Date completed
1	Humphrey Head Point		21	Stanley Ghyll Force	
2	Hampsfield Fell		22	Dunmallard Hill	
3	Whitbarrow Scar		23	Hallin Fell	
4	Gummer's How		24	Aira Force & Yew Crag	
5	Scout Scar		25	Harrop Tarn	
6	Biskey Howe		26	Latrigg	
7	Orrest Head		27	Keswick Railway Footpath	
8	Jenkins Crag		28	Friars Crag & Crow Park	
9	Stock Ghyll Force		29	Castle Head	
10	Rydal Falls and Park		30	Ashness Bridge & Surprise View	
11	White Moss Common		31	Lodore Falls	
12	Loughrigg Terrace		32	Taylor Gill Force	
13	Skelwith Force		33	Rannerdale Knotts	
14	Blea Tarn		34	Scale Force	
15	Tarn Hows		35	Lanthwaite Wood	
16	Latterbarrow		36	Ennerdale	
17	Grizedale Forest		37	Spout Force	
18	Coniston		38	Whinlatter Forest	
19	Swinside Stone Circle		39	Dodd Wood	
20	Birks Bridge		40	The Howk	

1 HUMPHREY HEAD POINT

Humphrey Head Point is something of a rarity in Cumbria as it is the only coastal limestone cliff of any height. The 150 foot high promontory protrudes one mile into Morecambe Bay and is a Site of Special Scientific Interest leased to Cumbria Wildlife Trust by the Holker Estates. Found in a cave at the bottom of the cliff were prehistoric and Roman remains including axes, spears and jewellery.

The headland was a popular destination in the eighteenth and nineteenth centuries because of its holy well, believed to be beneficial in relieving the effects of lead poisoning in miners. Humphrey Head is also said to be the place where Sir John Harrington of nearby Cartmel killed the last wolf in England.

MAP REF: **O.S. Landranger 96 388 747**

DIRECTIONS: *From the A590 near Haverthwaite, follow the B5278 to Flookburgh. From the centre of the village, bear left (signed Grange) for one mile to a right turn (signed Humphrey Head) just before the village of Allithwaite. After the railway crossing keep left to reach a small roadside parking area adjacent to the sign for the Humphrey Head Centre.*

A path out onto the headland is indicated on the nature reserve information board.

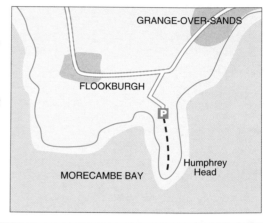

GRANGE-OVER-SANDS

FLOOKBURGH

P

MORECAMBE BAY

Humphrey Head

Humphrey Head. Val Corbett.

MINI WALKS, VIEWPOINTS & WATERFALLS

2   HAMPSFIELD FELL

WALK EASY GRADE

An excellent viewpoint and mini walk in the far south of the National Park, Hampsfield Fell (more generally known as Hampsfell) is another example of a limestone *'pavement'* (see Whitbarrow Scar) with an unusual innovation on its grassy summit: a hospice building. Built in 1834 by Rev T Remington, an incumbent of nearby Cartmel, the hospice is a four square tower used for the *"shelter and entertainment of wanderers over the fell"* and has been decorated with nineteenth century rhymes detailing the *"prospect rare"* and the reason for the construction of the building. Narrow steps up the side of the hospice give access to a roof top viewpoint across Grange-over-Sands and Morecambe Bay to the south and many of the key fells in southern Lakeland. A direction indicator helps pinpoint the views.

As described below, the 700 foot high summit is reached from the starting point in only about twenty minutes; the start point elevation of nearly 400 feet ensuring an easy climb of approx. 300 feet.

MAP REF: **O.S. Landranger 96 396 779**

DIRECTIONS: *From Cartmel follow signs to the outskirts of Grange-over-Sands. Pass the golf club and find a small roadside parking area near Meadowbank Lane.*

Opposite Meadowbank Lane, cross stone wall steps (public footpath sign to Hampsfell and Cartmel) and cross the field to an opposite stile. Cross the lane and further stile before turning right and walking with the wall boundary close by. At a wall corner (near a pump house like building) head uphill on an obvious grassy track. Pass over a stone stile next to a large metal gate and walk ahead on well defined paths, eventually crossing a wall via stone steps. The limestone pavement summit and hospice are soon reached. Return the same way.

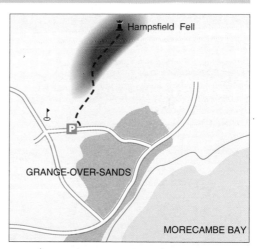

Hampsfield Fell. Val Corbett.

3 WHITBARROW SCAR

WALK MODERATE GRADE

Whitbarrow Scar's white carboniferous limestone cliffs provide some of the most far reaching vantage points in south eastern Lakeland and an enjoyable one hour long round walk, ideal if time is short or to supplement a longer walk completed earlier in the day. Views include the Pennines, Morecambe Bay and the Langdale Pikes. The public right of way to the top passes through an important nature reserve; a haven for birds and deer and a Site of Special Scientific Interest. The summit, known as Lord's Seat, is an excellent example of a limestone *'pavement'*, so called because the original limestone outcrop has been worn down into the flat table shape that can be seen today, by the immense weight and abrasive power of previous ice ages. Thousands of years of wind and rain have weathered the surface and enlarged hairline cracks inherent within the structure, into rectangular patterns resembling manmade pavements. A cairn at the top commemorates Canon G A K Hervey, founder of the Lake District Naturalists Trust.

MAP REF: **O.S. Landranger 97 435 860**

DIRECTIONS: From the A590 (signed to Barrow) in the far south of the National Park, head north signed to Mill Side and Beck Head. Pass through Mill Side and follow a country lane to reach a large T junction (Witherslack). Turn right and continue ahead to reach Witherslack Hall. A parking area for the start of the walk can be found by turning right in front of the hall.

After the kissing gate next to the information board, follow the path leading half left towards a football pitch, at the end of which is a stile which should be crossed to provide access to a route at the back of the goalposts. Now follow yellow waymarks climbing steadily before emerging from the trees to find a well defined path that soon leads right, marked by stone cairns. This path provides access to the summit where there is a large cairn with an inscribed stone.

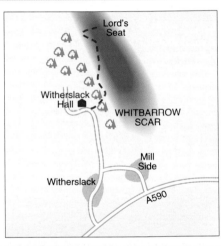

Whitbarrow Scar. Val Corbett.

From the exposed summit of Gummer's How there area excellent views across the southern half of Lake Windermere and the steamers at Lakeside. Standing at 1053 feet above sea level and one of the only hills of this height in the Windermere area (although the actual ascent is only some 400 feet due to the starting point), the rocky fell top is reached after a 20 minute walk on a well made path before a short scramble to the summit plateau.

MAP REF: **O.S. Landranger 96 391 885**

DIRECTIONS: From the A592 just south to the entrance to Fell Foot Country Park, take a minor road (signed Cartmel Fell and Gummer's How Picnic Area) that leads uphill to a Forestry Commission car park and picnic area on the right.

Turn right out of the car park and after about 100 yards look for a kissing gate on the left (signed to Gummer's How summit). A well marked path leads ahead to the summit.

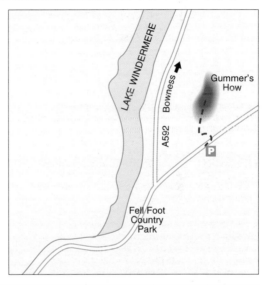

Windermere from Gummer's How. Val Corbett.

87

The carboniferous limestone escarpment of Scout Scar, running north to south just to the west of Kendal, provides an attractive alternative to central Lakeland. Although at 750 feet above sea level not as high as the central fells, Scout Scar's views are arguably just as far reaching. As well as Morecambe Bay, peaks such as Coniston's Old Man, Scafell Pike and Great Gable can all be recognised from here.

The walk to the summit, where a shelter was erected in 1912 to commemorate the coronation of George V, starts from around 500 feet above sea level so providing an easy and enjoyable walk.

MAP REF: **O.S. Landranger 97 487 894**

DIRECTIONS: *From the A590 west of Kendal, follow signs for Brigsteer to find a small roadside parking area, 30 yards from which is indicated a public footpath sign to Scout Scar. A kissing gate leads into the National Trust property of Helsington Barrows from where the obvious path can be followed.*

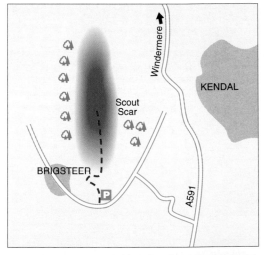

Scout Scar. Val Corbett.

6 BISKEY HOWE

A short (though uphill) walk from Bowness town centre past the Hydropathic Hotel (built in 1881) leads to the rocky precipice of Biskey Howe, an excellent viewpoint across Bowness Bay and the northern stretch of Lake Windermere. The viewpoint's proximity to the resort town of Bowness ensured it was a popular place to visit in the early days of tourism; today a directional viewfinder, erected to commemorate Queen Elizabeth's II's Silver Jubilee in 1977, details the magnificent panorama.

MAP REF: **O.S. Outdoor Leisure Map 7 (S.E. area) 407 969**

DIRECTIONS: Park in a suitable place at Bowness.

Walk uphill through Bowness as if heading for Windermere town before bearing right into Helm Road in front of a Lakeland clothing shop (signed to the Hydro Hotel). Continue up the hill for about half a mile. At the top, just as the road bears around to the left, notice some steps and a sign indicating the viewpoint.

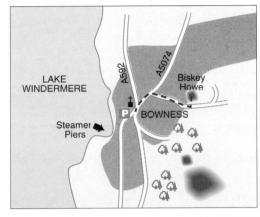

The stillness of nearby Windermere. Val Corbett.

ORREST HEAD

One of the best viewpoints for Lake Windermere and indeed often sited as one of the finest views in the whole of the Lake District, Orrest Head, with its 784 feet summit, is easily reached after a 20 minute walk from opposite the Windermere railway station. The summit has benches, in addition to a directional viewfinder to Coniston Old Man, Fairfield, the Langdale Pikes and Scafell Pike in the far distance. An inscription at the top reads:

"Thow who hast given me eyes to see
And loved this site so fair
Give me a heart to find out thee
And read thee everywhere"

MAP REF: **O.S. Outdoor Leisure Map 7 (S.E. area) 413 988**

DIRECTIONS: Head for the northern end of Windermere and park in a suitable place near to the railway station and Tourist Information Centre (a roadside parking area for around 10 cars is on the Kendal road near the Windermere Hotel). The walk starts on the opposite side of the road to the information centre near the Windermere Hotel.

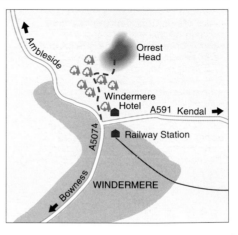

Cross the busy A591 to reach the footpath sign for Orrest Head. After only a few yards, turn left (signed to Troutbeck Rd) and continue to a large fork where you should bear right. Follow the wall that heads uphill and bears around to the right. Turn left at a waymark post and then zigzag up the hillside (views across northern end of Windermere), keeping the wall to your immediate left. Pass through a metal gate next to a memorial stone and walk up to the summit.

Orrest Head. Val Corbett.

MINI WALKS, VIEWPOINTS & WATERFALLS

8 JENKINS CRAG

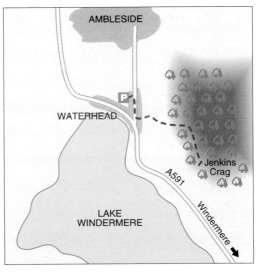

WALK MODERATE GRADE

The National Trust viewpoint of Jenkins Crag, reached after a 20 minute walk from Waterhead, provides an opportunity to see a greater part of Lake Windermere and the classic outline of Langdale Pikes just to the north. The crag consists of a rocky outcrop (the viewpoint is just under 600 feet high) backed by thickly wooded slopes; the path to it well made and easily followed. Because the start point car park is adjacent to the steamer terminus, the walk can easily be combined with a boat trip on the lake.

MAP REF: **O.S. Outdoor Leisure Map 7 (S. E. area) 378 033**

DIRECTIONS: Park in the main car park at Waterhead, next to the Tourist Information Centre (toilets here, refreshments available nearby).

Leave via the wooden steps at the top end of the car park and turn right on the main road. Immediately after the Ghyll Head Hotel notice a sign indicating a footpath to Jenkins Crag. Cross a wall stile at the top and a field before passing over a ladder stile which leads to a well defined path through the woods. Cross a beck and follow the path as it bears uphill to the left. Pass a National Trust sign for Kelsick Scar and after 100 yards, turn right to reach Jenkins Crag.

Jenkin's Crag. Val Corbett.

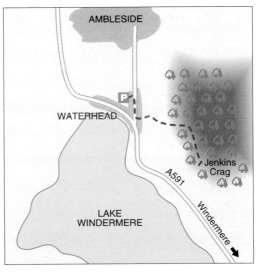
Map labels: AMBLESIDE, WATERHEAD, LAKE WINDERMERE, Jenkins Crag, A591, Windermere

MINI WALKS, VIEWPOINTS & WATERFALLS

91

9 STOCK GHYLL FORCE

Only fifteen minutes walk from the centre of Ambleside, this is one of Lakeland's loveliest and most accessible waterfalls, comprising a 70 foot cascade within two main steps, set in lush woodland.

Since the fifteenth century the steep gradient of the beck has been utilised to supply power for cotton, paper and bobbin mills, the latter being very widespread in the nineteenth century due to the massive demand from the Lancashire cotton industry. One such mill, parts of which have now been converted to provide accommodation, is located on the opposite side of the beck to the waterfall approach.

MAP REF: **O.S. Outdoor Leisure Map 7 (S.E. area) 385 046**

DIRECTIONS: Park in one of Ambleside's main car parks and head for the centre of the village (NB Ambleside gets very busy in the season, so try to go early to be sure of parking).

The waterfall can be reached from the centre of Ambleside by taking a lane to the right of Barclays Bank. Climb a tarmac road before bearing off left into a wooded area (falls sign). A woodland walk following red waymark posts leads to the waterfall. Cross the small wooden footbridge above the falls and descend following the waymark posts. A further footbridge re-crosses the stream, allowing a return to Ambleside via the original route.

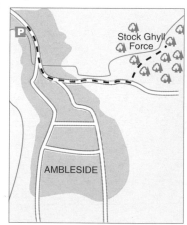

Stock Ghyll. Val Corbett.

WALK EASY GRADE

This mini walk is in real Wordsworth country, allowing a visit to Rydal Mount, William's home between 1813 and 1850. In addition, the walk passes through Rydal Park, a route Wordsworth would have used between his home and Ambleside where he had an office. Also included is a visit to Rydal Falls, situated on the private property of Rydal Hall. This is a conference retreat centre for the Diocese of Carlisle, although access to the Falls is allowed through a local agreement. Equally pleasurable is the excellent Ramblers Tearoom where tables overlook a smaller waterfall. The circular walk described takes approximately one hour without stops.

MAP REF: **O.S. Outdoor Leisure Map 7 (S.E. area) 366 060**

DIRECTIONS: The small National Park car park at Pelter Bridge, just before Rydal, is reached via the A591 north from Ambleside. Turn left across a stone bridge shortly after the Rydal village sign, an immediate right turn across a cattle grid leads to a parking area on the left (in low season it may be more convenient to park in the lane down from Rydal Mount).

From Pelter Bridge, return to the main road and turn left before bearing right to walk up past Rydal Church and Rydal Mount. Continue up the tarmac lane and pass through a wooden gate (sign indicates this is an access area courtesy of the Rydal Estate). Continue ahead, next to a wall, before turning right through a kissing gate to enter the Birk Hagg access area. An obvious path leads to a footbridge with views of the falls. From here, return back to Rydal Mount and turn left (signed as a private road and a public path) to reach the Ramblers Tearoom. Bear right and walk over the bridge before bearing right (signed as a footpath to Ambleside). Follow the gravel track that leads through Rydal Park before eventually reaching the main road. Turn right and follow the road back to your car.

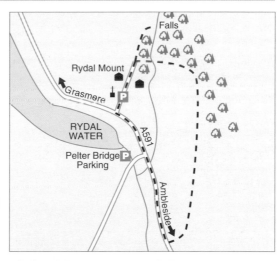

Rydal Hall Gardens. Val Corbett.

MINI WALKS, VIEWPOINTS & WATERFALLS

11 WHITE MOSS COMMON

An easily accessible but classic viewpoint of Rydal Water can be reached after just a 10 minute walk away from the National Trust run White Moss Common Quarry car park near Rydal village. The walk to the viewpoint is on the old Grasmere/Ambleside road (a route Wordsworth often used following his appointment as Distributor of Stamps for Westmorland), a short diversion through scrub allows access to several rocky knolls which provide superb views over Rydal and its islands. Exactly half a mile further on from the viewpoint is Dove Cottage and the Wordsworth Museum (see Attractions for details of opening hours etc.).

MAP REF: **O.S. Outdoor Leisure Map 7 (S.E. area) 347 066**

DIRECTIONS: The White Moss Common Quarry car park is located on the right hand side of the A591 (if heading north) between Rydal village and Grasmere.

Take the minor tarmac road which leads uphill from the northern end of the car park (not the busy A591 on which you arrived). At the top of an incline (opposite a much smaller parking area), notice a metal bench. Turn right, leaving the road to follow a path through undergrowth to the rocky viewpoints.

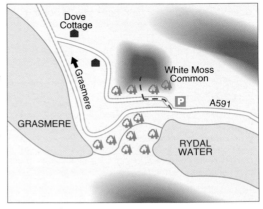

Rydal Water and White Moss Common. Val Corbett.

This walking area will be a big draw for Wordsworth devotees given its exploration of Loughrigg Terrace, just half a mile from Dove Cottage and a short drive from Rydal Mount, the poet's home until his death in 1850. The walk allows exploration of the southern shore of Grasmere (where there are usually ducks and swans waiting to be fed!) as well as lovely views towards Rydal Water. Loughrigg Terrace is generally regarded as the best viewpoint of Grasmere; in the far distance is Helm Crag, also known as The Lion and the Lamb because of a distinctive rock formation at its summit. The walk to Loughrigg Terrace takes about half an hour.

MAP REF: **O.S. Outdoor Leisure Map 7 (S.E. area) 347 066**

DIRECTIONS: Start from the White Moss Common Quarry car park on the right hand side (if heading north) of the A591 between Rydal village and Grasmere.

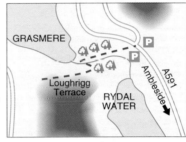

Leave the car park and cross the busy A591 to enter the National Trust property of White Moss Common. Ignore the wooden bridge that leads across the River Rothay and walk keeping the river on your left. Pass through a gate and follow the obvious path through woodland to reach a further wooden bridge that crosses the river and provides access to the shore of Grasmere Lake. To enjoy the splendid view from Loughrigg Terrace, proceed up the steps from the footbridge and follow the path that bears left (eventually joined by a wall) to reach a path junction where you should turn right (note view also to Rydal). A broad path leads away, the view gradually opening up over Grasmere with Helm Crag in the distance. Return to your car via the same route.

Grasmere. Val Corbett.

13 SKELWITH FORCE

Skelwith Force in height is one of the smaller Lakeland waterfalls, a fault in the underlying rock structure of the river bed causing a drop of about 20 feet. The attraction for visitors is the intensity of the fall as it has the greatest volume of water of any force in the Lake District. White water can be almost guaranteed as the River Brathay drains the whole of the Great and Little Langdale valleys. After rain, Skelwith Force can be a raging torrent.

Just down from the force are the Kirkstone Galleries and tearooms; the galleries providing an opportunity to purchase gifts fashioned from the attractive green slate sourced near the Kirkstone Pass.

MAP REF: **O.S. Outdoor Leisure Map 7 (S.E. area) 342 037**

DIRECTIONS: Take the A593 Coniston road through Clappersgate, turning right signed to Elterwater and Langdale on the B5343 just before the Skelwith Bridge Hotel. Park in the National Trust Silverthwaite car park reached after half a mile.

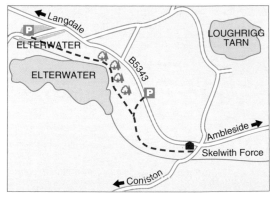

Cross to the opposite side of the road from the car park and pass through a gap in a low wall before descending through light woodland to cross a stile and enter a field. Turn left, heading for woodland to find a kissing gate in a stone wall next to a farm gate. Follow the obvious track ahead to reach Skelwith Force. (An alternative is to follow the riverside path from Elterwater village).

Skelwith Force. MDN.

MINI WALKS, VIEWPOINTS & WATERFALLS

WALK EASY GRADE

A classic high fell tarn that provides a very accessible short walk in the shadow of the distinctive profile of the Langdale Pikes. The walk is very suitable for families as it is mainly level and takes only an hour to complete the circuit with no chance of losing your way.

Blea Tarn is a typical corrie tarn, i.e. an upland hollow formed by ice, made all the more attractive, and unusual by the rhododendrons and conifers that are gathered around the south western shoreline. Wordsworth was certainly familiar with the tarn as it appears in his long poem *The Excursion*, *"Urn-like it was in shape, deep as an urn; with rocks encompassed, save that to the south...."* The tarn and approx. 292 acres surrounding it have been in the care of the National Trust since 1971.

MAP REF: **O.S. Outdoor Leisure Map 6 (S.W. area) 296 044**

DIRECTIONS: From central Lakeland follow the B5343 past Chapel Stile and through the Great Langdale Valley. After the Old Dungeon Ghyll Hotel the road turns left to become a minor road which heads for the Wrynose Pass and Little Langdale. A designated parking area for Blea Tarn will be found on the left.

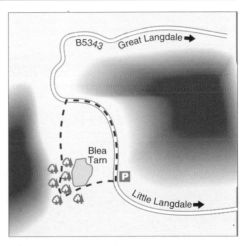

Leave the car park and pass through the kissing gate which provides access to a well made path (constructed by the National Trust to improve access for the partially mobile and quite suitable for wheelchairs). Follow the path around the tarn and after emerging onto open fell, continue ahead on a clear path until you reach the minor road on which you previously arrived. To complete a circular walk turn right and follow the road back to your car.

Blea Tarn. Val Corbett.

MINI WALKS, VIEWPOINTS & WATERFALLS

WALK EASY GRADE

Now in the care of the National Trust, the celebrated beauty spot of Tarn Hows is one of the most visited spots in Lakeland and in high season can be literally packed with people. The attraction is its sheer beauty, mirror like pools surrounded by thick woodland, and views towards the Helvellyn range and the Langdale Pikes. The 1.5 mile path around the tarn offers a lovely waterside walk and to the credit of the Trust, the level path is well maintained making it suitable for wheelchairs and push chairs.

Tarn Hows is essentially man made, having once been three separate tarns before being joined together in the nineteenth century. The National Trust has provided a dedicated disabled parking area close to the tarn. All other parking areas get very busy in all but the low season.

MAP REF: **O.S. Outdoor Leisure Map 7 (S.E. area) 330 000**

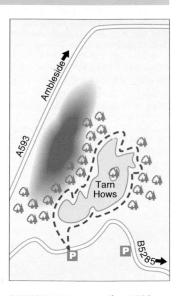

DIRECTIONS: *From the A593 just north of Coniston village, turn off onto the B5285 signed to Hawkshead and Tarn Hows. The parking areas at Tarn Hows are reached after approximately two miles and are well signed.*

Tarn Hows. Val Corbett.

MINI WALKS, VIEWPOINTS & WATERFALLS

16 LATTERBARROW

In the care of the National Trust since 1944, Latterbarrow is one of the best vantage points on the western side of Lake Windermere (primarily as it is one of the few upland tracts that has been left unplanted) and provides views across all the fells surrounding the head of the lake, as well as to the picturesque valley in which Hawkshead sits. The summit, topped with a well built cairn and reached after some twenty minutes walk, is 800 feet above sea level; the actual uphill distance roughly half that due to the height of the starting point.

MAP REF: **O.S. Outdoor Leisure Map 7 (S.E. area) 368 992**

DIRECTIONS: *From just outside Hawkshead on the Grizedale Forest to Windermere Ferry road, turn off to follow the signs for Wray Castle and Wray, passing through the hamlet of Colthouse. Half a mile further on, look out for a small roadside parking area on the right hand side with a wooden public footpath sign indicating the National Trust property of Latterbarrow.*

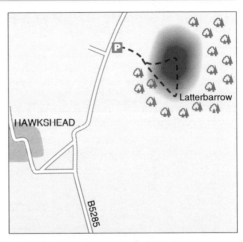

Pass through the gate and walk uphill. A broad path passes through a gap in a wall to reach a path junction. The official right of way actually proceeds ahead, although the majority of people appear to bear left here and follow a steep path to the large stone cairn at the summit.

View North from Latterbarrow. Val Corbett.

MINI WALKS, VIEWPOINTS & WATERFALLS

17 GRIZEDALE FOREST

WALK EASY GRADE   WALK MODERATE GRADE   WALK TOUGH GRADE

Grizedale Forest occupies a large area of land between the lakes of Coniston and Esthwaite. Originally part of the great monastic estates of Furness Abbey, Grizedale, acquired by the Forestry Commission in 1936, is an important working forest as well as a leisure area of some significance offering extensive visitor facilities and miles of footpaths and cycle trails. The excellent visitor centre includes a shop, crafts workshop, children's play area and tearooms as well as the famous 'Theatre in the Forest', housed in buildings that once belonged to the now demolished Grizedale Hall.

For the walker, it is advisable to head for the shop and buy the leaflet detailing the waymarked walks in the forest. There are many alternatives ranging from one to ten miles in length; whilst walking look out for examples of Grizedale's famous woodland sculptures that have been sited throughout the forest.

Walks from the visitor centre include:
Grizedale Tarn following white waymarks, 3.25 miles   **TOUGH**
Ridding Wood following blue waymarks, 1 mile   **EASY**
Carron Crag following red waymarks, 3 miles   **TOUGH**
Millwood Habitat Trail following yellow waymarks, 1.5 miles   **EASY**

Further south are three walks at Bogle Crag:
Yellow waymarks, 0.75 miles   **EASY**
Red waymarks, 3 miles   **MODERATE**
Blue waymarks, 3.75 miles,   **TOUGH**

as well as a further walk near the village of Satterthwaite:
The High Bowkerstead Walk, white waymarks, 2 miles   **MODERATE**

MAP REF: **O.S. Outdoor Leisure Map 7 (S.E. area) 335 945**

DIRECTIONS: *Grizedale Forest Visitor Centre is well signed from Hawkshead, west of Lake Windermere.*

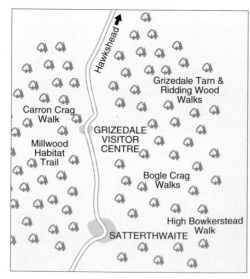

The Green Man, Grizedale. Val Corbett.

The Lake District's third largest lake has a long public access stretch on its western shore, running from Torver Common and as far as Coniston Hall before turning inland to reach the A593 south of Coniston village. Coniston Hall is the area's oldest building, dating from the thirteenth century when it was originally constructed as a pele tower (these were small square towers, built in this area during the thirteenth and fourteenth centuries as a defence against Scottish raids). The hall was originally owned by the de Flemings, Wordsworth's landlords at Rydal Mount; their wealth based on copper mined in the surrounding hills.

As you walk you may see a white plume of smoke out on the lake. This will be the National Trust owned '*Gondola*', a steam yacht dating from 1859, fully restored and providing a stylish way of viewing the lake.

MAP REF: **O.S. Outdoor Leisure Map 6 (S.W. area) 287 930**

DIRECTIONS: From the A593 south of Coniston, turn onto the A5084 in Torver. Use a parking area opposite a large Land Rover garage located on a bend in the road.

From the car park, turn left and walk down the road to find a left bearing path indicated as Torver Common. Pass through a kissing gate and descend with a wall on your right to reach the lake shore. Turn left and walk for whatever distance required before returning the same way (the woodland path heads north alongside the lake to Coniston Hall, a distance of approx. 2 miles).

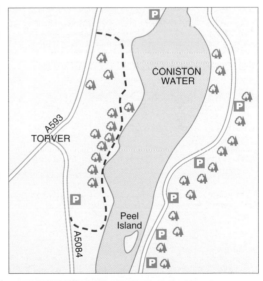

Gondola on Coniston Water. Val Corbett.

101

19 SWINSIDE STONE CIRCLE

One of the three most important stone circles in Cumbria (the others being Castlerigg and Long Meg and her Daughters), Swinside Stone Circle consists of 55 stones set in a ninety foot diameter round. Although the circle is located on private land, it can easily be viewed from the nearby public footpath. The walk from the parking area to the circle, located on the eastern flank of Black Combe, takes around half an hour there and back and passes through beautiful but rarely busy countryside using a partly made and easily followed track. Return views are towards the estuary of Duddon Sands, east of Millom.

MAP REF: **O.S. Landranger 96 181 874**

DIRECTIONS: From the A595 between Millom and Broughton-in-Furness, take a minor road signed to Broadgate and proceed to Cragg Hall where the road is wide enough to park without obstructing farm traffic.

Look for a public bridleway sign (about 100 yards from Cragg Hall in the direction of Broadgate) indicating the route to Swinside and Thwaites Fell. Follow the path uphill and continue on the clear track until you can see the circle. Return via the same way.

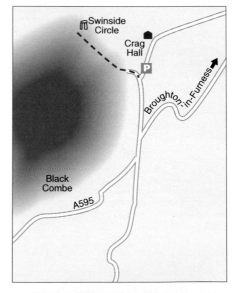

Swinside Stone Circle. Val Corbett.

WALK EASY GRADE

A number of waymarked woodland walks on Forestry Commission owned land at the head of the Dunnerdale Valley. Situated right in the heart of the fells, the beauty of Birks Bridge is in the rushing water of the River Duddon which has its source in the high fells around the Wrynose Pass, itself an area for a thrilling car journey through a stunning and unpopulated landscape.

MAP REF: **O.S. Outdoor Leisure Map 6 (S.W. area) 235 995**

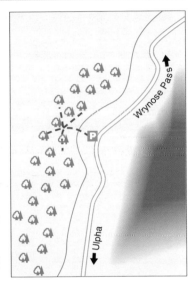

DIRECTIONS: Birks Bridge is reached after passing through the Wrynose Pass from central Lakeland and following the Dunnerdale road (signed Broughton via Duddon Valley). A Forestry Commission parking area is signed on the right hand side.

Birks Bridge, Duddon Valley. Val Corbett.

MINI WALKS, VIEWPOINTS & WATERFALLS

Stanley Ghyll Force (also known as Dalegarth Force) is a 60 foot high waterfall in a luxuriant narrow wooded gorge reached on a two mile circular walk in the beautiful Eskdale Valley. The start point for the walk is Dalegarth Station, the eastern terminus of the Ravenglass and Eskdale Miniature Railway, a narrow gauge service operating between Eskdale and Ravenglass, affectionately known as 'La'al Ratty'. Services run throughout the year (reduced service in winter) and provides an excellent way of seeing the Eskdale countryside.

MAP REF: **O.S. Outdoor Leisure Map 6 (S.W. area) 173 008**

DIRECTIONS: Dalegarth Station is on the main Eskdale road between the Hardknott Pass and Eskdale Green.

From Dalegarth Station car park (toilets and refreshments), return to the main road and turn right. Opposite the Eskdale Centre, turn left, crossing the River Esk onto an unsurfaced track. At a fork, bear left signed to Stanley Ghyll and follow a track between 2 stone walls. Pass through a gate to a woodland path and beckside walk. The falls are reached after a series of wooden footbridges. Return via the wooden footbridges and follow the beckside path to a large wooden footbridge. Cross and pass through a gate into light woodland before crossing the river via stepping stones in front of the church (if the river is in flood you will unfortunately have to return to your original route). Adjacent to the church, take the track to the main road before turning left to return to your car.

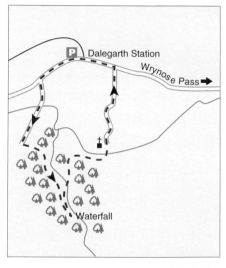

The approach to Eskale from central Lakeland is via the Hardknott Pass. Val Corbett.

WALK EASY GRADE **WALK MODERATE GRADE**

Situated at the foot of Ullswater, adjacent to the stone built crossing over the River Eamont that gives the village of Pooley Bridge its name, is the rounded mound of Dunmallard Hill. Topped by a hillfort (only a rough earthwork bank can now be seen) believed to be of Iron Age origin, the hill provides a short although at times steep circular walk on a permissive path that reveals views through the trees over Ullswater. Far less strenuous is a short bridleway that follows the River Eamont from Pooley Bridge; both can be used to work up a thirst for one of the many refreshment opportunities in the village.

WALK TERRAIN GRADE: Dunmallard Hill: **MODERATE**
Riverside walk: **EASY**

MAP REF: **O.S. Outdoor Leisure Map 5 (N.E. area) 469 245**

DIRECTIONS: Use the National Park Dunmallard car park at the northern end of Ullswater near Pooley Bridge.

From the entrance to the car park, pass through the kissing gate and follow the public footpath signed to Dacre. At a triple signpost follow the sign indicating the circular permissive path to Pooley Bridge.
The riverside path leaves the far end of the car park to follow the River Eamont.

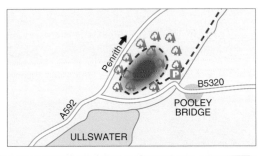

Ullswater. Val Corbett.

MINI WALKS, VIEWPOINTS & WATERFALLS

23 HALLIN FELL

WALK TOUGH GRADE

One of the classic viewpoints over Ullswater, reached after a twenty minute walk from the parking area adjacent to St Peter's Church in Martindale. Although 1270 feet high, the actual climb involves only 500 feet of direct ascent with the reward of extensive views both north and south across the lake.

MAP REF: **O.S. Outdoor Leisure Map 5 (N.E. area) 436 192**

DIRECTIONS: From Pooley Bridge at the north eastern end of Ullswater, follow the minor road on the lake's southern shoreline signed to Martindale. The parking area adjacent to the Parish Church of St Peter in Martindale is reached after approximately 4.5 miles.

With the church directly behind you, climb the path ahead adjacent to a stone wall. A well defined track leads to the cairn at the top of the fell.

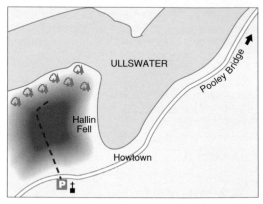

View south from Hallin Fell. Val Corbett.

MINI WALKS, VIEWPOINTS & WATERFALLS

A stunning combination of Lakeland's most popular waterfall together with possibly the best view of the head of Ullswater (certainly one of the most photographed views- if you own a copy of the 1:25,000 Outdoor 5 OS map, the view is shown on the cover). Aira Force has been drawing visitors since the inception of tourism in Lakeland and is still as popular today. Only the National Trust's careful path management and restoration in the area has curbed the damage that has been caused by the thousands of boots trampling the short walk to the falls every year. The force (taken from the Norse word *foss* meaning waterfall) falls 65 feet in two cascades with principal views from two stone footbridges.

Gowbarrow Fell, easily reached by bearing right from Aira Force, is an altogether different experience; craggy and wild with a well defined path which climbs a steady 300 feet across treeless terrain to reveal the splendour of Ullswater. Below can be seen Lyulph's Tower, built in 1794 appropriately as a hunting lodge as both Gowbarrow Park and Glencoyne Park nearby were originally set aside by the Normans as deer forests. The National Trust provides a cafe and toilets next to the car park.

WALK TERRAIN GRADE: Aira Force: **EASY** Gowbarrow Fell: **MODERATE**

MAP REF: **O.S. Outdoor Leisure Map 5 (N.E. area) 402 201**

DIRECTIONS: The Aira Force car park is well signed on the A592 between Glenridding and Pooley Bridge.

For Aira Force, follow the well made path from the National Trust Information point and cross a wooden footbridge to climb gradually with the beck below to your left. After ten minutes the falls are reached with viewing bridges located both above and below the cascade. A return path on the other side of the beck allows a circular route back to the car park.

For Yew Crag, follow the instruction for Aira Force and head up to the higher bridge to follow an obvious path that leads right away from the waterfall, in the direction of Ullswater. Proceed through a gate and follow the path that starts to climb up the lower crags. After a while, the path forks, take the left fork and continue straight ahead. Yew Crag is marked by a cairn and is accessed via a stile over a wire fence. The views across Ullswater to Hallin Fell and Place Fell make the short climb worthwhile.

To return to the car, retrace the route back from Yew Crag to Aira Force and descend via the clearly defined footpath.

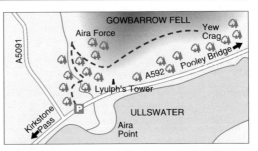

Aira Force. Val Corbett.

This mini walk presents an opportunity to visit the tranquil and picturesque Harrop Tarn, situated in the fells just to the west of Thirlmere. A well made and easily followed North West Water Authority path climbs past the attractive Dobgill waterfall before reaching Harrop Tarn (the falls are reached after approx. fifteen minutes, the tarn after twenty). A circular route, detailed below, takes around 1.5 hours and on the return descent provides views towards Thirlmere.

MAP REF: **O.S. Outdoor Leisure Map 5 (N.E. area) 315 140**

DIRECTIONS: From the A591 just to the south of Thirlmere, take the minor road (signed Armboth) that passes along the western side of the reservoir. Find the North West Water Dobgill car park (toilets here).

Follow the signed and well made footpath from the southern end of the car park. Pass through a tall kissing gate and zigzag upwards through woodland. Dobgill waterfall is soon reached before walking on through the woods to the tarn.

For a circular walk: Bear left to cross a wooden footbridge and proceed ahead (ignore Wythburn bridleway). After a short distance, bear left through a kissing gate and follow a clear path right, uphill, adjacent to a wall. At a meeting point of three walls, pass over the stile and walk ahead to pass through a gap in the wall. Turn left and follow the distinct descending path. Half way down, bear right on a grassy path to reach a gate in a wall. Do not go through the gate but turn left and walk with the wall on your right. Pass through the gate in the corner and descend to go left through a gate at the bottom. Proceed ahead through two gates before reaching a third gate leading on to the road. Turn left to return to the car.

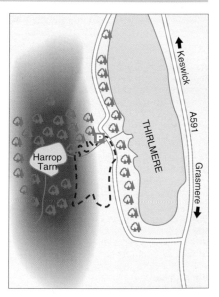

Harrop Tarn. MDN.

Latrigg, a foothill of Skiddaw, provides extensive views over Keswick, Borrowdale, Bassenthwaite, Derwentwater and much more besides, ideal if higher views are obscured by low cloud over Skiddaw or time/inclination prevents a longer walk. The 1200 foot high grassy summit is reached after an easy walk of around half a mile, the height of the car park ensuring only a modest climb of approx. 250 feet.

The underlying geology here consists of Skiddaw Slate, making for smooth rounded hills very different to the craggy slopes produced by the Borrowdale volcanics rock further to the south. The Skiddaw Slate is some of the oldest rock in the world, formed some 500 million years ago.

MAP REF: **O.S. Outdoor Leisure Map 4 (N.W. area) 282 254**

DIRECTIONS: From the A66 roundabout north of Keswick, take the A591 north (signed Carlisle and Mirehouse) and almost immediately turn right signed to Ormathwaite. Pass the Underscar Manor Hotel before turning right at the Applethwaite Country House Hotel (also signed Skiddaw by public footpath). The road gains height and becomes rougher before reaching a parking area at its end.

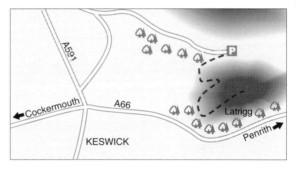

Pass through the gate following the well defined path that leads downhill. This soon levels out before forking left to take a gradual path that zigzags up to the top.

Keswick and Derwentwater from Latrigg. Val Corbett.

WALK EASY GRADE

MINI WALKS, VIEWPOINTS & WATERFALLS

A real treat for walking groups which include young children or those with reduced mobility, as the old Keswick railway line is flat and level allowing easy strolls through lovely countryside. The four mile long path crosses and re-crosses the River Greta, winding its way through woodland before passing south of the A66 to a further parking area near Threlkeld. The path also provides access to the mixed woodland of Brundholme Woods on the southern reaches of Latrigg.

In 1865, the railway line reached Keswick, linking Penrith with Cockermouth to bring an influx of tourists that helped to turn Keswick into the tourist resort it is today. During the early 1970's the line ceased to be used.

MAP REF: **O.S. Outdoor Leisure Map 4 (N.W. area) 272 237**

DIRECTIONS: *From central Keswick, follow brown tourist sign for the leisure centre. At the entrance to the leisure centre parking area, turn left and park in front of the disused railway station. The path starts at the far end of the old station platform.*

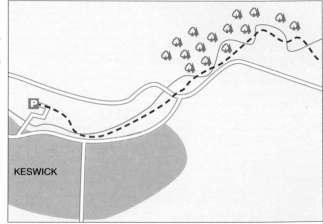

KESWICK

Keswick railway footpath. Val Corbett.

Two National Trust owned sections of the northern Derwentwater shoreline offering stunning views of the lake, islands and launches.

Friars Crag, which is suitable for wheelchairs and pushchairs, was bought by subscription for the National Trust in 1922 as a memorial to Canon Hardwicke Rawnsley, a local curate and one of the three founder members in 1895. Friars Crag was proclaimed by Ruskin, the nineteenth century critic and philanthropist, as one of the top three viewpoints in Europe; a memorial stone recounts the tale of it being one of his earliest memories following a childhood visit. The name Friars Crag is believed to derive from its use in the seventh century as a starting point for monks visiting St Herbert's Island, Derwentwater's largest and most southerly island.

Crow Park provides a 40 acre open space at the head of Derwent with views towards the '*Jaws of Borrowdale*'. Access is adjacent to the lakeside car park. Nearby Hope Garden offers ornamental gardens and miniature golf.

MAP REF: **O.S. Outdoor Leisure Map 4 (N.W. area) 266 229**

DIRECTIONS: The lakeside car park is signed from the B5289 on the southern edge of Keswick. Toilets are situated adjacent to the Century Theatre, refreshments available nearby.

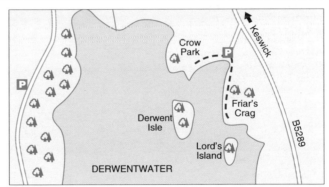

Friar's Crag and Crow Park. Val Corbett.

29 CASTLE HEAD

A fifteen minute walk to the 530 foot high wooded hill of Castle Head is rewarded with views across the whole of Derwentwater and surrounding fells, as well as across Keswick towards Skiddaw in the north. A view indicator and two benches are located at the top.

MAP REF: **O.S. Outdoor Leisure Map 4 (N.W. area) 266229**

DIRECTIONS: The lakeside car park is signed from the B5289 on the southern edge of Keswick. Toilets are situated adjacent to the Century Theatre, refreshments available nearby.

From the Lakeside car park at Keswick, head for a gap in the wall adjacent to the Century Theatre. A left bearing track through the National Trust owned woods is followed by a sharp left to follow a hedged path between two fields. Climb the steps, cross a stile and the main road, taking care as this road can be very busy. From a gap in the wall opposite, ascend via a left bearing path past a bench, before bearing right to the summit.

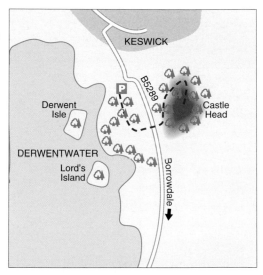

Derwentwater from Castle Head. Val Corbett.

Surprise View offers an excellent opportunity to see the whole of Derwentwater as well as the summit of Cat Bells, situated directly opposite (see Guided Walk 14 for a 4.5 mile route on this favourite fell). Clearly in view is the largest and most southerly of Derwentwater's islands; St Herbert's Island, an important destination for seventh century pilgrims visiting the hermitage there.

Ashness Bridge, reached from Surprise View by following the road back on which you arrived (approx. half a mile), is an attractive packhorse bridge, its backdrop of Derwentwater, Keswick and Skiddaw, competes only with Tarn Hows as Lakeland's most photographed view.

MAP REF: **O.S. Outdoor Leisure Map 4 (N.W. area) 268 196**

DIRECTIONS: From the B5289 south of Keswick, bear left signed to Ashness Bridge and Watendlath. After the narrow packhorse bridge, continue for a further half a mile to park in one of two parking areas adjacent to Surprise View.

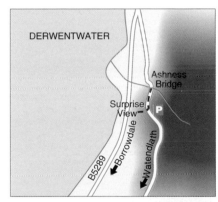

Ashness Bridge. Val Corbett.

MINI WALKS, VIEWPOINTS & WATERFALLS

31 LODORE FALLS

Lodore Falls is located behind the Stakis Lodore Hotel and best reached by using a footpath which starts a short walk away at the National Trust Kettlewell car park. The falls are situated on private property but an honesty box has been provided for those using this approach to Lodore. The waterfall, a must for Victorian tourists staying at Keswick, is formed by the beck from Watendlath Tarn cascading over huge boulders for a distance of some 100 feet. Although the waterfall is spectacular after spells of heavy rain, the falls dry to a trickle in periods of prolonged dry weather. Robert Southey's famous onomatopoeic poem *How does the water come down at Lodore?*, an extract of which is below, is quite unlike any other poem in the English Language:

'Rushing and lushing and brushing and gushing
And flapping and rapping and clapping and slapping
And curling and whirling and purling and twirling
And thumping and plumping and bumping and jumping
And dashing and flashing and splashing and clashing
And so never-ending, but always descending......'

The poet was responsible for the modern day spelling of the falls' name, its original derivation was from the Norse for Low-door referring to the gap in the ridge through which the falls gush.

N.B. The purchase of a National Trust car park ticket at Kettlewell, enables a visit without further parking charges, to the Bowder Stone, two miles further south (see Attractions).

MAP REF: **O.S. Outdoor Leisure Map 4 (N.W. area) 267 196**

DIRECTIONS: *From Keswick, head south on the Borrowdale road (B5289) and park in the lakeside National Trust Kettlewell car park, approximately half a mile after the Watendlath turnoff. Public toilets are located adjacent to the road near the Stakis Lodore Hotel.*

Leave the car park and cross the road to a gap in the wall (sign for the falls). A path through the woodland runs parallel with the road before descending a little towards the Stakis Lodore Hotel. Here, bear left to the falls viewpoint.

Lodore Falls. Val Corbett.

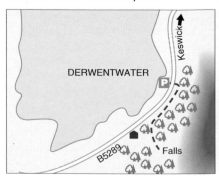

A spectacular 100 foot cascade set in a lightly wooded gorge one mile from Seathwaite, known as the place with the highest rainfall in England. The overall round trip to the force is approximately two miles.

MAP REF: **O.S. Outdoor Leisure Map 4 (N.W. area) 235 123**

DIRECTIONS: Follow the B5289 south from Keswick through Borrowdale. After passing through Rosthwaite, continue until turn off signed Seathwaite and Stylehead Pass, reached shortly before the hamlet of Seatoller. Park at Seathwaite.

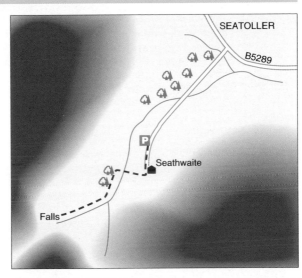

From the National Trust teashop in Seathwaite, follow the footpath sign at an entrance between two stone barns. A track leads between two stone walls and in the mountainside ahead can be seen the cascade of Sourmilk Gill. After the footbridge, turn left through a gate and follow the stream side track. Skirt a small wooded area before heading for a ladder stile over a wall on the fellside. A now less defined track bears ahead to the right towards further trees. After crossing a ridge by two large boulders, continue towards the tree lined gorge whereupon the waterfall appears as you round the fell. The best viewpoint, which can be reached after a short scramble, is adjacent to the gate next to a stone wall.

Seatoller and Great End. Val Corbett.

MINI WALKS, VIEWPOINTS & WATERFALLS

The Rannerdale Knotts, a small group of crags at the western end of a grassy ridge called Low Bank, are well worth seeking out for the excellent view of Crummock Water, one of the larger but less busy stretches of water in the Lake District.

The climb of about 800 feet to the 1165 foot summit justifies the effort for the tremendous viewpoint over the lake, Buttermere, Mellbreak and Grasmoor. The Rannerdale valley just to the north of the Knotts is said to have been the site of a Norman army massacre by the Saxons.

MAP REF: **O.S. Outdoor Leisure Map 4 (N.W. area) 164 185**

DIRECTIONS: Crummock Water and the Rannerdale Knotts are situated in the north western corner of Lakeland, accessed from Keswick via the B5289 through Borrowdale, the Honister Pass and Buttermere. After Buttermere village, proceed ahead on the road adjacent to Crummock for just over a mile to find a small parking area on the right hand side marked with a National Trust sign Rannerdale.

Return to the road, turn left and walk for about 50 yards to find a path bearing left up the hillside (a second path—marked as a bridleway— stays at low level to a rocky viewpoint suitable for picnics). Follow this path directly uphill to reach the summit. For a circular walk, follow the grassy ridge of Low Bank for about a mile before bearing right to follow a path which descends towards Buttermere village. On reaching the road, turn right and follow it back to the parking area (see map).

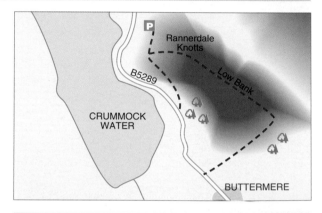

Crummock Water from Rannerdale Knotts. Val Corbett.

On National Trust property west of Crummock Water, Scale Force is tucked away in a narrow gorge on the way to the summit of Red Pike. It is the tallest waterfall in the Lake District with a single fall of 170 feet and two others of approximately 20 feet each. Wordsworth described it as *"a fine chasm, with a lofty, though but slender, fall of water"*. The force (from the Norse word *foss* meaning waterfall) is a spectacular sight even after fairly dry periods. Visitors have been drawn to the falls from the earliest beginnings of Lakeland tourism and to save the legs of early nineteenth century sightseers for whom Scale Force was a must, boats were hired to row across Crummock Water so saving the 2.5 mile return trip.

MAP REF: **O.S. Outdoor Leisure Map 4 (N.W. area) 176 171**

DIRECTIONS: From Keswick, follow the Borrowdale signs south on the B5289. Pass through the Honister Pass and alongside Buttermere Lake and park in Buttermere village.

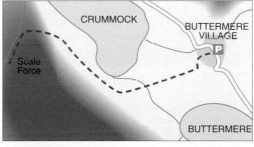

From the parking areas in Buttermere, follow the path next to the Bridge Hotel, signed as a public footpath to Scale Force. Follow the path ahead, bearing left to pass through a kissing gate before bearing right through a further kissing gate adjacent to a farm gate with a National Trust sign indicating the way to Scale Bridge and Scale Force. Walk adjacent to a wire fence before bearing right and crossing a stone bridge. Pass through a gate and follow the path off to the right, the path leads towards Crummock Water which gradually becomes visible on the right.

Cross several becks, including a larger one via a footbridge, the path now starting to bear off to the left away from the lake. At a large stone cairn, bear left for a short distance before returning to follow the cairn marked path ahead as it leads to Scale Beck Valley. As the northern end of Crummock Water starts to disappear from view, cross a beck and follow the path up steps to reach a gap in the stone wall. Lakeland's tallest waterfall can be viewed from the footbridge below.

Scale Force. MDN.

Situated at the northern end of Crummock Water in the far western corner of Lakeland is the National Trust owned Lanthwaite Wood, covering an area of nearly seventy acres. The woodland provides easy forest walking with access to the shoreline of the lake and views towards Grasmoor, Mellbreak and the Honister Pass beyond.

Lanthwaite Hill, a 682 foot treeless viewpoint reached after only a ten minute 200 foot gradual climb is worth a visit while you are here.

MAP REF: **O.S. Outdoor Leisure Map 4 (N.W. area) 149 216**

DIRECTIONS: From where the B5289 from Cockermouth heads south towards Crummock, Buttermere and the Honister Pass, take a minor road (signed Loweswater and Scales Hill) heading south west. After descending past the Scale Hill Hotel look for a National Trust car park on the left hand side just before the river bridge.

For Lanthwaite Wood, follow the well defined tracks from the parking area.

For Lanthwaite Hill, from the car park, walk up the hill towards the Scale Hill Hotel and then turn right, signed to Lanthwaite Green and Cinderdale Common. Follow the obvious track ahead before bearing left to emerge from the trees onto open ground; Lanthwaite Hill is the larger of the two mounds in front of you.

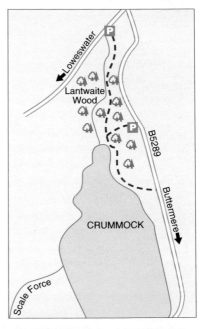

Loweswater Valley and Crummock. Val Corbett.

MINI WALKS, VIEWPOINTS & WATERFALLS

36 ENNERDALE

Ennerdale is rarely busy, its location far away from the tourist hotspots of central Lakeland sees to that, although it provides some of the finest walking country in the Lake District with miles and miles of path open to the public within the Forestry Commission woodlands. Ennerdale was first afforested in the 1920's; the rigid lines of single coniferous species were not without opposition although the forestry management today is much more imaginative, with the result that the environment has become more pleasing to the eye.

The Ennerdale Valley is fortunately remote; tall crags loom around the head of the lake where much of the early interest in rock climbing took place with Pillar Rock being a popular and challenging target. Deep inland at the head of the valley is the Black Sail Youth Hostel, easily the country's most remote and isolated hostel, reached only after a long walk.

Most walks start from the Bowness Knott car park (toilets available) where map boards and waymarks have been placed to help guide you (a detailed leaflet with a map of the walks can be obtained from any of the Forestry Commission visitor centres such as Whinlatter and Grizedale).

There are four main routes:

1) Smithy Beck Forest Trail Between 2 to 3.5 miles
Red waymarks **MODERATE**

2) Liza Path 9 miles Green waymarks **MODERATE**

3) Nine Becks Walk 10 miles Blue waymarks **TOUGH**

4) Round Lake Walk 7 miles **EASY**

MAP REF: **O.S. Outdoor Leisure Map 4 (N.W. area) 109 154**

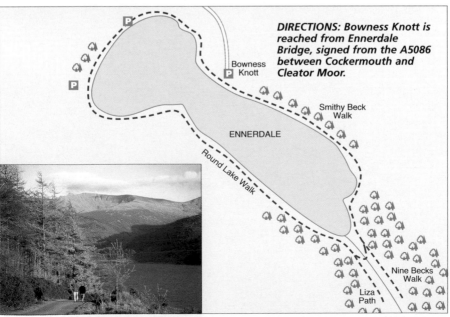

DIRECTIONS: *Bowness Knott is reached from Ennerdale Bridge, signed from the A5086 between Cockermouth and Cleator Moor.*

Bowness Knott

Smithy Beck Walk

ENNERDALE

Round Lake Walk

Nine Becks Walk

Liza Path

Ennerdale Forrest. Val Corbett.

MINI WALKS, VIEWPOINTS & WATERFALLS

Gushing through a narrow rocky cleft, the attractive 30 foot waterfall of Spout Force can easily be found within Forestry Commission woodland in the far north west of the National Park. Far away from the busier central fells, this waterfall is rarely crowded with visitors and can be reached via a waymarked circular walk of around 2 miles. Nearby is the Whinlatter Forest Visitor Centre, where many woodland walks are waymarked.

MAP REF: **O.S. Outdoor Leisure Map 4 (N.W. area) 182 257**

DIRECTIONS: *A car park with a sign indicating the waterfall is found at the western end of the Whinlatter Pass (B5292) between Keswick and Cockermouth.*

From the parking area, a track following yellow waymark posts leads across a stile and over fields . An obvious path through woodland reaches a wooden footbridge and then heads right alongside the beck signed to Spout Force. A small viewing platform will soon be found.

From the platform retrace your steps some 15 yards to follow the waymark posts which lead right through the woods, eventually turning right onto a tarmac road and back to the parking area.

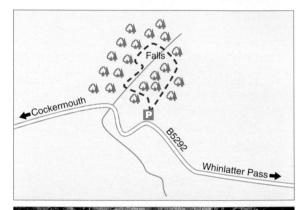

Spout Force. Val Corbett.

MINI WALKS, VIEWPOINTS & WATERFALLS

38 WHINLATTER FOREST

Set on the hills west of Keswick, Whinlatter Forest is the Forestry Commission's most northerly forest and one of their earliest in Cumbria, planting having started as a result of the timber shortage immediately after the first World War. Described as England's only mountain forest, Whinlatter, like Grizedale, has had considerable investment in order to turn the woodlands into a recreational resource with an interesting visitor centre and many waymarked woodland paths. To be sure of getting the most from your visit, it would be wise to obtain the most up to date leaflet from the visitor centre.

Walks include:

1) Revelin Moss 2 miles *Yellow waymarks* **EASY**

2) Comb Forest Trail 1.75 miles *Red waymarks* **EASY**

3) Comb Forest Conservation Trail 1.75 miles
Blue waymarks **MODERATE**

4) Lords Seat and Barf 5 miles
Follow relevant junction posts **TOUGH**

MAP REF: O.S. Outdoor Leisure Map 4 (N.W. area) **207 245**

DIRECTIONS: Head west from Keswick on the A66 before taking the B5292 at Braithwaite. The visitor centre is well signed.

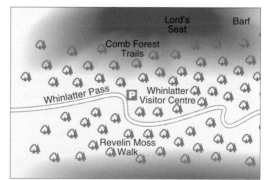

Whinlatter forest walks, viewpoint. Val Corbett.

MINI WALKS, VIEWPOINTS & WATERFALLS

Created at the end of the eighteenth century, Dodd Wood, just north of Keswick, was originally planted by the Spedding family, owners of nearby Mirehouse, before being leased by the Forestry Commission. The wood contains four walks indicated with coloured waymarks; a leaflet with detailed map and background information can be obtained from the Old Sawmill Tearoom which as its name suggests was once where the logs were cut using the waterpower of Skill Beck. The tearoom (017687 74317) is open 10am-5.30pm, seven days a week during the season (approx. two weeks before Easter through until November) and then at weekends in Nov./Dec. as well as Christmas and New Year.

1) The Sawmill Walk
A fifteen minute walk of approx. 400 yards adjacent to Skill Beck.
Follow yellow waymarks **EASY**

2) The Douglas Fir Trail
A 45 minute half mile walk which gives an opportunity to see magnificent specimens of the Douglas Fir, first planted here in 1927 and now growing at up to 120 feet in height. *Follow blue waymarks* **MODERATE**

3) The Skill Beck Trail
A one and a half mile circular walk which climbs to around a thousand feet above sea level rewarding the walker with lovely views over Bassenthwaite Lake. The tumbling waters of Skill Beck, its source some 1400 feet up on the western slopes of Carl Side, an attractive feature of the walk. *Follow red waymarks* **MODERATE**

4) The Dodd Summit Trail
The toughest of the four routes, comprising a 3 mile ascent of the 1647 foot high Dodd summit. The view from the top is magnificent and encompasses Derwentwater, Bassenthwaite and all the surrounding fells believed to embrace some 500 square miles! The informative Forestry Commission leaflet also indicates that Dodd Wood is an important nature reserve with 34 bird species, 7 mammal and 174 of plant identified.
Follow green waymarks **TOUGH**

MAP REF: O.S. Outdoor Leisure Map 4 (N.W. area) **236 282**

DIRECTIONS: *From the A66 roundabout north of Keswick, take the A591 north (signed Carlisle and Mirehouse). The entrance to Dodd Woods is opposite the entry point to Mirehouse.*

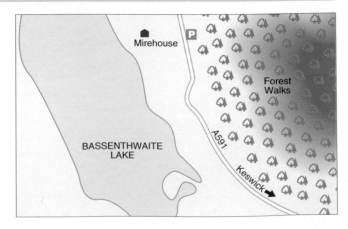

MINI WALKS, VIEWPOINTS & WATERFALLS

Caldbeck's picturesque limestone gorge is unique in the Lake District as limestone appears only on the periphery of the National Park; the well known waterfall easily reached after a 10 minute walk from the free car park in the village. Passed en route to the waterfall are the ruins of a bobbin mill which, at the time of its construction in 1859 had an overshot wheel with a diameter of some forty two feet and thought to have been the largest in the country. The mill ceased working in 1908 before being damaged by fire in 1959.

As well as the Howk, Caldbeck has much to offer the visitor. It includes the ornately carved gravestone of the renowned huntsman John Peel, buried here in 1854 and made famous by the song *'D'ye Ken John Peel'*, which was written by his friend John Woodcock Graves in 1832. The 'Beauty of Buttermere', Mary Robinson, is also buried in the same churchyard. Also worth a visit also is Priest's Mill, an award winning restored eighteenth century mill building containing a restaurant, small shops and an interesting mining museum (see Attractions for details of opening hours).

MAP REF: O.S. Landranger 90 **323 399**

DIRECTIONS: Caldbeck is situated on the far northern fringe of the National Park, use the main car park in the centre of the village near the beck. Refreshments and public toilets all within the village.

Leave the car park at the exit and turn left (large village duck pond and green in front of you), walking straight ahead to find a sign on a barn indicating the footpath to the waterfall. The Howk is reached shortly after passing the ruins of an old bobbin mill.

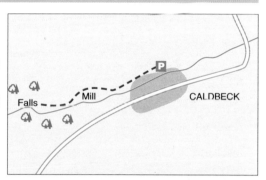

The Howk, Caldbeck. Val Corbett.

123

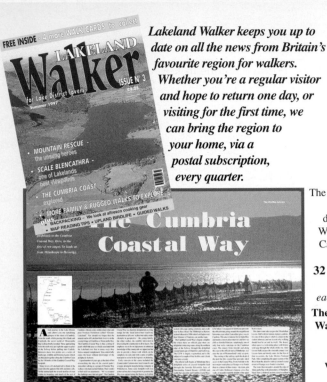
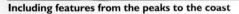

Keswick Railway footpath. Val Corbett.

Rydal from White Moss Common. Val Corbett.

THE LAKE DISTRICT NATIONAL PARK AUTHORITY

by Mike Cain

The Lake District National Park Authority was established by Parliament in 1951 to safeguard the area's outstanding beauty and to help people enjoy it. As a local authority, we also take into account the needs of the 40,000 or so people who live inside the National Park boundary. In short, we are here to look after the National Park, helping people to enjoy its beauty whilst fostering the well-being of those who live and work here.

The protection and conservation of what is widely regarded as the finest upland scenery in England is the National Park Authority's main responsibility. This has a fundamental influence on a wide range of policies and activities. Employing around 180 staff in Planning, Park Management, Visitor Services and Administration,

we try to ensure development is appropriate to the landscape and to the needs of the local community. We prepare sensitive management plans, repair and improve footpaths, fund town and village enhancement schemes and offer specialist land management, built environment, landscape design, ecology and recreational planning advice. Our Local Plan guides development to ensure housing, commercial and conservation needs are compatible with the landscape. We give grants to create new access opportunities, maintain and improve hedgerows, plant trees, stock proof wild flower meadows and woodlands, regenerate and protect lakeshore habitats and repair dry stone walls. As a plethora of lakes and tarns provide both recreational opportunity and support important wildlife

Brockhole Gardens. David Ward.

habitats, we apply bylaws, provide boat launching areas and maintain the lakeshore footpaths to balance recreation with conservation. We own 9000 hectares of fells and woodland and carry out sensitive management to sustain wildlife habitats.

The fact that the NPA does not own all the land within the National Park is a fundamental difference with National Parks overseas, particularly in the USA. The Lake District National Park Authority owns approximately 3.9% of the land with the remainder being in the hands of other agencies such as the National Trust, North West Water plc, Forest Enterprise, and a vast range of private landowners. Therefore, as well as depending on the controls that are available, such as the development control system, consultation of farm grants and forestry proposals, we work closely with landowners and other environmental agencies to establish management agreements and to ensure the 2,300 miles of bridleways and footpaths are accessible to all.

Working closely with English Heritage we help protect historical monuments such as Castlerigg Stone Circle and Hardknott Roman Fort for everyone's enjoyment.

Hundreds of Voluntary Wardens provide invaluable support, repairing damage to the fragile landscape - an expensive and never-ending task. Our Lake District Tourism and Conservation Partnership with Cumbria Tourist Board, the National Trust and several leading players in the local tourism industry raises money for the essential practical conservation projects in the National Park. To ensure continued protection of the National Park we must bring about changes in attitudes. Our network of information centres, the National Park Visitor Centre, Brockhole, near Windermere, a comprehensive events programme and a wide range of publications all help raise awareness and understanding of the National Park

and the work done to protect it.

Recognising that children are our future, we provide a wide range of educational resources, activities and opportunities for youth and school groups. A varied programme of tutored activities, Learning through Experience, offers an unrivalled opportunity to discover issues facing the Lake District and our Blencathra Centre, near Keswick, run with the help of the Field Studies Council, is one of the most important centres in northern England for environmental education.

All this work and more is achieved with a limited budget. A grant from the Department of the Environment of around £3m, supplemented by a levy on local taxpayers and the NPA's own income, has to be made go a long way. Decisions on how that money is spent and how the National Park is managed fall to a 26-member board, consisting of Secretary of State appointees and representatives of Cumbria County Council and the district and parish councils within the Park boundary.

It is in no small part due to the NPA's work that the Lake District remains as beautiful as it is today. The Authority's achievements are as much apparent in what is not there as in what is. Complacency, however, is not in the Lake District National Park Authority's vocabulary. With the help of our partners, local residents and the visiting public, we will continue to ensure the Lake District gives as much pleasure to future generations as it gives to us.

For full details of Brockhole Visitor Centre, see Attractions section.

Ranger.

Scafell range from Hardknott Fort. Val Corbett.

Castlerigg. Val Corbett.

Seathwaite Bridge, Duddon. Val Corbett.

by Mark Norton

BEATRIX POTTER

B eatrix Potter competes hard with William Wordsworth as the most famous literary figure in Lakeland, although, unlike Wordsworth, she was not Cumbrian by birth. Nor did she spend her early life here, having been born in London and moving to the Lake District permanently only after her marriage at the age of 49. Beatrix Potter and Lakeland's relationship is of course due to the influence of the Cumbrian landscape and even more importantly the animals contained within it, each one combining to inspire the development of her writing. Similarly, the last 30 years of her life were spent as a large landowner and Lakeland farmer doing much to conserve and preserve the landscape that had influenced her earlier creativity.

Born to wealthy professional parents in Kensington in 1866, Helen Beatrix Potter had a rather closeted and somewhat lonely childhood. Her barrister father and heiress mother believed in a rather strict upbringing, though it is possible that these lonely days in her nursery may have first led to the development of her drawing and story telling skills. Annual summer holidays appear to have been the only relief from this rather isolated and cramped existence. The family and servants would decamp for periods of three months at a time to Scotland before increasingly spending summers in the Lake District. Stays at Wray Castle overlooking Lake Windermere were followed by holidays at Lingholm on the shores of Derwentwater.

Hill Top. Val Corbett.

Beatrix Potter outside Hill Top. National Trust.

These excursions seem to have inspired the young Beatrix. Her interest in nature and animals led in 1900 to the publication of her first book, *'The Tale of Peter Rabbit'*. This charming tale of Flopsy, Mopsy, Cottontail and Peter, with illustrations by her own hand, proved to be extremely popular. Three years later, 50,000 copies of the book were in print; an increasingly streetwise Beatrix registering a Peter Rabbit doll at the London Patent Office in the same year.

The period 1900-1905 saw Potter at her most prolific with *'The Tale of Squirrel Nutkin'*, *'The Tailor of Gloucester'*, *'The Tale of Benjamin Bunny'* and *'The Tale of Mrs Tiggy Winkle'* published to public acclaim.

Beatrix remained in London with her parents who had by now started to holiday near Esthwaite Water. Much to the annoyance of her parents, she used some of her early royalties to purchase land nearby at Near Sawrey. *'The Tale of Two Bad Mice'* in 1904 saw a relationship develop with Norman Warne, son of her publishers Frederick Warne. Her engagement the following year and purchase of Hill Top Farm (now owned by the

The World of Beatrix Potter Attraction.

National Trust) was marred by Norman's death shortly afterwards. Hill Top became more and more a welcome escape from her parents: characters such as Tom Kitten, Samuel Whiskers and Jemima Puddleduck were all created here and based on animals around the farm.

It was not until 1913, aged 49, that she finally left London and her parents to settle permanently in her beloved Lakeland. Her marriage to a Hawkshead solicitor, William Heelis, marked the end of her 13 years of creative writing, a relatively short period given the effect she was to have on children's publishing. The couple moved to Castle Cottage where they stayed until their deaths. Potter spent her time here developing a

knowledge of farming and animal husbandry, becoming a devotee in particular of the Herdwick sheep, a tough hardy breed native to Cumbria.

Following her death in 1943, her considerable land holdings including 15 farms were bequeathed to the National Trust, the only proviso being that Hill Top should remain untouched and only her precious Herdwicks be allowed on her land.

Her books continue to be as popular as ever with millions of copies sold each year and every conceivable type of merchandise bear her characters. A far cry indeed from 'Peter Rabbit's' first print run of only 250 copies, available for one shilling and two pence each!!

Derwentwater, an early inspiration for the writing of Beatrix Potter. Val Corbett.

BEATRIX POTTER ATTRACTIONS IN LAKELAND

Please refer to Index for page ref.

■ Hill Top
■ World of Beatrix Potter Exhibition
■ Beatrix Potter Gallery

Gosforth Cross. Val Corbett.

Ambleside. Val Corbett.

MOUNTAIN RESCUE!

A look at the work of the
Keswick Mountain Rescue Team

by Mark Norton

Mountain rescue? Never happen to me! Probably quite true, but for a significant number of people each year, the Mountain Rescue Service is a life saving facility in every sense of the word, run by unpaid volunteers, out in all weathers and at all times of the day, often for many hours at a time. The Lake District has 11 Mountain Rescue Teams as well as a specialised mines rescue unit, each one staffed by volunteers who can be called on at any time by the police to assist in search and rescue operations. Teams are based at Furness, Millom, Kendal, Kirkby Stephen, Coniston, Penrith, Patterdale, Langdale, Wasdale, Cockermouth and Keswick.

1997 sees the 50th anniversary of the Keswick rescue team with some 1,500 callouts since the team's inception in 1947. The increasing popularity

Courtesy of Dave Willis, Mountain Sport Photography.

of the fells at all times of the year ensures that the team's yearly callout average has grown to an all time high. From less than 20 annually in the 40's and 50's, callouts doubled during the 70's and early 80's. 1995 (the latest year for which figures are available at time of publishing) proved to be the busiest year on record with 87 rescues (not including 6 animal rescues and some 20 or so alerts for overdue walkers which did not develop into full team callouts). All this means that the Keswick team is now the busiest in Britain. Their patch covers some 400 square miles of mountainous terrain, stretching from Scafell Pike to Skiddaw, Grisedale Pike to Thirlmere and Helvellyn to Bassenthwaite, including three of the highest peaks in England.

The team, with an average age of 40, consists of over 40 members (including four female colleagues) on the callout list, made up of police constables, hoteliers, doctors, rangers, teachers and builders as well as a dentist, solicitor, baker and many others. All volunteers undergo an initial probationary period of one year. Becoming a member of the service is dependent upon at least 75% of fellow team members approving, essential, given the team nature of their work and the close co-operation between personnel. Members undergo a continuous training schedule to ensure they are able to cope with all kinds of rescue situations, thus minimising the danger to themselves when out on the fells.

The team relies on two Defender Landrovers, each fully equipped with stretchers, first aid kits, painkillers and communications gear. The team's latest piece of equipment is the PROPAQ, which enables monitoring of a casualty's temperature, blood pressure and level of oxygen in the blood. This costly piece of equipment was donated by an anonymous benefactor. In extreme cases, the team will liaise with RAF Boulmer in Northumberland and RAF Leaconfield in Yorkshire to effect helicopter evacuation.

Courtesy of Mike Scott, North News.

Although October was the peak month in 1995 and the majority of callouts occurred from around midday to early evening, a look at the incident log for the year shows the sheer diversity of callouts that the team has to deal with. On the first day of the year, at nine o'clock in the evening, the team was called out to 2 people after flashing lights were reported near the Rigg Head Quarries. The couple, which included a woman who had fallen whilst ice climbing on Goat Crag, were escorted down from the area. February 23rd saw a walker brought down from the Sty Head path near Taylor Gill. A broken ankle had resulted from the wearing of wellies. July 2nd, mid afternoon, the team called to rescue a paraglider (aged 39) who had been dumped 40 feet after hitting turbulence. The man, with internal injuries, was flown to Carlisle Hospital. On 15th September, during the late afternoon, a walker came across the body of a lady in How Gill. The police were alerted and the body was recovered by the team. The casualty had died from neck injuries sustained in a fall. October 21st, 10pm, two walkers became lost whilst descending from Scafell in darkness. They rang the police on their mobile

telephone to say that they were lost and didn't know where they were. Keswick Team members and dogs found them and brought them down. Christmas Eve, 1.55pm saw the team called to Latrigg after a passer-by heard shouts of help from the fellside. The area was searched but nothing was found.

Running costs for the Keswick Team are around £30,000 per annum, all raised by public donation, fund-raising events and legacies. A high profile £200,000 appeal for funds in 1995 for a much needed purpose built HQ on the outskirts of Keswick saw considerable local effort and support, made all the more difficult by a surprising refusal for funding from the National Lottery. Although the team has now taken occupation of their new HQ, fund-raising continues to ensure the service can carry on.

Whilst it is true statistically, that you may never need the services of one of Lakeland's Mountain Rescue Teams, the next time you see a collection box, remember the brave volunteers and the excellent work they do in saving lives, helping broken bodies, rescuing stranded walkers and reuniting loved ones.

GUIDED WALKS

The 20 walks in this section have been divided into these three grades:

SAFETY WARNING

When walking in the Lake District, particularly in the fells or upland areas, it is vigorously recommended that strong walking shoes or preferably boots are used. These will keep your feet dry in boggy areas and prevent accidents when walking on loose rock or terrain which is not level. Always check that there will be enough daylight to complete your route and avoid walking in upland areas during poor weather conditions including low visibility. Leave details of your route and estimated return time if heading up into the hills and always be aware of weather forecasts. Always wear and carry the correct equipment including waterproofs. In the event of an emergency, call the police on 999 who will alert the nearest mountain rescue team.

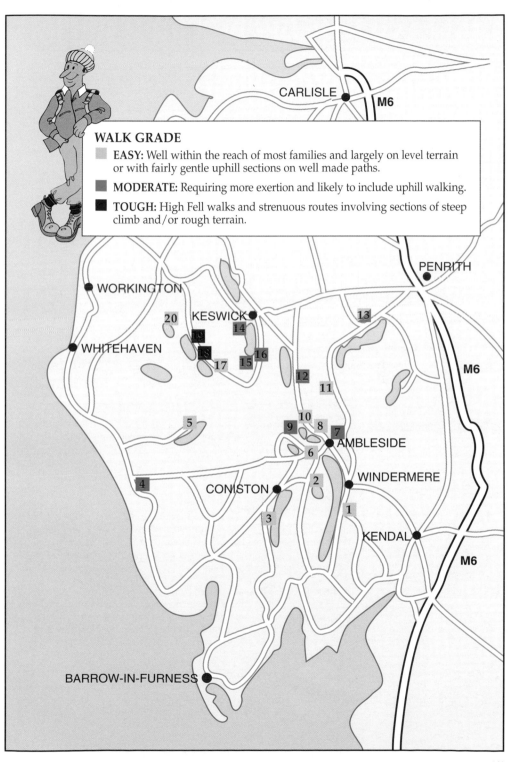

WALK GRADE

EASY: Well within the reach of most families and largely on level terrain or with fairly gentle uphill sections on well made paths.

MODERATE: Requiring more exertion and likely to include uphill walking.

TOUGH: High Fell walks and strenuous routes involving sections of steep climb and/or rough terrain.

CARLISLE **M6**

PENRITH

WORKINGTON

KESWICK

WHITEHAVEN

20 · 19 · 14 · 18 · 17 · 16 · 15 · 13 · 12 · 11

WINDERMERE

AMBLESIDE

10 · 9 · 8 · 7 · 6

5

CONISTON

4 · 2 · 3 · 1

M6

KENDAL

M6

BARROW-IN-FURNESS

LAKELAND EXPLORED GUIDED WALKS

All twenty walks in this section have been thoroughly researched to confirm accurate instructions and the existence of public rights of way and permissive paths. Once the initial research had been completed, the instructions were 'test walked' to ensure ease of use and language employed.

A major difference when walking in the Lake District are the different names for geographical features, mainly as a result of the Nordic influence during settlement by them in the tenth century. Below are a few definitions of words that may come in useful:

FORCE	means waterfall, from Norse word *foss*.
BECK OR GILL	refers to mountain or upland streams.
TARN	is a stretch of water similar to a small lake created as a result of glacial erosion during the Ice Age.
FELL	is the Lakeland word for mountain.

Other terms used in the text include:

CAIRN	is a pile of stones, usually loose and small in height and acting as guides to the main path in upland areas. Fell summits usually have one marking the highest point.
SHEEP FOLDS	are usually stone structures on fellsides built to hold sheep.
PITCHED PATHS	refer to the use of stone to construct a hard wearing path, usually in areas of high erosion (the article on the National Trust has a picture as an example).
KISSING GATE	refers to a hinged gate which allows passage without the use of a latch or bolt.

DISTANCE: Rounded to the nearest half mile.

REFRESHMENTS & TOILETS

REFRESHMENTS/TOILETS: Reference is usually made to only those facilities which are encountered within the immediate course of the walk. In general, only those facilities that are available all year have been included although be aware that there may be limited opening during the winter.

TIME: Rounded to the nearest half hour.

ELEVATION

ELEVATION: This information can be used to determine the amount of uphill walking within the route by subtracting the start point height from the highest elevation reached. This is of course a more accurate assessment of the climb involved than using the highest elevation figure only.

WALK GRADE: The walk grades have been included to help guide you to the walk most suited to your needs. It is wise to use them in conjunction with the elevation details which indicate the amount of uphill walking within the route. Although the grades naturally are somewhat subjective, the following criteria was used to help determine the grading:

MAP REF.: Refers to the start point car park.

- **EASY:** Well within the reach of most families and largely on level terrain or with fairly gentle uphill sections on well made paths.
- **MODERATE:** Requiring more exertion and likely to include uphill walking.
- **TOUGH:** High Fell walks and strenuous routes involving sections of steep climb and/or rough terrain.

YOUR WALKS RECORD

Use this page to record the dates on which you completed each walk:

NO.	TITLE	DATE COMPLETED
1	Bowness-on-Windermere	
2	Hawkshead	
3	Torver Back Common	
4	Ravenglass to Eskdale Green	
5	Wasdale Head	
6	Skelwith Force and Elterwater	
7	Ambleside and High Sweden Bridge	
8	Rydal Water and Nab Scar	
9	Grasmere and Alcock Tarn	
10	Wordsworth's Grasmere	
11	Brothers Water	
12	Thirlmere and Great How	
13	Aira Force and Yew Crag	
14	Cat Bells	
15	Borrowdale and Castle Crag	
16	Watendlath and Dock Tarn	
17	Buttermere	
18	Haystacks	
19	Scale Force and Red Pike	
20	Loweswater	

The Publishers have tried throughout the course of this book to use language and descriptions within the walk instructions that can be understood by all. Whilst very confident walkers who regularly use maps might find some of the descriptions over detailed compared to existing walks books, we make no apology for this as it will ensure that even the most inexperienced walker can enjoy the scenery through which the routes explore without fear of getting lost.

As with all walks books, Lakeland Explored will stay in pristine condition if you avoid getting the book wet. Lakeland Explored has been designed to fit into most map holders; a cheap and effective alternative is to use one of the supermarkets' produce bags which are thin enough to allow you to read your walk directions!

If you prefer to carry an Ordnance Survey map with you, there are four Outdoor Leisure maps (yellow covers) covering the Lake District:

Map 4 The English Lakes, North Western Area. **Map 5** The English Lakes, North Eastern Area. **Map 6** The English Lakes, South Western Area. **Map 7** The English Lakes, South Eastern Area.

Bowness. Val Corbett

BOWNESS-ON-WINDERMERE

This walk starts from central Bowness before passing through a rather gentle landscape of farmland and open countryside. The seclusion and solitude, given its nearness to bustling Bowness, is surprising but rewarding. The walk also offers two excellent viewpoints across Lake Windermere, close to the start and end of the walk.

ELEVATION
Highest elevation reached: 430 ft (130m). Start height: 160 ft (50m).

REFRESHMENTS & TOILETS
In Bowness.

DIRECTIONS TO START
Park in any one of the indicated car parks in the town and head for the church just up from the steamer piers.

WALK DIRECTIONS

From the steamer piers, head up into Bowness and walk past the church, uphill, as if walking to Windermere town. Turn right into Helm Road (there is a large Lakeland Clothing Company shop on the corner) and walk up past the Windermere Hydro Hotel, climbing away from the town. Where the road bears around to the left,

note a number of steps by a lamppost and a small slate sign indicating Biskey Howe viewpoint. This offers magnificent views across Lake Windermere - a view indicator details points of interest.

From the viewpoint, return to the road and turn right before turning left up a tarmac lane marked as a private road and *Deloraine*. Ascend into an area of light woodland and large detached properties.

The lane continues ahead to a sign indicating Helm Farm and cottage only (both left and right forks are marked as private). At Helm Farm, just before the track bears around to the right, turn left through a kissing gate and continue through a second kissing gate. At a path junction, take the right hand path (i.e. straight ahead) towards a number of houses adjacent to a wire fence. Pass over a stone stile and bear right, following the path between a hedge and the fence. Proceed up a gentle slope until a path junction and public footpath sign is reached. Here, turn sharp right (i.e. the second of two paths on the right signed to Windermere) and follow the track around to the left and through a kissing gate to pass beside some houses.

Continue through the small field which climbs gently ahead to a metal kissing gate. Cross the lane to a stone stile next to a public footpath sign. Continue ahead along the edge of the field until the point where the stone wall leads away to the right. Here, descend ahead to the bottom of the field to find a ladder stile adjacent to a small stream. Cross the stile and footbridge before passing up some steps and turning right onto a tarmac lane. Continue ahead, gradually gaining height to reach a sharp right turn in the lane. Here, pass through a large farm gate onto the rough track

leading ahead. Cross the field to another gate, continuing over a stream to follow the track ahead. At a path junction, walk ahead (the Dalesway path leads left) to pass through a further 4 gates before the now tarmac lane reaches a main road (the B5284 road to Kendal).

Turn right and walk past the Windermere Golf Club. After a short distance downhill, turn right into a road signed to Heathwaite. At a junction turn left. After approximately 300 yards the road descends to two indicated footpaths. Take the second footpath which is reached via stone steps over a wall next to a metal gate.

The track leads around the right hand side of Brant Fell (627 feet, 191m). Just before the farm buildings, bear left uphill, keeping the stone wall to the right. Cross a stile and head downhill between the wall and a fence. At the bottom, cross over a stile on the left and continue ahead to the viewpoint of Post Knott offering views across Lake Windermere.

Turn right from the knoll to a gate and follow a path to the left through woodland. Just before a large opening in a wall ahead, turn left through a gate onto a footpath that goes down a field to another gate. Pass through the gate and follow the road downhill back to Bowness.

DISTANCE

4

MILES

TIME

2

HOURS

MAP REF.
ORDNANCE
SURVEY
OUTDOOR
LEISURE 7
SE AREA

404
969

WALK EASY GRADE

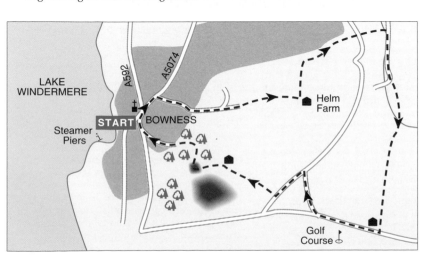

Hawkshead. Val Corbett

HAWKSHEAD

A walk from historic Hawkshead, one of the most attractive and popular villages in Lakeland, via farm tracks and Forestry Commission land providing views across Esthwaite Water. On the return to Hawkshead, the house is passed where Wordsworth lodged whilst at school.

ELEVATION   Highest elevation reached: 720 ft (220m). Start height: 260 ft (80m).

REFRESHMENTS & TOILETS   In Hawkshead village.

DIRECTIONS TO START   Park in the main Hawkshead car park, reached from either the Lake Windermere ferry or from Coniston via the B5285.

WALK DIRECTIONS

From the car park, head towards Hawkshead village, past the coffee shop and National Park information centre. Cross the road and pass through two posts indicating both the grammar school and church. Pass the grammar school and continue straight ahead through the church gate to reach a gate at the end of the churchyard. Go straight on, through a kissing gate before turning left (signed as a public footpath to Roger Ground). Pass through another kissing gate and proceed ahead with a wire fence to your immediate right. Crossing fields, pass through two further kissing gates before the narrow track reaches a minor road.

Turn right, heading uphill for a short

distance before turning left down a lane indicated as a public footpath to Howe Farm. Descend to a small footbridge, cross, and go through a gate, continuing across the field following the line of the fence on your left. Note views across to Esthwaite Water.

Pass through a metal gate in the wall on the left and another gate to the immediate left of the farm. Turn left down the farm track and then right onto the main road. After a short distance, turn right up a track indicated as a public footpath, just to the right of a low white cottage. The track continues between a number of cottages; leave via the left hand side to ascend a beckside track. Pass out of the woodland via a stile and follow the track across a beck before bearing left to a small ridge. Continue the steady climb via waymarked posts to reach a stile. Now walk ahead to pass a line of trees.

After the trees, bear right and pass through gates and stiles next to a cottage before following a broad track up to a road.

Cross the stile turning right and then almost immediately left across a road to the Forestry Commission property of Moor Top. Continue along the broad.track as it bears right (also waymarked with red cycle posts), note views across towards the

northern end of Lake Windermere. As the track descends away from woodland, turn right down a path following yellow waymarks (also a no bikes sign), walking parallel with a broken stone wall.

Cross a beck and through a kissing gate, descending adjacent to a wall. Eventually you will reach a tarmac lane that leads back to Hawkshead village (note en route Anne Tyson's house - not open to the public - where William Wordsworth boarded whilst at Hawkshead Grammar School).

WALK
2

DISTANCE
3.5
MILES

TIME
2
HOURS

MAP REF.
ORDNANCE
SURVEY
OUTDOOR
LEISURE 7
SE AREA
354
981

Originally a Norse settlement, Hawkshead developed under the control of the monks of Furness and became one of their largest and most valuable land holdings. Hawkshead Court House, to the north of the village, was the grange or outlying abbey farm of the Furness estate and is over 500 years old. The development of Hawkshead into an important woollen centre in the eighteenth century saw the settlement's greatest prosperity and

much of the architecture that can be seen today dates from this period.

The imposing parish church of St Michael and All Angels dates from the fifteenth century although a religious building existed here some 500 years previously. The size of the church indicated the medieval prosperity of the village. In Wordsworth's day the church was whitewashed, hence his description of the church as "snow white on a hill" and standing "like a throned lady".

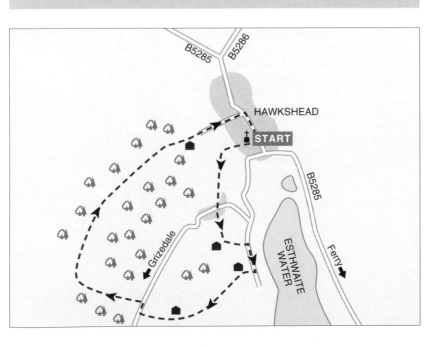

Torver Back Common. Val Corbett

TORVER BACK COMMON

An outward journey across the open moorland and woodland of Torver Back Common with views over Coniston Water and to the Old Man Mountain range. Return is via the lakeside path on the western shore of Coniston.

ELEVATION   Highest elevation reached: 490 ft (150m). Start height: 330 ft (100m).

REFRESHMENTS & TOILETS   None within immediate course of the route.

DIRECTIONS TO START   From the A593 south of Coniston, turn onto the A5084 in Torver. Use a parking area opposite a large Land Rover garage located on a bend in the road.

WALK DIRECTIONS

Staying inside the parking area, leave via the track at the top. Head north to a kissing gate next to a farm gate and sign indicating Torver Commons. Take a left hand path away from a beck, proceeding ahead to the left of a small tarn. Follow the path across to run parallel with a wall on the left. From the wall corner, look ahead to a marshy tarn and follow the path up the hill to the right of the tarn.

As the path gains height, Coniston Water appears below and on clear days the Old Man Mountain range visible to the left. From the hill, take the path that bears left at the head of the tarn and which can be seen continuing on to the ridge ahead, crossing several becks en route. Once this ridge is reached, follow the obvious path that descends through the bracken gradually bearing right to walk near a beck. Walk over the beck at a crossing point, the path on the other side leading off adjacent to a wall and climbing slightly away from the gully.

After a short distance, bear right from the wall to follow a clear path that meanders ahead towards woodland. Several paths through the trees lead to a distinct broad track that crosses left to right in front of you. Once on this track, turn right and head down through an entrance in a wall to reach the shore of Coniston Lake.

Turn right to follow a woodland lakeside path which leads south for approx. 1 mile. The path eventually bears right in front of a stone wall (at the bottom of the wall is a boathouse). Proceed uphill next to the wall. At a clearing and path junction, keep to the central path which climbs to pass through a kissing gate. Follow the farm track back to the main road, turn right and return to the parking area.

WALK
3

DISTANCE
3.5
MILES

TIME
2
HOURS

MAP REF.
ORDNANCE SURVEY OUTDOOR LEISURE 6 SW AREA
287
930

Coniston Water is the third largest lake in Lakeland, 5.5 miles in length and very straight. It is this latter attribute that has been a factor in Coniston becoming so popular with world speed record attempts. Sir Malcolm Campbell first set the record of 142 m.p.h. shortly before the outbreak of World War Two. His son, Sir Donald, following the tradition, pushed the record to 276 m.p.h. in Bluebird. However the same qualities that made Coniston suitable for speed records, also makes it treacherous. The long narrow valley can at times accentuate the effect of northerly winds making the water surface choppy and unstable. On January 4th 1967 whilst believed to be travelling at over 320 m.p.h., Bluebird became airborne and disintegrated. Sir Donald's body was never recovered.

The Old Man of Coniston (2631 feet) is one of the more popular fell climbs in Lakeland. The routes from Coniston village ascend via the Church Beck Valley, a site of intensive copper mining in the last century resulting in the alternative name of Copper Mines Valley. It is believed that some form of copper mining has taken place here since Roman times, though mining peaked towards the end of the last century when hundreds of men were employed.

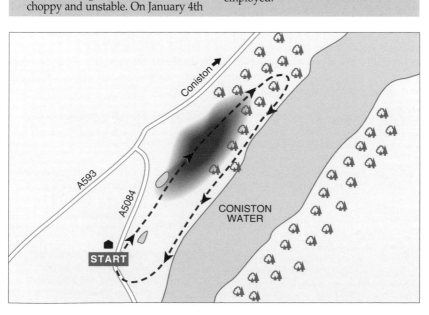

149

La'al Ratty. Val Corbett

RAVENGLASS TO ESKDALE GREEN

This walk starts at the National Park's only coastal village, Ravenglass, passes the remains of a Roman Bath House, and heads inland for Eskdale Green via Muncaster Fell. The walk can also include a visit to Muncaster Castle, the entrance of which is passed in the course of the walk.

N.B. This is not a circular walk; the return journey is via 'La'al Ratty', the Ravenglass and Eskdale miniature railway that runs a service throughout the year. Ring 01229 717171 or contact your nearest Tourist information Centre to confirm the times of trains returning from Eskdale Green to Ravenglass.

ELEVATION — Highest elevation reached: 760 ft (231m). Start height: Sea level.

REFRESHMENTS & TOILETS — At Ravenglass Station and Muncaster Mill.

DIRECTIONS TO START — From central Lakeland via the Wrynose and Hardknott passes into Eskdale. Proceed to Ravenglass to find Miniature Railway car park.

WALK DIRECTIONS

From Ravenglass Miniature Railway Station, leave, passing the train turntable to cross the bridge over the main British Rail lines. Continue ahead down the lane (Murray Field Terrace) and turn left along the main street, heading for the beach. At the beach, turn left and follow the stone wall, taking the path bearing up to the left next to a North West Water metal gate.

The path passes up the side of a field before going through a kissing gate and under a small bridge. Afterwards, bear right before turning right onto a tarmac lane that leads to the remains of the Ravenglass Roman Bath

House.

Leaving the Bath House, head up a tarmac track into a wooded area. Just inside the woods, follow a footpath sign left. After passing under power lines, the track bears around to the right. A short distance later, proceed left on a signed footpath marked by a yellow arrow. Continue through woodland, the track climbs gently before passing through a gate and continuing ahead between open fields. Through a metal gate, cross a stile and through a further metal gate before turning left to pass to the side of Muncaster Home Farm and reach the main road. Cross the road and turn right, passing Muncaster Castle entrance to leave the road at the next right hand bend.

Continue straight ahead up Fell Lane signed to Muncaster Fell. The path climbs ahead before passing through two gates. Where the path splits into two, keep right (i.e. straight on) and follow the footpath sign to Eskdale. Pass through a kissing gate next to a gate and onto the open fell land of Muncaster Fell. The path proceeds ahead with a conifer wood to the left. Continue to the Trig. Point on Hooker Crag (760 feet - 231m) before you.

From Hooker Crag, head for the two hillocks in front of you. Once between them, follow the path up over the next hill and onto a third. From here, a path gradually bears left down to a gap in a stone wall. Pass through the gap in the wall, the wall now runs parallel with the path for some distance. Eventually, the path bears off to the right and over the right hand side of the hill before you (Silver Knott). From Silver Knott, follow the well defined path which descends to go through a kissing gate and through an area of gorse bushes. Once through the gorse, turn left on a track which runs in front of a stone wall and walk ahead (if there is any danger of you missing the last train from Eskdale Green, the track straight ahead leads to Irton Station - see map).

For Eskdale Green, after a short distance turn right to follow a path, with a path sign, next to a wire fence. Go through a kissing gate and cross a beck before passing over the railway line and up to a gap in the wall. Once through, turn left along a track, bearing right at a junction near some houses shortly after a cattle grid. Walk uphill and then follow the lane to Eskdale Green Station, from where you can catch 'La'al Ratty' back to Ravenglass.

DISTANCE

5 MILES

TIME

2.5 HOURS

MAP REF.
ORDNANCE SURVEY OUTDOOR LEISURE 6 SW AREA
084 964

WALK MODERATE GRADE

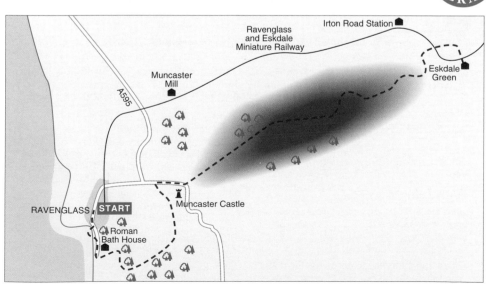

WASDALE HEAD

An easy and enjoyable walk with no climbing, but, nonetheless, offering a real mountain location - the summits of Great Gable, Kirk Fell, Lingmell and Sca Fell tower above the route. This, coupled with views across the moody barrenness of Wastwater and The Screes makes this location a must for those wanting to experience the Lake District at its best.

ELEVATION — Highest elevation reached: 330 ft (100m). Start height: 250 ft (75m).

REFRESHMENTS & TOILETS — Wasdale Head Inn and the adjacent Barn Door shop near start.

DIRECTIONS TO START — From the Wrynose and Hardknott Pass proceed through Eskdale to Santon Bridge. Follow signs to Nether Wasdale and alongside Wastwater to Wasdale Head.

WALK DIRECTIONS

Park on the green in front of the hamlet and proceed back down the road towards Wastwater. At the first bend in the road, cross the stile signed as a public bridleway (Eskdale/Miterdale). *This part of the walk can sometimes be in flood. In these circumstances, do not cross this stile, but stay on the main road until reaching the road bridge. Once there, resume the instructions from *.*

Follow the path diagonally across the fields with Lingmell and Sca Fell towering above

to the left. Cross two becks via stepping stones, go through a kissing gate next to a farm gate and follow the track through the gorse bushes. Pass through a further gate, crossing the dried up river bed to reach the path on the left hand side. Proceed over a stile by a gate into the camp site. Continue ahead until the track bears right. Here, bear left through a kissing gate signed for the Scafells and Eskdale. Take the right hand path alongside a wire fence, turning right down the farm track with views across Wastwater to the left.

Pass the National Trust car park and cross a bridge, walking on to reach the Wasdale Head road. Turn right and continue ahead for a short distance with Kirk Fell directly ahead and Great Gable just to the right.

* At the bend in the road, before the bridge, pass through the kissing gate and follow the path which runs ahead parallel with the beck. Proceed through a gate and walk on, before bearing off to the right to cross the beck via a slender stone arched bridge. Here, fork left walking beckside towards Great Gable. As the path begins to climb, leave the main track, turning right along a path between a stone wall and a beck.

After crossing the beck in four places, pass through a gate, the path now bearing around to the right towards Burnthwaite Farm. Cross a wooden footbridge and follow the path between two stone walls, turning right through a gate at the farmhouse. From here there is an obvious track back to Wasdale Head; the tiny church of St Olaf's, surrounded by trees, is passed en route. The church is usually open and well worth a visit; the surrounding graves record the treachery of the surrounding mountains.

WALK
5

DISTANCE
3
MILES

TIME
1.5
HOURS

MAP REF.
ORDNANCE SURVEY OUTDOOR LEISURE 6 SW AREA
187
085

When approaching Wasdale by road on the northern shore of Wastwater, you will be encountering what many regard as perhaps the greatest dalehead in Lakeland. Wasdale is literally walled in by the mighty forms of Yewbarrow, Kirk Fell, Great Gable and Lingmell. Great Gable, symbol of the National Park, was largely responsible for the hamlet's reputation as the birthplace of British rock climbing. The magnificent crags forming the Great Napes were the principal target for climbers, following Haskett-Smith's famous first ascent of Naples Needle in 1886. A cave high on Gable Crag was reputedly the refuge of a legendary whisky smuggler. This route through the mountains, Moses Trod, can still be followed on maps today.

WALK EASY GRADE

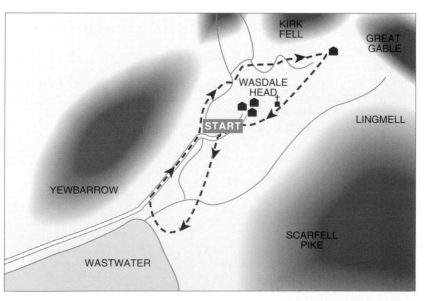

153

River Brathay. Val Corbett

SKELWITH FORCE AND ELTERWATER

Skelwith Force Waterfall, although only 20 feet high, is well known as having the greatest volume of water of any of the waterfalls in the Lake District. This walk goes on to pass the attractive tree fringed water of Loughrigg Tarn before skirting Elterwater and returning via a path alongside the attractive River Brathay.

ELEVATION Highest elevation reached: 330 ft (100m). Start height: 200 ft (60m).

REFRESHMENTS & TOILETS Skelwith Bridge and Elterwater village.

DIRECTIONS TO START From Coniston, take the A593 north through Clappersgate, turning right signed to Elterwater and Langdale on the B5343 just before the Skelwith Bridge Hotel. Park in the National Trust Silverthwaite car park reached after half a mile.

WALK DIRECTIONS

From the car park cross to the opposite side of the road and pass through a gap in a low wall before descending through light woodland to cross a stile and enter a field. Turn left, heading for woodland to find a kissing gate in a stone wall next to a farm gate. Follow the obvious track ahead to reach Skelwith Force. Head downstream through the slate quarry buildings (the Kirkstone Galleries and tea rooms are off to the right).

Once the main road is reached, turn left in front of the Skelwith Bridge Hotel to cross the B5343 and proceed up a minor road with a 1 in 4 gradient, between a white cottage and bus shelter.

Continue to a T junction and turn right over a bridge signed to Ambleside and Coniston. Shortly after, turn left up a tarmac lane before bearing right in front of cottages. Take the track indicating a N.T. footpath to the tarn. Continue past a cottage on the left to a further track, taking an immediate left to pass through a gate signed N.T. Loughrigg Tarn and Grasmere.

Follow the broad track around the tarn, passing cottages before eventually reaching the end of the lane at a gate. Pass onto the road, turning left to descend through the hamlet of Oaks. On reaching a road junction, go right and descend to a further junction, this time going straight on.

The road eventually meets the main Langdale road. Turn right and walk ahead with views towards the famous Langdale Pikes. Cross over a cattle grid before turning left down the minor road into Elterwater village. At the centre of the village you will find a pub, shop and toilets in the National Trust car park located to the left.

Go through the car park, leaving via a kissing gate (sign for Skelwith). Walk ahead, adjacent to a wall, on a scenic riverside path. Continue through light woodland, glimpses of Elterwater are to the right. The path emerges via a kissing gate to cross open fields. After passing through a further kissing gate, fork left before a tree lined mound to a stile. Return to the car park via the path used earlier.

WALK
6

DISTANCE
3.5
MILES

TIME
2
HOURS

MAP REF.
ORDNANCE
SURVEY
OUTDOOR
LEISURE 7
SE AREA
342
037

WALK
EASY
GRADE

In height, Skelwith Force is one of the smaller Lakeland waterfalls, a fault in the underlying rock structure of the river bed causing a drop of about 20 feet. For visitors, the attraction is its intensity and force as it has the greatest volume of water of any waterfall in the Lake District. White water can almost be guaranteed as the River Brathay drains the whole of the Great and Little Langdale valleys. Particularly after rain, Skelwith Force can be a raging torrent.

The name Elterwater is derived from the Norse word for Swan; Whooper Swans can often be seen wintering here before returning to their native Scandinavia. As a lake it is somewhat limited, with an ill defined shape and low lying reedy shores. The depositing of material from upstream is gradually reducing the size of the lake which in thousands of years hence is likely to be little more than a marsh.

Elterwater village was once an important centre for the Lake District's gunpowder industry. Stickle Tarn was dammed to provide a regular supply of water to the works which remained until the 1920's before being eventually converted into a time-share complex.

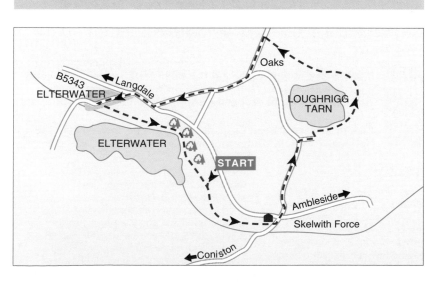

High Sweden Bridge. Val Corbett

AMBLESIDE AND HIGH SWEDEN BRIDGE

This walk heads north from Ambleside to follow a woodland path, much of which is alongside Scardale beck, before passing over the old packhorse crossing of High Sweden Bridge. The second half of the walk provides far reaching views across Ambleside and towards Lake Windermere.

ELEVATION Highest elevation reached: 920 ft (280m). Start height: 165 ft (50m).

REFRESHMENTS & TOILETS Toilets in start point car park. Refreshments throughout Ambleside.

DIRECTIONS TO START Park in the Rydal Road car park in Ambleside, located near the National Trust Old Bridge House.

WALK DIRECTIONS

Cross the bridge at the top of the car park and turn right towards the main part of Ambleside. Pass the much photographed National Trust Old Bridge House, curiously positioned astride Stock Ghyll. Cross the road and head up the path signed to North

Road and marked with a yellow arrow. Turn left at the top into North Road before passing the Unicorn Inn to reach a T junction. Here, proceed straight ahead, slightly uphill and past the Chapel House Hotel. Shortly afterwards, turn left (signed Sweden Bridge lane) and continue on to pass through a gate. The path climbs ahead

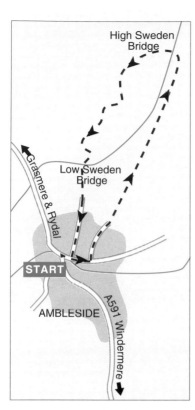

WALK
7

DISTANCE
3
MILES

TIME
2
HOURS

MAP REF.
ORDNANCE
SURVEY
OUTDOOR
LEISURE 7
SE AREA
377
047

Windermere behind you as you ascend. The path proceeds onwards for some distance, latterly through an area of trees, before passing through a gate; Scardale Beck below to your left. Go through a gate and after emerging from the woodland, proceed through a farm gate in the stone wall. Ahead bearing to the left, the path crosses the beck via High Sweden Bridge.

Immediately after the bridge, pass through a gate and turn left to follow a path uphill just to the left of the low stone wall. At the top of the rise, cross the wall via a ladder stile and proceed in an upward direction, gradually bearing left to cross a ladder stile next to a stone sheep fold.

Descend via the obvious path back in the direction of Ambleside, encountering two ladder stiles next to gaps in the wall. The path eventually bears to the left before passing through a large gate and descending left to Low Sweden Bridge. Cross, turn right and follow the path through a farm gate into a farmyard. Go through the kissing gate before descending on a tarmac lane back to Ambleside and the car park.

between two stone walls with increasingly attractive views of Lake

The Old Bridge House, astride Stock Ghyll, dates from the sixteenth century and now serves as a small National Trust Information Centre. Its original purpose was as a summerhouse and apple store for nearby Ambleside Hall although it is traditionally said that it was built by a man too mean to purchase land!

The single arch of the photogenic High Sweden Bridge clearly reveals its original arch as a crossing point on the packhorse route from Ambleside to Patterdale via the Scandale Pass. Nowadays, the route is popular with walkers completing the Fairfield Horseshoe, a long but rewarding circular ridge walk to the Fairfield summit via Dove and Hart Crags. The return route is via Greatrigg Fell and Rydal Fell before returning to Ambleside via Rydal Park.

Ambleside's prosperity was dependent upon the water power obtained from Stock Ghyll. At one time there were at least six mills on the Ghyll with the manufacture of wooden bobbins for the textile factories of Lancashire a key industry. Near the start of the walk is a seventeenth century corn mill which has a reconstruction of the original water wheel.

The principal view on the climb to High Sweden Bridge is across Rydal Water to the distinctive humped outline of the Langdale Pikes. The views on the return are across Ambleside to Lake Windermere. Note the spire of St Mary's Church, unusually tall for the Lake District.

Rydal. MDN

RYDAL WATER AND NAB SCAR

This walk passes alongside Rydal Water in an area rich in Wordsworth connections, this being a favourite of the poets. The second half of the route uses woodland paths before passing Rydal Mount, Wordsworth's home from 1813 until his death in 1850.

ELEVATION — Highest elevation reached: 460 ft (140m). Start height: 160 ft (50m).

REFRESHMENTS & TOILETS — Ramblers Tearoom near the end of the walk at Rydal Hall. Toilets half way around at White Moss Common car park.

DIRECTIONS TO START — The small National Park car park at Pelter Bridge is reached via the A591 north from Ambleside. Turn left across a stone bridge shortly after the Rydal village sign, an immediate right turn across a cattle grid leads to a parking area on the left. If full, the walk can be started from the National Trust White Moss Common Quarry car park on the right hand side (if heading north) of the A591 midway between Rydal and Grasmere.

WALK DIRECTIONS

From the car park, walk on to the tarmac lane, turn left and walk past a small terrace of cottages. After reaching a second terrace, pass through a gap ahead next to a farm gate (signed as a public bridleway). This descends between two stone walls before passing through another gate. At this point, bear right (marked as a bridleway) towards the lake shore. Follow the lakeside path and near the end of the lake, cross a beck and gradually gain height following a path next to a wall (a slate sign indicates White Moss, Grasmere and Red Bank). Cross a further beck and continue alongside the wall. The path gains height before turning right through a kissing gate in the wall into an area of woodland (if you would like a view of Grasmere at this stage, proceed to the ridge viewpoint ahead. Afterwards return to the kissing gate in the wall).

Descend on a woodland path, bearing to the left to cross a long wooden footbridge. Turn right and walk ahead, following a path that gradually bears left up to the main road (toilets are available in the parking area to the right).

Cross the main road, walking towards the car park before turning left to take the minor road on the right climbing away from the main road.

If starting the walk from White Moss Common Quarry car park only: Facing towards the main road, turn right out of the car park up a tarmac lane as it climbs away from the main road.

As the road reaches a summit and starts to bear around to the right (there is a small parking area on the left), turn right from the road and take a path past a metal park bench to a viewpoint across to Rydal Water. Return to the road, turn right and continue ahead to the junction at How

Top Farm, noting the views to the left across the wall to Grasmere Water.

Turn right and follow the tarmac road uphill (slate sign indicating path to Rydal). After an initial climb, the tarmac road levels out and passes a marshy pond on the left. At this point, do not bear right but continue ahead adjacent to a wall on an unmade track that runs below the looming crags of Nab Scar. Pass a house (Brockstone) on the left and go through a gate. Follow the path through two further gates before emerging from the trees to find clear views across Rydal Water on the right.

Pass through two further gates before descending between two stone walls and on to a further farm gate. Emerge onto a tarmac track, turning right to descend past Rydal Mount. Just before the main road is a left turn to Rydal Hall and the Ramblers Tearoom (marked as a private road).

At the main road, turn left and then right to cross Pelter Bridge. Turn right and walk over a cattle grid back to the car park.

DISTANCE
4
MILES

TIME
2
HOURS

MAP REF.
ORDNANCE
SURVEY
OUTDOOR
LEISURE 7
SE AREA
366
060

WALK EASY GRADE

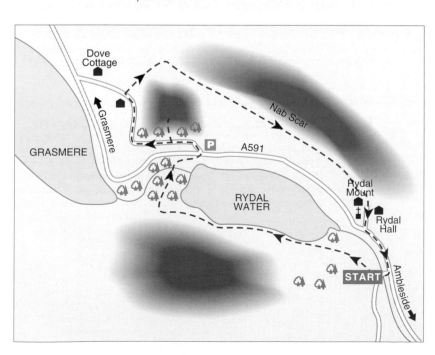

Dove Cottage

Grasmere

Nab Scar

GRASMERE

P

A591

RYDAL WATER

Rydal Mount

Rydal Hall

Ambleside

START

159

Alcock Tarn. Val Corbett

GRASMERE AND ALCOCK TARN

A climb to Alcock Tarn offering views across Grasmere Water and Helm Crag. Descent is adjacent to the attractive Greenhead Gill before finishing with a riverside walk in the much loved village of Grasmere, famous as the burial place of William Wordsworth.

ELEVATION — Highest elevation reached: 1200 ft (360m). Start height: 200 ft (60m).

REFRESHMENTS & TOILETS — In Grasmere village. Toilets also at Stock Lane car park near the start of the walk.

DIRECTIONS TO START — From the A591 Windermere to Keswick road, turn on to the B5287 to Grasmere village. Park in the Red Bank Road car park, signed opposite the church.

WALK DIRECTIONS

From the Red Bank Road car park, turn right and head for the church. Turn right along the main Grasmere village road, passing the Stock Lane car park and up to the A591. Cross to head up the lane bearing left past Dove Cottage. With a stone wall on your left, climb steadily away from the hamlet of Townend. The road bends around to the left to reach the pond at How Top

Farm. Immediately after the pond, bear uphill (left from the road) on a lane marked with a public footpath sign to Alcock Tarn. After approximately 100 yards of uphill walking, bear left next to a park bench onto an unmade track, signed to Alcock Tarn.

At a fork next to a door marked Wood Close, bear right past the National Trust Brackenfell sign. A steep path bears to the right of a stone wall before continuing between two stone walls and passing through a kissing gate in the right hand corner. The path climbs, bearing to the left and staying close to the wall on the left. As the path is routed up between two walls, note the views behind you over Grasmere, and a little further on, to your left the view towards Helm Crag. Keep walking ahead, climbing steadily with the wall on your left to reach a stile. Turn left across the stile and over a narrow beck, on clear days, views southwards are as far as Lake Windermere.

Walk on with the tarn to your right, passing over a stile in the stone wall ahead. Keeping to the left of a marshy area, proceed ahead with a stone wall on your left. After a large stone cairn, walk on to a rocky outcrop which provides excellent views across the valley below.

From the outcrop, continue on the original course with the dramatic ravine of Greenhead Gill on the fellside above to the right. The path descends into the ravine formed by the gill, zigzagging downwards. At the bottom, do not cross the gill

immediately, instead follow the wall down to the left of the gill before passing over a footbridge.

Turn left through a gate and proceed down the lane before turning left on to a minor road and following it downhill to the A591. Turn left and walk towards Our Lady of the Wayside Church before turning right across the road to find a public path signed between two fields. Emerge into Grasmere village and turn left, crossing the road bridge to walk past the Rothay Garden Hotel. Shortly afterwards, turn left through a gate and follow the path around the park adjacent to the river. Pass through Broadgate car park before turning left across a wooden bridge. Follow the path (stay on the left side of the river at a path junction) before going over another footbridge to emerge by St. Oswald's Church.

Turn left into the churchyard; a small sign indicates Wordsworth's grave. Continue through the churchyard to the main road, turning right and then left, back to Red Bank car park.

WALK
9

DISTANCE
3.5
MILES

TIME
2
HOURS

MAP REF.
ORDNANCE
SURVEY
OUTDOOR
LEISURE 7
SE AREA
337
074

WALK
MODERATE
GRADE

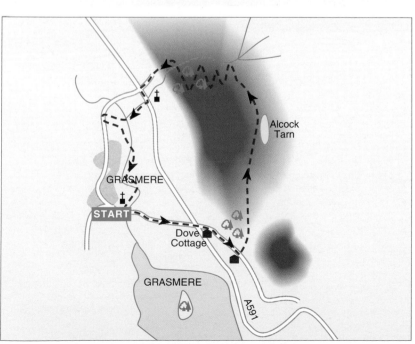

Dove Cottage. Val Corbett

WORDSWORTH'S GRASMERE

A 4 mile exploration of Wordsworth country, including the western shore of Grasmere, before a short climb to a superb viewpoint across Rydal Water. The return route passes Wordsworth's home, Dove Cottage, and St. Oswald's church where the poet and his family are buried.

ELEVATION Highest elevation reached: 460 ft (140m). Start height 200 ft (60m).

REFRESHMENTS & TOILETS In Grasmere village. Additional toilets found half way around the route at White Moss Common car park.

DIRECTIONS TO START From the A591 Windermere to Keswick road, turn onto the B5287 to Grasmere village. Park in the Red Bank Road car park, signed opposite the church.

WALK DIRECTIONS

From the Red Bank Road car park, turn left and walk along the road past the Gold Rill Country House Hotel. After a short distance, go past a refreshment kiosk, the site from where boats can be hired. Keep to the road and after a short uphill section, pass on the left a cottage with a post box in the wall before rounding a left hand bend.

Turn left and go through a gap in the wall. Walk down a few wooden steps at a National Trust sign and descend with a stone wall on your left to the lakeshore.

At the bottom, turn right and proceed along the lakeshore path to the far end where there is a weir and a wooden footbridge. Cross the footbridge and follow a woodland path (leading right) before passing through three gates. Follow the track which bears left up to the main A591 road (if toilets are required at this point, bear to the right from the third gate - the parking area reached has a toilet block).

With the National Trust White Moss Common Quarry car park opposite, cross the road towards the car park and turn left for a few yards before taking the minor road that climbs away from the main road. As the road reaches a summit and starts to bear around to the right (a small parking area is on the left), turn right off the road and take a path past a metal park bench to a viewpoint across Rydal Water.

Returning to the road, turn right and continue ahead to the junction at How Top Farm. Turn left from How Top Farm and descend to pass Dove Cottage.

Cross the main road and take the road back, past the Stock Lane car park (toilets here also) to Grasmere village. Turn right into St. Oswald's churchyard - Wordsworth's grave is easily found. Return from the churchyard to the road, turning right and then left back to Red Bank Road car park.

Grasmere Sports Day has been held since 1852 and is the nearest equivalent in England to a Scottish Highland Games. Held on the Thursday closest to August 20th, Grasmere Sports is the biggest in the Lake District with Cumberland wrestling, fell racing and pole jumping. One of the highlights is hound trailing, a popular pastime in this area which involves hounds following a fellside trail made with a cloth soaked in aniseed. Spectators with binoculars, follow the breakneck progress around the fellside.

Wordsworth's fascination with water, as revealed in much of his work, stemmed partly from his boyhood; his schooling at Hawkshead developing a love of nearby Esthwaite Water. Ice skating in particular was a passion and within days of moving into Dove Cottage in December 1799, he recorded skating on Grasmere and Rydal. Also the summers allowed the Wordsworths to indulge in a passion for boating, particularly to the central island of Grasmere where they picnicked and wrote letters to their friends.

DISTANCE
4
MILES

TIME
2
HOURS

MAP REF.
ORDNANCE SURVEY OUTDOOR LEISURE 7 SE AREA
337
074

WALK EASY GRADE

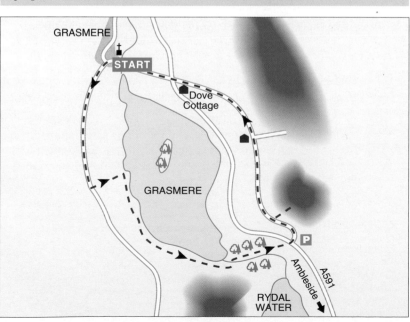

GRASMERE

START

Dove Cottage

GRASMERE

RYDAL WATER

Ambleside

A591

P

Brotherswater. Val Corbett

BROTHERS WATER

A lowland walk around the picturesque Brothers Water before passing through the attractive hamlet of Hartsop and skirting low fells to Angletarn Beck where there is a delightful waterfall.

ELEVATION
Highest elevation reached: 690 ft (210m). Start height: 525 ft (160m).

REFRESHMENTS & TOILETS
Refreshments available at the Brothers Water Inn or in the Sykeside Camping Barn Shop.

DIRECTIONS TO START
Start from a small parking area at Cow Bridge just to the north of Brothers Water, reached from the A592 between the Kirkstone Pass and Ullswater.

WALK DIRECTIONS

Cross the bridge and turn left through a kissing gate next to a National Trust information sign. The woodland path proceeds ahead alongside the river before running along the shore of Brothers Water. Continue past the end of the tarn and pass through a kissing gate next to a farm gate and a further kissing gate at Hartsop Hall Farm. Follow the track all the way around to the left of the farm to find another kissing gate, next to a cattle grid. Proceed ahead on a broad track. Cross a bridge and carry on through a kissing gate into the campsite ahead. Continue right past the Sykeside Camping Barn and where the lane forks right to the Brothers Water Inn, continue straight on via the tarmac lane. Before the lane reaches the main road, bear left through a gate next to a National Trust sign indicating a permissive path. This path skirts the eastern shore of the lake before passing through a kissing gate and bearing right from the lake to a kissing gate in the wall on the right.

Cross the road and pass through the gate opposite, marked as a public footpath. The path climbs gradually between two stone walls before passing some cottages and crossing a footbridge. Bear right onto a tarmac lane and climb through the hamlet, taking a left turn near the end of the hamlet up a steep track marked with a public footpath sign. Pass through a farm gate, following the concrete track.

At a three way path junction (Brothers Water now directly left), continue straight on past Grey Rigg Cottage, passing through a kissing gate to follow a now narrower, rocky track. The track leads ahead under wooded crags before crossing a ladder stile to the delightful Angletarn Beck waterfall. Pass through the gate adjacent to the footbridge, proceeding ahead between two stone walls.

After some distance, turn right onto the main road and return to the car park.

DISTANCE

3.5
MILES

TIME

2
HOURS

MAP REF.
ORDNANCE
SURVEY
OUTDOOR
LEISURE 5
NE AREA

404
134

The Kirkstone Pass, its name is said to derive from the churchlike slope of rocks nearby; 'Kirk' meaning church, is Lakeland's highest road pass, reaching 1489 feet by the Kirkstone Inn, England's third highest inn. The inn was a coaching stop for travellers recovering from the aptly named 'struggle' from Ambleside which was so steep that passengers had to alight and walk to enable the horses to recover.

The hamlet of Hartsop was once a small mining community based around two lead mines. Nowadays, it is well known for its splendid examples of spinning galleries, a once common architectural style in the Lake District. The galleries date from the seventeenth century and were constructed to provide a covered area, allowing sheep fleeces to dry before spinning.

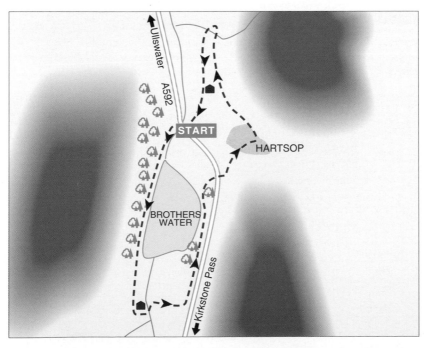

Great How. Val Corbett

THIRLMERE AND GREAT HOW

A walk along the eastern side of Thirlmere before an ascent to the viewpoint of Great How. The return journey on the opposite fells visits the attractive waterfall of Fisherplace Gill; the views from here confirm that although basically a reservoir, Thirlmere has a beauty all of its own.

ELEVATION — Highest elevation reached: 1050 ft (320m). Start height: 620 ft (190m).

REFRESHMENTS & TOILETS — Toilets in start point car park. The Kings Head Hotel is on the A591 just a short drive from the start point.

DIRECTIONS TO START — On the A591 between Grasmere and Keswick, is the North West Water Swirls car park approx. 2.5 miles north of the most southerly part of Thirlmere.

WALK DIRECTIONS

Turn right out of the car park onto the main road and walk for 100 yards before crossing to the National Park Station Coppice car park. From here, descend via wooden steps onto a left bearing path and through a kissing gate signed to Great How. A grassy path descends next to a wire fence before reaching a kissing gate and passing into woodland. Bear right and follow the woodland path (occasionally marked with white waymarks) for approximately 1 mile northwards, keeping Thirlmere on your left.

On the way the route encounters several footbridges and kissing gates (at one point, the path appears to come to an end next to a rocky outcrop. Here, bear right and zigzag upwards to rejoin the main path).

On reaching a path junction, continue ahead (i.e. uphill, signed as a permitted path to Great How) climbing a fairly steep track to the summit viewpoint. This provides far reaching views before descending back via the same route to the path junction. This time, turn left (signed Legburthwaite) and follow a descending track as it bears around to the left to run parallel with the main road on your right. Descend to a gate and cross the main road, turning right along the road for a short distance before descending to a stone stile on your left marked with a public footpath sign.

Cross the field adjacent to the stone wall before passing through a gate and turning right onto the minor road. This passes through the hamlet of Legburthwaite. Shortly before the road descends to the main road, bear left by a telephone box (bridleway sign indicating Glenridding via Sticks Pass). Walk up the minor road, passing farm buildings on your left.

Cross a wall via a ladder stile and continue uphill, crossing a stile on the right in front of a rocky outcrop. Turn left across the man made watercourse and through a gate by

Sty Beck Fall. Cross in front of the fall and follow the public footpath sign left towards Swirls car park. The path follows the wall along the valley side before crossing a beck and reaching a footpath sign that indicates the path leads away from the wall.

A footbridge crosses in front of the attractive Fisherplace Gill Waterfall to continue on a path ahead, just above the wall. Cross two becks to reach a junction of paths. Here, continue straight ahead before rejoining the wall and eventually descending to pass over a footbridge across a further waterfall.

Continue to a T junction in front of a wood, here turn right, crossing the footbridge and kissing gate and descending through trees. Pass through a second gate and return to the car park.

WALK
12

DISTANCE

4

MILES

TIME

2.5

HOURS

MAP REF.
ORDNANCE
SURVEY
OUTDOOR
LEISURE 5
NE AREA

316
168

Whilst still regarded as one of the 16 lakes in the Lake District, Thirlmere is in fact a reservoir, created in 1879 by Manchester Corporation Water Works to supply the increasing water needs of the city. The dam built at the northern end raised the water level in the valley by 50 feet; previously there had been two small lakes with a crossing between them. Two hamlets, Armboth in the north and Wythburn in the south were lost in the flooding of the valley with only Wythburn church, standing on higher ground, surviving.

Although the creation of Thirlmere was bitterly opposed by campaigners such as Ruskin, Canon Rawnsley and Octavia Hill, parliamentary approval was given in 1879. However, the storm of protest over the action provided a catalyst to the conservationist cause and was instrumental in the formation of the National Trust in 1895. The 2000 acres of conifers planted in 1908 were similarly opposed though time has softened their appearance and modern day forestry management includes more deciduous woodland species.

Ullswater. Val Corbett

AIRA FORCE AND YEW CRAG

Aira Force is one of Lakeland's most popular waterfalls, a classic seventy foot 'hanging valley' cascade set in a wooded gorge close to the north west shore of Ullswater. The return journey allows a detour to Yew Crag on National Trust owned Gowbarrow Fell, an excellent viewpoint with stunning views across Ullswater and to the fells beyond.

ELEVATION — Highest elevation reached: 980 ft (300m). Start height: 490 ft (150m).

REFRESHMENTS & TOILETS — Cafe in Aira Force car park. Hotel also in Dockray, half way round the walk.

DIRECTIONS TO START — The National Trust Aira Force car park is on the A592 along the northern shore of Ullswater.

WALK DIRECTIONS

Go through the gate at the top of the car park next to a National Trust information sign. Follow the clear broad path ahead, turning right through a gate and past a large hollow tree trunk into an area of woodland. Cross the beck via a footbridge and turn left up the broad path to the falls.

Cross the small stone bridge in front of Aira Force and take the stone steps leading off to the left.

The path turns back in the direction of the falls allowing a diversion to the stone bridge above the falls. Do not cross the bridge but stay on the path to the left of the beck, passing two further attractive but less impressive falls. At the third fall, High

Force, just past a wooden bridge, turn left up an inclined path to a gap in the wall. After the gap in the wall, turn right and pass through a gate before crossing the field, keeping to the right of the rocky outcrops. Pass through a gate in the wall and proceed, ascending to the village of Dockray.

Cross the bridge bearing right and opposite the Royal Hotel, turn right down a public footpath signed to Aira Force and Ulcat Row. This leads past some farm buildings before bearing to the right and passing through a gate. The broad track descends to cross two becks before going through a gate adjacent to a farm gate. Continue ahead ignoring the permissive path to the left.

Follow the path into woodland passing through a gate. Emerge from the trees and carry straight on, crossing a beck and following the path to reach Aira Force once again. Take the path to the left leading away from the falls. After 150 yards, the path forks. Keep left through a gate and start to climb the path up the lower crags. After a while, the path forks - take the left fork again. Yew Crag is marked by a cairn and is accessed via a stile across a wire fence. The views across Ullswater to Hallin Fell and Place Fell make this detour worth the short climb.

To return to the car, retrace the route back from Yew Crag to Aira Force and descend via the clearly defined footpath.

Aira Force has perhaps the best setting of any waterfall in Lakeland. Its seventy foot cascade below a stone bridge can after heavy rain become a torrent. Wordsworth described it as a *"powerful brook, which dashes among rocks through a deep glen, living on every side with a rich and happy intermixture of native wood"*. The falls can be viewed from footbridges built both below and above the cataract, with the lower bridge in certain conditions, providing the amazing sight of three concentric rainbows in the spray of the waterfall.

WALK
13

DISTANCE
4
MILES

TIME
2
HOURS

MAP REF.
ORDNANCE
SURVEY
OUTDOOR
LEISURE 5
NE AREA
401
201

WALK
EASY
GRADE
Aira Force

WALK
MODERATE
GRADE
Yew Crag

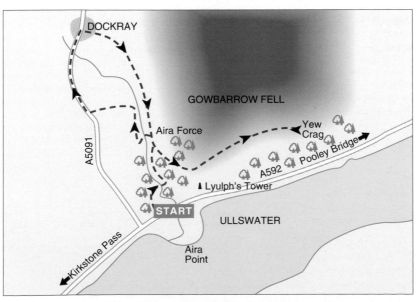

DOCKRAY

GOWBARROW FELL

Aira Force

A5091

Yew Crag

Pooley Bridge

A592

Lyulph's Tower

START

ULLSWATER

Aira Point

Kirkstone Pass

169

Cat Bells. Val Corbett

CAT BELLS

An ascent of the Cat Bells ridge allows rewarding views across Derwentwater and towards Borrowdale. The return via the south western shore of Derwent affords many places to stop and enjoy the view across the 'Queen of the Lakes'.

ELEVATION
Highest elevation reached: 1480 ft (450m). Start height: 360 ft (110m).

REFRESHMENTS & TOILETS
None.

DIRECTIONS TO START
From the A66 south of Keswick, turn off signed to Portinscale and Lingholm Gardens. Follow signs towards Grange. After crossing a cattle grid, take a right turn (signed Skelgill) to find a small roadside parking area.

WALK DIRECTIONS

From the parking area, follow the inclined path which, after only a short distance reveals fine views across Derwentwater. The incline gradually becomes steeper as it zig zags its way to the initial summit of Skelgill Bank (1108 feet, 340m). An obvious path leads to the summit of Cat Bells which stands before you. Summit views include Bassenthwaite Lake in the north as well as Skiddaw overlooking Keswick, Derwentwater and Borrowdale.

Descend from the summit on the path ahead. Before the path starts to climb to the next summit, turn left and descend via a fairly steep incline. The path heads to the right hand edge of a wooded area to reach a gate and stile, after which descend to reach a tarmac road. Now turn sharp left and follow the main road past the National Trust Low Manesty 'no parking' sign. Shortly, a small National Trust parking area at Manesty Woods becomes apparent. Continue through the gate and follow the well made track. Proceed past a house following the National Trust Brandlehow sign. Pass through a kissing gate next to a wooden garage - there is a shoreside picnic area here.

From here, bear right across a stile and proceed on a woodland path which skirts the lakeshore northwards for some distance. Next to the Hawes End landing stage, pass through a kissing gate in the wall and turn left to walk alongside the wall. Go through a gate, noting Cat Bells summit to your left.

Continue through two kissing gates before turning right onto a tarmac lane. After the Hawes End Centre sign, follow the lane for a few more yards before bearing left up a woodland track. This leads up to the main road. Walk on, crossing the cattle grid and back to the parking area.

The present day tranquillity of the Newlands Valley, lying to the west of the Cat Bells ridge, belies a history of intense mining activity. The Goldscope Copper Mine was worked from the thirteenth century although it was not until the setting up of the Society for the Mines Royal by Elizabeth I in the sixteenth century that output rose to any appreciable level. The mines were eventually abandoned in the 1860's due to increased competition from cheap imports.

Brandlehow Park was the first National Trust property in the Lake District. The 108 acres of woodland and adjacent foreshore were bought by subscription in 1902 and Manesty Park, just to the south, was bought by the Trust between 1908 and 1928. Brackenburn (not open to the public) is where the novelist Sir Hugh Walpole lived from 1924 to 1941.

Derwent Isle, Derwentwater's most northerly island was once home to Joseph Pocklington, an eighteenth century eccentric who constructed a number of follies, including a fort, battery and chapel. He was also responsible for organising the Keswick Regatta from 1780 which included mock sea battles.

WALK
14

DISTANCE
4.5
MILES

TIME
2.5
HOURS

MAP REF.
ORDNANCE SURVEY OUTDOOR LEISURE 4 NW AREA
246
212

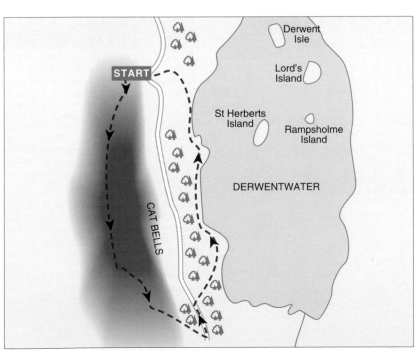

Borrowdale. Val Corbett

BORROWDALE AND CASTLE CRAG

This walk commences alongside the picturesque River Derwent before climbing to the rocky viewpoint of Castle Crag, which offers lovely views across Derwentwater and the Borrowdale Valley.

ELEVATION

Highest elevation reached: 950 ft (290m). Start height: 295 ft (90m).

REFRESHMENTS & TOILETS

In Rosthwaite (start point).

DIRECTIONS TO START

From Keswick, follow the Borrowdale signs south on the B5289. At the village of Rosthwaite, turn right to the indicated National Park Authority car park (a small overflow car park is located next to the Borrowdale Institute).

WALK DIRECTIONS

Turn right out of the car park and proceed up the lane in front of small cottages. At Yew Tree Farm, bear right (footpath signed to Grange) and follow the track between two stone walls. The path bears to the right to run alongside the River Derwent and passes over an attractive stone packhorse bridge before reaching a pair of gates. Cross the stile adjacent to the right hand gate and follow the path alongside the river.

The track crosses a small stream before passing to the left of a small wooded knoll. Follow the track around to the right to a kissing gate next to a farm gate, proceeding into High Hows Wood. The woodland path eventually comes to a path junction, take the left path. It passes through a small disused quarry - continue past some slate cairns and through a gap in a wall which crosses the quarry.

Once away from the quarry, proceed uphill into a wooded area. At a path junction, bear right and drop downhill through the trees. At a gap in a wall, bear right for a short distance before bearing to the left and down to a small grassy clearing. The path again runs close to the river before climbing gently to a stile adjacent to a gate. Once across the stile, descend downhill but do not cross the watercourse of Gowder Dub. Instead, turn left following a bridleway sign to Seatoller and Honister which heads upstream.

After a short distance, cross the Gowder Dub and follow the track uphill through a wooded area. Upon reaching a gate, pass through, Goat Crag is above on the right.

Continue uphill past a large slate scree on the left to a stone cairn. At the cairn, bear left up an indistinct path, keeping to the left of the beck. The path climbs to a stone wall which is crossed via a stone stile (a seat is on the right, shortly after the wall). Head uphill and just before a slate scree, climb a ladder stile and pass over an adjacent stile over a wire fence.

Follow the footpath, initially right and then left up the slate scree slope. The path is quite steep, eventually a stone cairn is reached. Resume the path to the left up the slate slope, a small plateau is soon reached. From the plateau continue on a short distance to the actual summit of Castle Crag which offers views to the north across Derwentwater to Keswick and Skiddaw as well as across Borrowdale to Rosthwaite in the south. (At the summit is a war memorial to the men of Borrowdale).

From the summit, retrace your steps to the previously reached stone cairn. From here, cross to a ladder stile over a stone wall and fork left downhill to a further stone wall and gate. The path continues downhill into some trees - once out of the trees, descend across a field to a gate. Cross the adjacent stile and bear right (you are now back on the path used earlier). Follow the path back along the river, across the bridge to the parking area at Rosthwaite.

WALK 15

DISTANCE

3 MILES

TIME

2 HOURS

MAP REF.
ORDNANCE SURVEY OUTDOOR LEISURE 4 NW AREA
257
148

WALK MODERATE GRADE

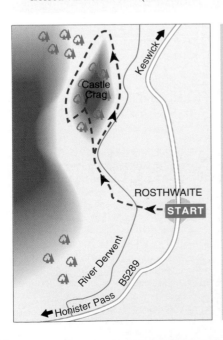

Castle Crag is in the ownership of the National Trust, the summit given in 1920 by Sir William Hamer in memory of his son John and the men of Borrowdale, killed in the Great War of 1914-18. The lower slopes of Castle Crag were given to the Trust in 1939 by Lady Hamer as a memorial to Sir William; a seat commemorating this is passed en route to the top.

There was once a hillfort on the summit, used as a defensive fortification by the Brigante tribe at the time of the Roman invasion in the first century. Hence, the name Borrowdale, given to the whole of the valley in which Castle Crag stands, meaning 'valley of the fort'. Castle Crag forms part of the western side of the 'Jaws of Borrowdale'.

WATENDLATH AND DOCK TARN

Quite simply the best way to observe the scenery and the remote hamlet of Watendlath, its inky black tarn providing a sharp contrast to the surrounding landscape. The return journey climbs to Dock Tarn before arriving at Rosthwaite via the Stonethwaite Valley.

ELEVATION Highest elevation reached: 1400 ft (430m). Start height: 295 ft (90m).

REFRESHMENTS & TOILETS In Rosthwaite (start point) and Watendlath.

DIRECTIONS TO START From Keswick, follow the Borrowdale signs south on the B5289. At the village of Rosthwaite, turn right to find the signed National Park Authority car park (a small overflow car park is located next to the Borrowdale Institute).

WALK DIRECTIONS

Turn left from the car park, heading towards Rosthwaite village stores before turning left onto the main road (B5289). After approx. 30 yards, turn right up a lane signed to Hazel Bank Country House (also signed as a public bridleway to Stonethwaite and Watendlath). Proceed over a stone bridge and turn immediate left up a public bridleway signed to Watendlath. Cross two small becks via a concrete ramp before passing through a gate and turning right.

Follow the path uphill before going through a gate in a stone wall. The path climbs to the left to another stone wall. Pass through the kissing gate, cross the beck to follow the path uphill, a stone wall to your left. Walk past a kissing gate on your left and continue uphill, ignoring the grassy track leading off to the left, keeping to the main path as it leads off to the right next to a gorge.

Cross over a beck and proceed uphill to a further stone wall, passing through a kissing gate next to a farm gate. The well made path continues ahead with a marshy area on the right before eventually descending to give views across Watendlath and its tarn. A kissing gate and packhorse bridge provide access to the village (tearooms and toilets available here).

Turning back from Watendlath, retrace your steps back across the packhorse bridge and turn left to pass through the kissing gate used earlier, following the footpath signed to Dock Tarn as it heads off with Watendlath Tarn to your left. Follow the path through the gate and continue straight ahead between the two stone walls, passing over a stone stile next to a gate and beck.

After approx. 70 yards, cross another beck and follow the path to the right, adjacent to the beck. Follow the course of the wall around to the left. At the end of the wall, cross the beck once again and proceed uphill keeping the beck and the stone wall off to the right.

Pass through a kissing gate adjacent to a gate, following the footpath to the left indicated by a National Trust sign. The path, gradually ascending left climbs towards Dock Tarn. This area can be boggy, though the worst part is traversed by a series of large stepping stones. The path climbs gradually to a stone wall with a kissing gate. From here, continue ahead, on a by now steep climb. Once you have reached the top, walk onwards through the

heather following a cairn marked path to eventually reach Dock Tarn.

The path passes along the right hand side of Dock Tarn. Near the beck that drains the tarn, the path bears off to the right following the direction of the outlet beck downhill.

Cross a stile in a stone wall, a gentle climb is followed by a descent past a ruined stone building. The path descends very steeply into light woodland before reaching a stile in a stone wall close to the beck. Continue to the valley bottom, turning right through a gate and walking ahead alongside a stone wall. Pass through another gate and turn left to cross a bridge over Stonethwaite Beck. After reaching houses, turn right and follow the lane away from the hamlet. After passing a terrace of houses, follow the road right to reach the main road.

Cross ahead to take a lane (signed Longthwaite). Where the road bears left, pass through a gate to walk in front of Foxwood Cottage. Cross a stile and keep to the right hand side before bearing right through a gate in the corner. Walk directly across the field to cross a stile and continue on with houses off to the right. Pass through a gate, turn right and then left to return back to the car park.

WALK
16

DISTANCE
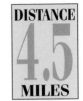
MILES

TIME

HOURS

MAP REF.
ORDNANCE SURVEY OUTDOOR LEISURE 4 NW AREA

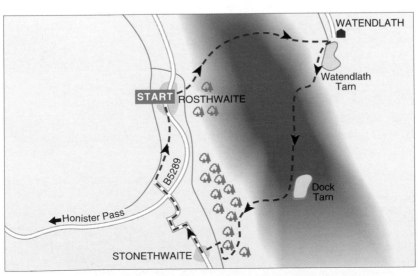

Buttermere. Val Corbett

BUTTERMERE

Buttermere is rightly considered one of the Lake District's gems with a mile and a half long lake surrounded by high crags. The walk is reached via the Honister Pass, a straightforward but thrilling car ride from Keswick and Borrowdale.

This walk is a low level circuit around the lake, see walks 18 and 19 if you wish to get up into the fells of Haystacks and Red Pike above Buttermere.

ELEVATION — Highest elevation reached: 330 ft (100m). Start height: 330 ft (100m).

REFRESHMENTS & TOILETS — In Buttermere village.

DIRECTIONS TO START — From Keswick, take the B5289 south signed to Borrowdale. Continue through the Honister Pass and park on the right at Gatesgarth Farm.

WALK DIRECTION

From the parking area, turn right onto the road, crossing a bridge and proceeding ahead towards the lake. The lakeside path becomes apparent after a short distance and is marked with a small wooden sign. The path follows the shoreline in an anticlockwise direction. Across the lake you will see running from left to right the 2500 foot (760m) high summits of High Crag, High Stile and Red Pike.

Continue through a rocky tunnel (occasionally this tunnel has to be repaired - if this is the case, follow the indicated diversion before rejoining the main path once again). As the lake starts to narrow, leave the main path and cross a small stile adjacent to the shoreline (*N.B. during the months of April and May, this permissive path around the end of the lake is closed due to the lambing season. If undertaking this walk during these months, simply follow the well signed diversion into Buttermere village before returning to the lakeside via tracks next to the Fish Hotel*). A National Trust sign indicates that it is a permitted footpath and instructs walkers to "Please keep to the lake edge". Continue towards the head of

the lake, crossing a small stream and four stiles. At the head of the lake a wooden bridge leads across the Buttermere Dubs to start the return on the western shore.

Follow the path back along the lake, keeping to the shoreline path whenever faced with an alternative woodland route.

Once out of the woods, the dramatic beauty of Fleetwith Pike and Haystacks dominate the view. After the lake follow the path and turn left, a broad track returns you back to Gatesgarth Farm and the parking area.

Buttermere's name derives from the first owner of the lake, a Norseman called *Buthar*, hence 'Buthar's Mere'. Fortunately, the whole of the lake, Burtness Woods and much of the surrounding area is now in the hands of the National Trust.

The vale was famous in the eighteenth century as the home of the 'Beauty of Buttermere'. Mary Robinson, the fifteen year old daughter of the innkeeper of the Fish Inn who was 'discovered' by J. Budworth whilst researching 'A fortnights ramble in the Lakes'

published in 1795. His description of her beauty resulted in her becoming a tourist attraction, bringing many visitors, including in 1802 a future husband, the Hon. Alexander Hope M.P. Unfortunately all was not what it appeared and he was subsequently revealed as plain John Hadfield, a bigamist wanted for fraud (then a capital offence). Hadfield was eventually caught and hung at Carlisle for his crimes. Mary later married a farmer and went to live in Caldbeck, where she is now buried.

WALK
17

DISTANCE
4.5
MILES

TIME
2
HOURS

MAP REF.
ORDNANCE
SURVEY
OUTDOOR
LEISURE 4
NW AREA
196
150

WALK
EASY
GRADE

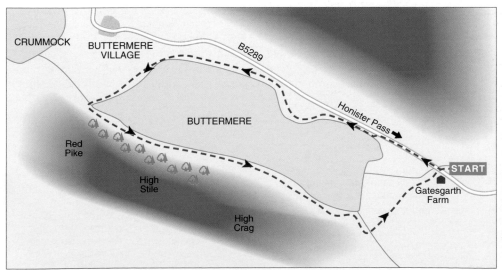

HAYSTACKS

A high fell walk involving a fairly steep initial climb into the hills above Buttermere and onto the summit of Haystacks. From here there are excellent views across Buttermere and Crummock on one side and towards Ennerdale Water and Forest on the other. The descent is via an old quarry track alongside Warnscale Beck. The start point is reached by way of a drive through the Honister Pass, a delight in itself.

ELEVATION	Highest elevation reached: 1960 ft (597m). Start height: 330 ft (100m).
REFRESHMENTS & TOILETS	There is usually an ice cream van at Gatesgarth Farm. Refreshments and toilets in Buttermere village.
DIRECTIONS TO START	From Keswick, follow the Borrowdale signs south on the B5289. Pass through the villages of Rosthwaite and Seatoller and through the Honister Pass. At the bottom of Honister park on the right near Gatesgarth Farm.

WALK DIRECTIONS

From the car park at Gatesgarth Farm, cross the road and pass through a gate signed as a public bridleway to Ennerdale and Buttermere. Follow the clear path straight ahead with Buttermere to your right, passing through several gates. Continue across a footbridge over a beck and through a kissing gate adjacent to a farm gate in a stone wall.

At a path junction ignore the right fork (to Buttermere) and continue straight ahead signed as a public bridleway to Ennerdale via Scarth Gap. At a further path junction, turn left keeping the wire fence to your immediate left. Cross a small beck via a wooden footbridge and continue straight ahead up the stone covered track until you reach a stile and gate in a wire fence. A well defined track, marked by a series of small stone cairns, climbs towards Scarth Gap.

Cross another small beck and head for the broken wall. Pass through a gap in the wall, following a now less distinct but still traceable route. Once the grassy plateau of Scarth Gap is reached, the path bears around, off to the left, with the summit of Haystacks now looming ahead.

Near a large stone cairn (and an isolated detached metal gate!), bear to the left and start the ascent of Haystacks. The route, marked by stone cairns, is steep in places and includes some short rocky scrambles.

Summit views are to Buttermere and Crummock as well as to Ennerdale Forest (N.B. you have not reached the summit until you can see the small summit tarn).

With your back to Buttermere, leave the summit of Haystacks on the path to the left of the summit tarn. This bears around to the left and starts to descend left down a well defined path through the heather towards Innominate Tarn. The path passes to the left of the tarn, marked by cairns. Continue ahead, following the stone cairns to cross the beck which drains Blackbeck Tarn. From the beck, take the pitched path that gradually climbs (a fainter path is off to the left) to reveal views to the right over Blackbeck Tarn. Continue ahead, following small stone cairns, keeping the summit rocks of Green Crag to your left.

The path winds ahead following cairns - the slate quarry workings on Fleetwith Pike now come into view. Cross a further small beck before descending on a well defined stone path to Warnscale Beck. Once across, bear left and rise to a defined path heading down the valley, parallel with the beck, back towards Buttermere Water. Continue down following the route of the beck back to the parking area at Gatesgarth Farm.

DISTANCE
4.5
MILES

TIME
3.5
HOURS

MAP REF.
ORDNANCE
SURVEY
OUTDOOR
LEISURE 4
NW AREA
196
150

WALK TOUGH GRADE

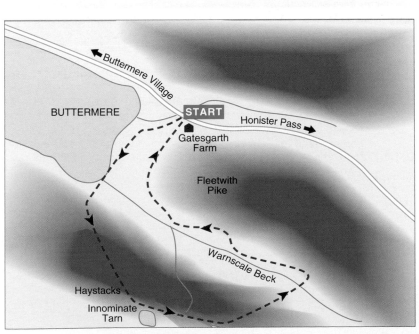

View from Red Pike. MDN.

SCALE FORCE AND RED PIKE

A walk to Lakeland's loftiest waterfall and on via Lingcomb Edge to the summit of Red Pike. Rewarding views across Crummock, Buttermere and Ennerdale Waters. The descent is by way of the attractive Bleaberry Tarn and National Trust Burtness Woods.

ELEVATION
Highest elevation reached: 2475 ft (755m). Start height: 360 ft (110m).

REFRESHMENTS & TOILETS
Tea shop and hotels in Buttermere village.

DIRECTIONS TO START
From Keswick, follow the Borrowdale signs south on the B5289. Pass through the Honister Pass and alongside Buttermere Lake and park in Buttermere village.

WALK DIRECTIONS

From the parking areas in Buttermere, follow the path next to the Bridge Hotel, signed as a public footpath to Scale Force. Proceed on the path ahead, bearing left to pass through a kissing gate before bearing right through a further kissing gate adjacent to a farm gate which has a National Trust sign indicating the way to Scale Bridge and Scale Force. Walk beside a wire fence before bearing right to cross a stone bridge. Go through a gate and follow the path off to the right; the path leads towards Crummock

Water which gradually becomes visible on the right.

Cross several becks, including a larger one via a footbridge, the path now starting to bear off to the left away from the lake. At a large stone cairn, bear left for a short distance before returning to follow the cairn marked path ahead as it leads to Scale Beck Valley. As the northern end of Crummock Water starts to disappear from view, cross a beck and follow the path up steps to reach a hole in the stone wall. Take a few minutes to view Lakeland's tallest waterfall from the footbridge below.

From the footbridge, head back to the wall and take the stepped path that leads uphill to the left of the waterfall. Continue up the valley for some distance, adjacent to the beck. Gradually, the distinct rocky path leads away from the beck into more open ground to follow a steep rocky track that leads left uphill. Head for two large rocks visible on the horizon, after which continue on the obvious path along Lingcomb Edge with the summit of Red Pike before you. The path zig zags its way up to the summit, the latter part of the climb being fairly loose under foot. The views from the summit are across Buttermere, Crummock and Ennerdale, a reward for the exertions.

From the summit, do not take the path leading on to the next summit (High Stile), instead, continue across the summit, descending on a cairn marked path towards Bleaberry Tarn below.

Ignore the alternative path to the smaller summit in front of you (Dodd 2100 feet, 641m.), and pass over a ruined wall adjacent to the tarn. Cross the outlet beck (this will eventually become Sourmilk Gill which will be passed later) and bear left descending away from the tarn. The path eventually bears to the right from a stone wall - Buttermere Water again starts to come into view. Pass through a gap in the wall and rejoin the main track leading off to the right.

Descend via the zig zag path towards Burtness Woods. Pass through a gate in a wire fence and bear left to follow the path down into the woodland. Upon reaching the path by a National Trust sign indicating Red Pike, bear left through a gate and cross a footbridge to proceed back to Buttermere village on the clearly defined path.

DISTANCE
5
MILES

TIME
3.5
HOURS

MAP REF.
ORDNANCE
SURVEY
OUTDOOR
LEISURE 4
NW AREA
176
171

WALK TOUGH GRADE

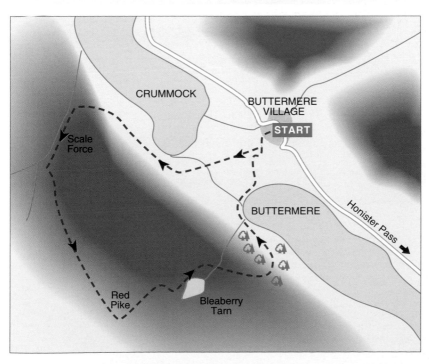

Loweswater. Val Corbett

LOWESWATER

The 'leafy lake' of Loweswater is often forgotten due to its position in the far north west of the lakes. This lowland circular walk around the lake involves no climbing and is a welcome alternative to some of the more popular lake circuits.

ELEVATION
Highest elevation reached: 410 ft (125m). Start height: 410 ft (125m).

REFRESHMENTS & TOILETS
None encountered within the immediate course of the walk.

DIRECTIONS TO START
The most attractive route to Loweswater is on the B5289 from Keswick via Borrowdale, the Honister pass, Buttermere and Crummock (after Crummock, turn left signed to Scale Hill). Alternatively follow the A5086 south from the A66 Cockermouth bypass towards Cleator Moor. Pass through the village of Mockerkin and continue ahead to reach Loweswater. In both cases, start from a roadside parking area at the northern end of the lake near a phone box.

WALK DIRECTIONS

From the parking area, continue along the main road with Loweswater on your right. After half a mile, there is a small lay-by with a National Trust sign detailing fishing rights. Here, take the lakeshore path that runs parallel to the road. After a short distance, rejoin the main road and continue ahead past the end of the lake and

Thrushbank House.

Turn right down a narrow tarmac lane opposite a farm gate. At the bottom, pass through a small National Trust car park and gate indicating Watergate Farm. Follow a broad track in the direction of the lake. Pass through a series of gates before bearing off to the right, close to Watergate Farm at the foot of the lake.

Go through a gate into the National Trust Holme Wood. Walk ahead and shortly after a small footbridge, do not bear right towards the stone building, instead, continue ahead on a broad track through the woods.

Cross a beck and proceed to the end of the woods, passing through a gate in a stone wall.

Follow the track uphill and over a stile next to a gate before turning right after a gate next to Hudson Place Farm. Proceed downhill on a tarmac lane to cross a stile adjacent to a metal gate where the lane bears off to the left. Head across the field to the opposite stile and cross a footbridge before heading for a stile in the right hand field boundary. Follow the path left, through a kissing gate and onto the main road. Turn right to return to the parking area.

DISTANCE
4
MILES

TIME
2
HOURS

MAP REF.
ORDNANCE
SURVEY
OUTDOOR
LEISURE 4
NW AREA
122
224

WALK
EASY
GRADE

Loweswater is unique in that it is the only lake where the water flows eastwards towards the centre of the Lake District. The Dub and Park Becks flow into Crummock before resuming a seaward journey via the Rivers Cocker and Derwent. This relationship harks back to a time when Loweswater was joined with Crummock and Buttermere as one lake.

The whole lake, Holme Wood as well as Watergate and High Nook farms are in the care of the National Trust which in total owns nearly 1000 acres in the immediate vicinity.

The name Loweswater means 'leafy lake', a reflection no doubt of its afforested western shore This has resulted from the underlying geological circumstances of Skiddaw Slate; colonisation by woodland easier here than further south in the central fells. An alternative meaning is also attributed to a previous Norse owner, *Loghi*. This is a common enough phenomenon with Ullswater, belonging at one time to a Norseman called *Ulph* and the original name of Lake Windermere also resulted from the name of a landowner called *Vinand*, hence Vinand'smere.

Loweswater is one of the smallest of Lakeland's principal 16 lakes with only Rydal and Elterwater smaller and Grasmere of a similar size.

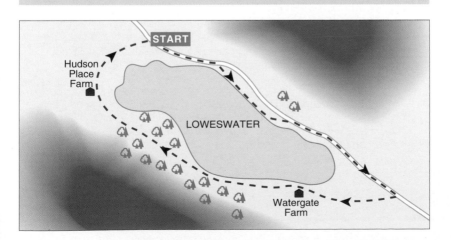

START

Hudson
Place
Farm

LOWESWATER

Watergate
Farm

MAN & THE LAKELAND LANDSCAPE

by Mark Norton

Although the Lake District is visited by people from all over the world seeking a 'natural' landscape, the physical appearance of the region today is largely a result of man's activity. The most obvious example is that 10,000 years ago, the lower fells of the Lake District National Park were covered in deciduous forest, with coniferous species such as pine, crowning the upper fell tops. Over the centuries vast areas of forest have thus been systematically cleared, at first to allow cultivation and animal raising, but more recently as a result of the vast needs for charcoal, used in the smelting of iron ore from the fifteenth century.

The history of man's occupation of the area dates from around 5000 years ago. At first, this was limited to the western coastal plain, but gradually settlement of central Lakeland increased and small communities little by little cleared lowland forests to allow animal domestication and crop cultivation. An important confirmation of Neolithic presence was the discovery in the 1940's of 'axe factories' in the Langdale and Scafell mountain areas. Not of course factories in the modern sense, but rather mass evidence of the fashioning and shaping of hard volcanic rock outcrops into

axeheads that could be polished into fearsome cutting tools. This trade in axeheads was considerable with Cumbrian examples found as far away as Kent, Sussex and even Ireland.

The quality of the Neolithic axes ensured that by the time the Romans arrived, the clearing of the forests had already started to change the landscape. To the Romans, Cumbria was something of a military outpost, the edge of their empire and known world rather than an area for civilian occupation such as southern England. The building of the 73 mile long Hadrian's Wall from AD120 to hold back the Scots, and the construction of forts, resulted in the need for strong and permanent communication routes. The High Street ridge route between their fort of Galava at Ambleside and their military centre at Brougham can still be enjoyed today, though by far the most important route was driven across the fells west, to their supply port at Ravenglass. Traces of this route as well as their fort of Mediobogdum can still be found in the Hardknott Pass.

After Roman withdrawal from around AD400, a Celtic tribe, the Cymry, prospered and controlled the area before being colonised by settlers and

Wastwater. Val Corbett.

farmers from Northumbria who arrived in the seventh century. One of the most important impacts on the Cumbrian landscape however, was to begin some 200 years later with the arrival of Norse settlers from the ninth century. Evidence of their distribution is found in name endings such as '-*thwaite*', meaning clearing, indicating the continued disappearance of woodland for farming. The Vikings were second and third generation settlers who had arrived in Cumbria after establishing themselves in Scotland, Ireland and the Isle of Man and were largely peaceful in nature. It is believed that they were also responsible for the introduction of the Herdwick

strain of sheep, suited to the hard Lakeland winters and upland grazing.

The Norman conquest of England from the eleventh century led to the establishment of large estates and baronies, with castles constructed as a defence to the ever present threat from the north. This period also saw the emergence of monastic ownership of vast swathes of land. The Cistercian monks of Furness Abbey, for example, laid claim to estates from modern day Barrow-in-Furness, through Windermere and Coniston and as far north as Hawkshead and Borrowdale. The monks accentuated the forest clearance in order to establish a woollen industry, once again based on

The Old Courthouse, Hawkshead. Val Corbett.

the Herdwick sheep; the felled timber being used to make charcoal, an essential requirement of the smelting process for the rapidly growing iron industry.

It was, from the thirteenth century onwards, a time of exploitation of Cumbria's natural resources. Extensive copper deposits in the Newlands Valley, south west of Keswick, as well as near Coniston and Caldbeck saw the growth of industrial activity in the Lake District. Graphite for example, discovered and mined at Borrowdale, lead to the establishment of a pencil industry at Keswick. The discovery of lead near Glenridding saw an industry that would continue until the

1960's; slate production, still quarried in Borrowdale near the Honister Pass, dates from 1643. The effect of all this on the landscape included the building of small settlements to house workers, the utilisation of water courses for power and even the artificial deepening of natural tarns to be used as reservoirs such as Levers Water in the Coniston copper mining area and Keppelcove Tarn near Glenridding. At the same time farming was undergoing change. The redistribution of monastic lands after the dissolution in the sixteenth century saw the appearance of 'statesman' farmers who owned smaller areas of land, farming it intensively. The dry stone walls of Cumbria, so part of the

Town End House, Troutbeck. Val Corbett.

Wasdale. Val Corbett.

landscape that is loved today, were instigated by these farmers who used the available labour during the eighteenth century to turn the open fells into a network of fields.

The effect of modern man on the landscape is of course more obvious. Population growth during the nineteenth century saw an increasing demand for water and the resultant construction of Thirlmere and Haweswater reservoirs. The coming of the railway age in the 1850's and the writings of the lake poets ensured the growth of tourism in the Lake District. Resort towns such as Bowness and Windermere quickly developed; the large houses built by rich northern industrialists on the lake shore of Windermere gradually turning into hotels and spas.

The escalating industrialisation of northern towns and the unchecked growth of tourism in the late nineteenth and early twentieth centuries could so easily have destroyed the Cumbria we know today. Fortunately, visionaries such as

Wordsworth, Ruskin and Canon Rawnsley, one of the founders of the National Trust, ensured that man's ultimate effect on the Lakeland landscape would be controlled and its beauty preserved. The National Trust's first purchase in Lakeland, Brandlehow Wood near Derwent Water in 1902, and the creation of the National Park in 1951 guaranteed that the Lake District landscape would be safeguarded for those who live and work in the region as well as the millions of visitors, captivated by the area's beauty.

Nowadays, and for the first time since forest clearance began 5,000 years ago, forests are now planted rather than destroyed with approximately 10% of the National Park now covered by trees. The National Trust plants between 20,000 and 25,000 trees each year; the original plantings of coniferous species by the Forestry Commission are now increasingly complemented by the slower growing but more aesthetically pleasing deciduous woodland.

Grasmere. Val Corbett.

Duddon Valley. Val Corbett.

Lakeland without a car

Picture courtesy of National Trust.

The following information is designed to help guide you in the exploration of the Lake District without the use of a car.

A good source of information is the **Cumbria County Council Public Transport Team** who can be contacted care of **Cumbria County Council, Citadel Chambers, Carlisle, Cumbria CA3 8SG.**
For all public transport enquiries, phone **Journey Planner** on **01228 606000**, Mon.-Fri. 9am-5pm, Sat. 9am-12noon. The excellent **'To and through Cumbria'** map is well worth asking for if you intend to use public transport a lot during your stay in the Lake District. From May 1997, Cumbria County Council will be operating a public transport information system on the internet.
To find out more visit the following site:
http://www.wwwebguides.com/pubtrans/cumbria/info.html
The principal bus operator is **Stagecoach Cumberland** which provides a detailed bus timetable booklet called **Lakeland Explorer** (contact number **01946 63222**, Mon.-Sat. 7am-7pm, Sun. 9am-5.30pm, contact address is **Stagecoach Cumberland, PO Box 17, Tangier Street, Whitehaven, Cumbria CA28 7XF**). One day and four day Explorer tickets can be purchased to allow unlimited travel on all Cumberland Services in Cumbria (1 day tickets available at time of boarding the bus, 4 day tickets available from Cumberland offices and various company agents).
Below is a brief summary of the principal bus routes (correct as at June 1997, please call the bus company or obtain an upto date timetable booklet if uncertain). The routes described are usually both ways, i.e. the Bowness to Grasmere service bus returns from Grasmere to Bowness, allowing return trips to be made.
Please be sure to check that the bus calls at your chosen destination before boarding.

Bowness to Grasmere *Open top bus- Service No 599*
Departing from Kendal and calling at: Windermere, Bowness, Troutbeck Bridge, Brockhole, Waterhead, Ambleside, Rydal and Grasmere.

Carlisle to Lancaster *Service No 555*
Departing from Carlisle and calling at:
Keswick, Grasmere, Rydal, Ambleside, Waterhead, Brockhole, Troutbeck Bridge, Windermere, Staveley and Kendal before continuing on to Lancaster.

Keswick to Buttermere *Service Number 77 and 77A*
Departing from Keswick and calling at:
Whinlatter, Lorton, Buttermere, Honister, Seatoller, Grange and back to Keswick.

The Coniston Rambler *Service No 505 and 506*
Departing from Kendal and calling at:
Windermere, Bowness, Windermere Steamboat Museum, Brockhole, Waterhead, Ambleside, Skelwith Bridge, Hawkshead and Coniston.

Ambleside to Ulverston *Service No 515*
Departing from Ambleside and calling at:
Hawkshead, Grizedale Visitors Centre, Satterthwaite, Force Forge, Rusland Cross, Newby Bridge and Ulverston.

The Langdale Rambler *Service No 516*
Departing from Ambleside and calling at:
Skelwith Bridge, Elterwater, Chapel Stile and Dungeon Ghyll Old Hotel.

Kendal to Cartmel *Service No 530, 531 and 532*
Departing from Kendal and calling at:
Helsington Lumley Road, Levens Bridge, Levens village, Lindale, Grange-over-Sands, Kents Bank Station, Allithwaite, Flookburgh, Cark and Cartmel. Some services also continue to Newby Bridge, Bowness and Windermere.

Cartmel to Lakeside *Service No 534*
Departing from Cartmel and calling at:
Grange-over-Sands, Allithwaite, Flookburgh, Cark, Holker Hall, Haverthwaite, Backbarrow, Newby Bridge, Lakeside, Stott Park and Finsthwaite.

Kendal to Barrow-in-Furness
Service No X35 - Shoppers Express
Departing from Kendal and calling at:
Grange-over-Sands, Newby Bridge, Haverthwaite, Ulverston, Dalton and Barrow-in-Furness.

The Patterdale Bus *Service No 108*
Departing from Penrith and calling at:
Yanwath Cottages, Pooley Bridge, Gowbarrow Cottages, Park Brow Foot, Glenridding and Patterdale.

Keswick to Patterdale *Service No 37*
Departing from Keswick and calling at:
Threlkeld, Troutbeck Hotel, Park Brow Foot, Glenridding and Patterdale. (NB First bus of the day starts at Workington and calls at Embleton and Cockermouth before reaching Keswick. Last bus of the day, vice versa).

Picture courtesy of Lakes Supertours.

The Kirkstone Rambler *Service No 517*
Departing from Bowness and calling at:
Windermere, Troutbeck, Kirkstone Pass Inn,
Brotherswater, Patterdale and Glenridding.

The Borrowdale Bus *Service No 79*
Departing from Keswick and calling at:
Lodore Hotel, Grange, Rosthwaite and Seatoller.

The Caldbeck Rambler *Service Number 73*
Departing from Keswick and calling at:
Castlerigg Stone Circle, Threlkeld, Mungrisdale, Mosedale,
Hesket Newmarket and Caldbeck.

The Kentmere Rambler *Service No 519*
Departing from Kendal and calling at:
Crook, Staveley and Kentmere.

The Haweswater Rambler *Service No 111*
Departing from Penrith and calling at: Eamont Bridge,
Yanwath, Askham, Helton, Bampton, Bampton Grange,
Burnbanks, Haweswater Hotel and Mardale Car Park.

Keswick to Muncaster Castle *Service No 11A*
Departing from Keswick and calling at:
Whinlatter Visitors Centre, Cockermouth, Crossgates,
Rowrah, Arlecdon, Frizington, Cleator, Egremont,
Sellafield Visitors Centre, Calderbridge, Gosforth,
Holmrook, Ravenglass and Muncaster Castle.

Whitehaven to Penrith *Service No X5*
Departing from Whitehaven and calling at:
Distington, Harrington, Workington, Clifton Hotel,
Bridgefoot, Broughton Cross, Cockermouth, Embleton,
Brathay Hill, Castle Inn, Bassenthwaite, Millbeck Road
End, Thornthwaite, Braithwaite, Keswick, Threlkeld,
Troutbeck Hotel and Penrith.

*There are also several companies offering guided
tours in the Lake District using minibuses:*

RELAX AND RIDE *The National Trust*
All services operate between May and October only:

LANDSCAPE TOURS Half day tours of the south and
north lakes running from Bridge House, Ambleside and
from Lakeside in Keswick. Book via the relevant National
Trust information centre at Ambleside **(0831) 725962** or
Keswick **(01768) 773780**.

THE TARN HOWS TOURER This is a free Sunday
service between Hawkshead and the beauty spot of Tarn
Hows *see Mini Walks section for further details*.

WATENDLATH WANDERER This is a free Sunday
service operating between Keswick and the celebrated
National Trust beauty spot of Watendlath. The return
service calls at Lakeside Information Centre, Lake Road
Car Park, Lakes Food Store, Moot Hall, Great Wood Car
Park, Ashness Gate Car Park, Ashness Bridge Car Park,
Surprise View Car Park and Watendlath Bridge.

*These last two services are part of a commendable
initiative by the National Trust to promote exploration of
the Lake District by alternative means to the car. Although
the service is free, the National Trust's charitable status
ensures all donations are gratefully received.*

LAKELAND SAFARI *Tours*
Full day, half day or evening safaris in a six seater vehicle
with the local owner/driver, a Cumbria Tourist Board Blue
Badge Guide. Various options such as Photo-Romantic,
Hadrian's wall etc.
*Book direct or at any Tourist Information Centre. For a
free brochure contact Lakeland Safari (Tours), 23
Fisherbeck Park, Ambleside LA22 0AJ* **(01539) 433904.**

LAKES SUPERTOURS Luxury mini coaches visiting
stately homes, lakes, churches and mountain passes.
Small informal groups and friendly driver/guides. Book at
any Tourist Information Centre or at your hotel.
For details contact **Lakes Supertours, 1 High Street,
Windermere LA23 1AF (01539) 488133.**

MOUNTAIN GOAT TOURS Pioneers of the *'Off the
beaten track touring'* using luxury mini coaches with
panoramic windows and seat belts. Tours are of half or full
day duration with friendly PSV trained driver/guides. Tours
include Hardknott and Wrynose Passes, Northern Lakes
and Tarn Hows and Langdales. Tours operate all year
round from Windermere and Keswick. Book direct or at
any Tourist Information Centre.
For details contact **Mountain Goat Tours, Victoria
Street, Windermere LA23 1AD (01539) 445161 or
(01768) 773962.**

CUMBRIAN DISCOVERIES Personalised and special
interest tours on foot, by car, minibus or coach for
individuals and groups of any size. Specialist in walking,
driver guided and study tours using professional Blue
Badge Guides. *Contact* **(01768) 362200.**

CUMBRIA TOURIST GUIDES General or specialist
interest tours by coach, minibus, car or on foot. Full, half
day and evening tours available using friendly and
knowledgeable Blue Badge Guides. *For details contact*
**Mickle bower, Temple Sowerby, Penrith CA10 1RZ
(01768) 362233.**

ALISTAIRS OF WINDERMERE Driver/guided tours of
the Lake District including visits to Beatrix Potter and
Wordsworth homes and the northern counties. *For
details contact* **Alistairs of Windermere, PO Box 4,
Windermere LA23 1JY (01539) 488191**

Made in Cumbria is a Cumbria County Council economic development initiative promoting craft and giftware. The scheme helps local craftspeople to sell their work throughout the county, British Isles and overseas.

For further details on Made in Cumbria, please contact Cumbria County Council, County Offices, Kendal, Cumbria LA9 4RQ (01539) 732736. E-mail: enq@madecumb.demon.co.uk

The county has a rich cultural life, reflecting the traditions of old Cumberland, Westmorland, Lancashire and Yorkshire. Crafts are an important part of this historical legacy, preserving practical skills and techniques for generations to come. Whilst some craftspeople continue to use time honoured techniques, once a part of everyday life, others develop their own artistry and explore modern technologies. Cumbria, as a result, is home to a wealth of talented craftspeople and artists, producing a glorious array of products, ranging from baskets to batik, figurines to furniture and turned wood to wall hangings.

The following are just a selection of the many craft workshops and craft and gift shops found in Cumbria:

CUMBRIA CRYSTAL LTD

Address	Lightburn Road, Ulverston, LA12 0DA (01229) 584400
Directions	Park in town centre and follow signs to Crystal factory and shop.
Opening Hours	**Factory** Mon-Thurs, 9am-4pm, Fri 9am-3pm. **Shop** Mon-Fri, 9am-5pm and Sat 10am-4pm.
Details	Experience the unique skills of craftsmen producing the finest quality full lead crystal. See glass blowing and hand cutting with thousands of pieces for sale in the factory shop.

PIXIE PINE DESIGN

Address	40 Challoner Street, Cockermouth, CA13 9QU. (01900) 822575
Directions	Off main street behind Brysons Bakery.
Opening Hours	Mon-Sat, 9.30am-5.30pm and Sun, 12 noon-4pm.
Details	An Aladdin's cave of childhood memories. Children's furniture from wardrobes to chairs, lovingly handpainted as well as traditional wooden toys, rocking horses, dolls houses and trains etc.

ALBION GLASS

Address	3 The Old Brewery, Craw Hall, Brampton CA8 1TP (01697) 73780
Directions	5 minutes from Brampton town centre on Craw Hall Road
Opening Hours	All year, Mon-Sat, 9am-5pm.
Details	Workshop and showroom producing traditional hand made leaded stained glass windows and door panels using classical and individual patterns.

Hare Moon Panel, Albion Glass.
Courtesy of Richard Knowles, Made in Cumbria.

HERON GLASS

Address	54 The Gill, Ulverston, LA12 7BL. (01229) 581121.
Directions	From A590, follow brown signs for glass blowing factory.

Opening Hours Mon-Sat, 8.30am-5pm.

Details Using traditional methods, highly skilled glass makers transform molten glass into truly unique pieces of art glass, all on display in the factory shop alongside other local crafts.

MADE IN CUMBRIA GIFT SHOP

Address Windermere TIC, Victoria Street, Windermere, LA23 1AD. (01539) 446499

Directions Next to Windermere railway station.

Opening Hours Apr-Oct, daily, 9.30am-4.30pm. Nov-Mar, daily on demand.

Details Open daily for a wide range of crafts and gifts. Groups welcome.

Made in Cumbria Gift Shop, Windermere.
Courtesy of Richard Knowles, Made in Cumbria.

GOSFORTH POTTERY

Address Gosforth, CA20 1AH. (01946) 725296

Directions Leave A595 north of village.

Opening Hours Summer: Daily, 10am-5.30pm. Winter: Jan, Thurs-Sun, 10am-5.30pm, Feb-March, Tues-Sun, 10am-5.30pm.

Details A busy country pottery selling their own earthenware and stoneware pots . Demonstrations and 'have a go' during holidays.

THE TEAPOTTERY

Address Central Car Park Road, Keswick, CA12 5DF. (01768) 73983

Directions Keswick's central car park, off Heads Rd.

Opening Hours Daily, 9am-5pm.

Details Internationally known for its unique, hand made teapots, The Teapottery in Keswick enables visitors to watch craftspeople at work and browse in the shop upstairs.

THE HEATON COOPER STUDIO

Address The Studio, Grasmere, LA22 9SX. (01539) 435280

Directions Central Grasmere, opposite village green.

Opening Hours Easter-October, Mon-Sat, 9am-6pm and Sun, 12noon-6pm. November-Easter, Mon-Sat, 9am-5pm and Sun, 12noon-5pm.

Details A changing exhibition of watercolours and the largest collection of reproductions of the Lake District by W. Heaton Cooper and A. Heaton Cooper. Paintings, greetings cards, books, sculptures and art materials.

THE KIRKSTONE GALLERIES

Address Skelwith Bridge, Ambleside, LA22 9NN. (01539) 434002

Directions Skelwith Bridge is on the A593 between Ambleside and Coniston.

Opening Hours Daily, 10am-6pm (closes 5pm Nov-Mar).

Details Kirkstone is a unique sea green stone made in to everything from earrings to worktops and displayed alongside an unusual collection of home furnishings, crafts and gifts. Excellent coffee shop also.

ADRIAN SANKEY

Address Rydal Road, Ambleside, LA22 9AN. (01539) 433039

Directions By the Old Bridge House.

Opening Hours Daily, 9am-5.30pm.

Details Created from fire - fashioned by hand. Watch glass blowing in the open studio as well as browse a distinctive collection of traditional and contemporary lead crystal studio glass. A working watermill is now the award-winning Glass House Cafe Restaurant.

LOWES COURT GALLERY

Address 12 Main Street, Egremont, CA22 2DW. (01946) 820693

Directions Follow information centre signs.

Opening Hours Jan-Feb, Mon-Fri (10am-1pm) and Sat (10am-5pm). Mar-Dec, Mon-Tues (10am-1pm & 2pm-5pm), Wed (10am-1pm) and Thurs-Sat (10am-5pm).

Details Gallery showing a wide range of paintings, prints and craft work. Changing displays of work for sale by Cumbrian makers as well as Tourist Information.

SEATOLLER BARN

Address   Borrowdale, near Keswick, CA12 5XN. (01768) 777294

Directions   Take B5289 from Keswick for 7 miles to reach Seatoller.

Opening Hours April to October, 10am-5pm.

Details   Featuring interpretative displays, tourist information and a wide range of books and maps. Products from several local crafts people are featured including ceramics, glassware, pottery, honey and jewellery.

CONISTON INFORMATION CENTRE

Address   Ruskin Avenue, Coniston, LA21 8EH. (01539) 441533

Opening Hours April to October, 9.30am-5pm.

Details   Situated in the centre of Coniston, this brand new purpose built Information Centre provides a comprehensive service for those visiting the area, as well as a range of locally produced crafts.

Derwent Bay Bears.
Courtesy of Richard Knowles, Made in Cumbria.

DERWENT BAY BEARS

Address   Derwent Bay Sawmill, Portinscale, Keswick CA12 5UB (01768) 774788

Directions   Off A66 to Portinscale and left hand side at Swinside Lodge Hotel.

Opening Hours April-Oct, daily, 9am-6pm. Nov-Mar, Tues-Sat, 10am-4pm

Details   Visit the Derwent Bay Bears; Barney, Bruno, Bertie, Honey, Fleur and Boris. They live on the edge of Derwentwater at the Sawmill where they were sculpted by chainsaw from Cumbrian timber. Demonstrations daily.

SERENDIPITY

Address   12 Market Place, Brampton, CA8 1RW. (01697) 741900

Directions   Next to the Moot Hall.

Opening Hours Easter to September, Mon-Sat, 9am-5pm and Sun, 10am-4pm.

Details   Cumbria's finest and most popular craftsmen compete to exhibit in this northernmost Made in Cumbria shop in the pretty little market town on the Roman wall.

GOSSIPGATE GALLERY

Address   The Butts, Alston, CA9 3JU. (01434) 381806

Directions   Signed, behind Market Cross.

Opening Hours Summer: daily (10am-5pm). Winter: Sat (10am-5pm), Sun (11am-4.30-pm). Weekdays variable and by appointment.

Details   In the heart of the North Pennines the gallery specialises in showing quality art and craft from the north if England. A continuous programme of exhibitions complements a great variety of totally regional craftwork and pictures.

KENNEDYS FINE CHOCOLATES

Address   The Old School, Orton, Penrith CA10 3RU (01539) 624781

Directions   3 miles from the M6, junction 38 on the B6260.

Opening Hours Mon-Sat, 9am-5.30pm and Sun 12 noon-5pm.

Details   Hand made chocolates using natural ingredients and cream from the local farm. Visit our chocolate factory, chocoholics welcome!

Kennedys Fine Chocolates.
Courtesy of Richard Knowles, Made in Cumbria.

Attractions

The Lake District has a wide variety of quality attractions, from historic houses to wildlife parks, steam railways to museums. These are of a very high standard and offer an exciting day out for all the family.

For ease of reference, each attraction has been put into one of four colour coded groups.

The attractions are organised broadly south to north from Morecambe Bay to Carlisle. This allows you to locate attractions concentrated together in particular parts of the county. Alternatively, the attraction numbers can be found on the map on page 196, allowing a straight forward indication of its location. If one particular attraction is required, use the index. Golf courses, horse riding, cinemas and leisure centres are detailed separately.

- **MUSEUMS & ART GALLERIES**
- **HISTORIC BUILDINGS & GARDENS**
- **LEISURE, WILDLIFE & THEME PARKS**
- **OTHER**

A SHORT NOTE ON THE ENTRY DETAILS:

DIRECTIONS In most cases, the directions are detailed from the nearest 'A' class road.

OPENING HOURS Though all opening hours have been verified with the attractions concerned, in the winter it will often be worthwhile to ring before making a long journey.

DISABLED ACCESS If in doubt, ring prior.

ACTIVITIES/FACILITIES As well as the primary activities at the attraction, the details include ancillary facilities such as coffee shops etc.

🐕 Dog access OK 🐕 Dog access prohibited

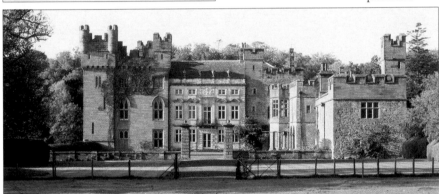

Hutton in the Forest.

Lanercost Priory. Val Corbett.

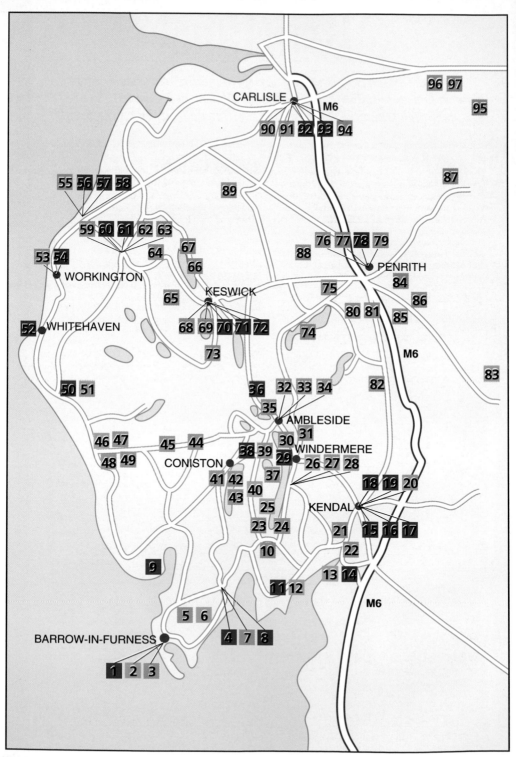

CARLISLE

M6

96 97
95

90 91 92 93 94

87

55 56 57 58

89

59 60 61 62 63

76 77 78 79

88

84

64

67

66

PENRITH

53 54

WORKINGTON

75

65

KESWICK

80 81

85

86

52 WHITEHAVEN

68 69 70 71 72

74

M6

73

50 51

82

83

36

32 33 34

35

AMBLESIDE

46 47

45 44

31

30

WINDERMERE

48 49

CONISTON

38 39

29

26 27 28

37

18 19 20

41 42

40

43

25

KENDAL

23 24

21

15 16 17

10

22

13 14

9

11 12

5 6

4 7 8

BARROW-IN-FURNESS

1 2 3

1 THE DOCK MUSEUM

ADDRESS & TELEPHONE North Road, Barrow-in-Furness, LA14 2PW. (01229) 870871

DIRECTIONS Follow A590 to Barrow. Well signed.

OPENING HOURS Easter to Oct, Wed-Fri, 10am-5pm and weekends 11am-5pm. Nov-March, Wed-Fri, 10.30am-4pm and weekends 12noon to 4pm

DISABLED ACCESS Yes.

ACTIVITIES/FACILITIES The spectacular Dock Museum, built over a Victorian graving dock, provides a fascinating insight into the industrial history of Barrow, with of course much reference to the importance of the town's shipbuilding tradition. The museum has a fine collection of ship models and the *Emily Barratt*, the last wooden trading schooner to be built in Britain. **FREE ADMISSION.** **Dogs:** Access In the grounds only please.

Dock Museum, Barrow. Val Corbett

2 PARKHOUSE ANIMAL FARM

ADDRESS & TELEPHONE Parkhouse Road, Barrow-in-Furness, LA13 0PL. (01229) 827300

DIRECTIONS Follow brown tourism signs.

OPENING HOURS Daily, 10am-5pm.

DISABLED ACCESS Yes also lift in the Cafe.

ACTIVITIES/FACILITIES Animal farm with a host of friendly animals and chances to hug a bunny and feed the baby lambs. Donkey rides, birds of prey, full playground facilities, indoor play area, mini amusement arcade, tractor rides and cafe/licensed restaurant. **Dogs:** Certain areas only.

■ MUSEUMS & ART GALLERIES	■ LEISURE, WILDLIFE & THEME PARKS
■ HISTORIC BUILDINGS & GARDENS	■ OTHER

3 FURNESS ABBEY

ADDRESS & TELEPHONE   Near Barrow-in-Furness. (01229) 823420

DIRECTIONS   1.5 miles north of Barrow-in-Furness.

OPENING HOURS   Easter to Oct, daily, 10am-6pm (or dusk if earlier in Oct).
Nov to Mar, Wed to Sun, 10am-4pm (closed 24-26 Dec and 1pm-2pm in winter).

DISABLED ACCESS   Limited access to around 75% of site.

ACTIVITIES/FACILITIES   Discover one of the richest Cistercian monasteries in England. Explore the soaring ruins of red sandstone and soak up the grandeur of this 700 year old site. Located in a peaceful valley, the majestic remains of Furness Abbey once housed the flourishing community of a wealthy order. Stroll around the site and enjoy the inclusive audio-tour. View fine stone carvings in the museum and learn the story of the fascinating religious community through an informative exhibition.
Dogs: Yes on leads.

4 GLEASTON WATERMILL

ADDRESS & TELEPHONE   Gleaston, near Ulverston, LA12 0QH. (01229) 869244

DIRECTIONS   Follow brown tourism signs from the A5087 (Ulverston to Barrow coast road).

OPENING HOURS   Easter to October, Tues-Sun, 11am-5pm. November to Easter, Wed-Sun, 11am-4pm. Open Bank Holidays also.

DISABLED ACCESS   Yes and toilets.

ACTIVITIES/FACILITIES   Working water mill with a five metre diameter wheel. Impressive wooden machinery dating from 1770's. Working most days. Milling and farming displays. Adjacent archaeological site has digs most summers with finds from Mesolithic period to modern times on display. Fully licensed cafe and restaurant. During the summer a store sells gifts and local produce including flour. Also highland cattle, rare breed pigs, geese, ducks and hens and a leather workshop where you can watch craftsmen at work.
Dogs: Only in grounds if on a lead.

5 DALTON CASTLE

ADDRESS & TELEPHONE   Dalton-in-Furness. (01539) 435599

DIRECTIONS   Follow signs in Dalton.

OPENING HOURS   Easter to end September; Saturdays only 2pm-5pm.

DISABLED ACCESS   No.

ACTIVITIES/FACILITIES   Built about 1340 as the manorial courthouse of Furness Abbey and later held by successive lords of the manor of Furness. Includes recently restored armour belonging to the castle. Admission is free but donations welcome (note open Saturday afternoons only).

ATTRACTIONS

6 SOUTH LAKES WILD ANIMAL PARK

ADDRESS & TELEPHONE   Dalton-in-Furness, Cumbria, LA15 8JR. (01229) 466086

DIRECTIONS   Signed on the A590 with brown 'Elephant' tourism signs.

OPENING HOURS   Daily, 10am-6pm.

DISABLED ACCESS   Yes

ACTIVITIES/FACILITIES   The Lake District's only zoological park is recognised as one of Europe's leading conservation zoos. The rolling 17 acres are home to the rarest animals on earth, they are participants in co-ordinated breeding programmes to save them from almost certain extinction in the wild. Many of the animals have complete freedom to wander at will, such as lemurs, kangaroos, wallabies and exotic deer. It is also the only zoo in Britain to hold both Amur and Sumatran tigers, the biggest and smallest tigers left in the world. There is also a safari railway, children's farm, cafe, gift shop and picnic areas.

7 GRAYTHWAITE HALL GARDENS

ADDRESS & TELEPHONE   Estate Office, Graythwaite, Ulverston, Cumbria, LA12 8BA.

DIRECTIONS   From the A590 at Newby Bridge follow signs for Lakeside & Hawkshead. Graythwaite Hall is approx. 4.5 miles north of the A590.

OPENING HOURS   April 1st to June 30th, daily 10am-6pm.

DISABLED ACCESS   Not good because of terrain.

ACTIVITIES/FACILITIES   The gardens date from 1889 when Thomas Mawson of Windermere was commissioned to redesign six acres around Graythwaite Hall (not open to the public). The resultant garden is essentially a spring phenomenon with rhododendrons, azaleas and spring flowering shrubs and although over the years there have been minor changes in layout and species, the basic conception is as Mawson finished it in 1895. An arboretum has been planted to the west of the pond to commemorate family births and marriages.   **Dogs:** Yes, on a lead.

8 THE LAUREL AND HARDY MUSEUM

ADDRESS & TELEPHONE   4c Upper Brook Street, Ulverston, LA12 7BH. (01229) 582292

DIRECTIONS   Follow brown tourism signs to Town Centre. Turn into Upper Brook Street from King Street.

OPENING HOURS   Open 7 days a week, 10am-4.30pm including Bank Holidays. Closed January.

DISABLED ACCESS   Full disabled access and toilets.

ACTIVITIES/FACILITIES   The world's only museum devoted to Laurel and Hardy, in Ulverston, the town where Stan was born on 16th June 1890. Everything you want to know about them is here. Bill Cubin, owner and curator of the museum has devoted his life to the world-famous comedians and has collected an amazing variety of memorabilia, believed to be the largest in the world, including letters, photographs, personal items and furniture. A large extension opened in 1992 gives ample room to browse. There is also a small cinema showing free films and documentaries all day.

9 MILLOM FOLK MUSEUM

Millom Folk Museum. Penny Moreton.

ADDRESS & TELEPHONE
St George's Road,
Millom, LA18 4DJ.
(01229) 772555

DIRECTIONS
A595 to Millom, over
the railway bridge,
through traffic lights.
Park opposite.

OPENING HOURS
May to September,
Monday to Saturday,
10am-5pm.

DISABLED ACCESS
Yes.

ACTIVITIES/FACILITIES A truly 'local' museum covering the important development and decline of the iron mining and steel making of the Millom area over the last 150 years. Displays include a full scale reconstruction of a drift from the Hodbarrow Iron Ore Mine and a miner's cottage kitchen. Historic photographs and mining equipment are displayed alongside material devoted to the Millom writer Norman Nicholson.
Dogs: Depending on the size of dog or numbers at a time.

10 THE LAKESIDE & HAVERTHWAITE RAILWAY

Lakeside and Haverthwaite Railway. Val Corbett

ADDRESS & TELEPHONE
Haverthwaite Station,
Ulverston, LA12 8AL. (01539)
531594

DIRECTIONS
Haverthwaite Station is situated
on the A590, 2 miles beyond
Newby Bridge.

OPENING HOURS
Easter and May to October. Also
weekends in April. Obtain
timetable for details of services.

DISABLED ACCESS Yes

ACTIVITIES/FACILITIES
Originally the Furness Railway
branch line, the only part
remaining is the 3.5 mile
section from Haverthwaite
through Newby Bridge to the terminus at Lakeside (connections made with Windermere Lake Cruises boats). The steam locomotives haul the trains on this steeply graded railway, comfortable coaching stock ensures that passengers have a pleasant and leisurely journey through contrasting lake and river scenes of the Leven Valley. Station restaurant and tearoom available April to Dec.

11 LAKELAND MOTOR MUSEUM

ADDRESS & TELEPHONE   Holker Hall, Cark-in-Cartmel, Grange-over-Sands LA11 7PL.
(01539) 558509.

DIRECTIONS   Located on the B5278, 10 mins drive south of Newby Bridge
(follow brown tourism signs for Holker Hall).

OPENING HOURS   April to October, Sunday to Friday 10.30am-4.45pm.

DISABLED ACCESS   Yes.

ACTIVITIES/FACILITIES   Over 150 classic and vintage cars, motor-cycles, tractors, cycles
and engines plus rare motoring automobilia. 1930's garage re-creation and the Campbell
Legend Bluebird exhibition, featuring the lives and careers of Sir Malcolm Campbell and
son Donald who captured 21 land and water speed records for Great Britain. Highlights
include full size detailed replicas of the 1935 Bluebird car and the famous K7 Jet
Hydroplane in which Donald Campbell was killed on Coniston Water in January 1967. 🐕

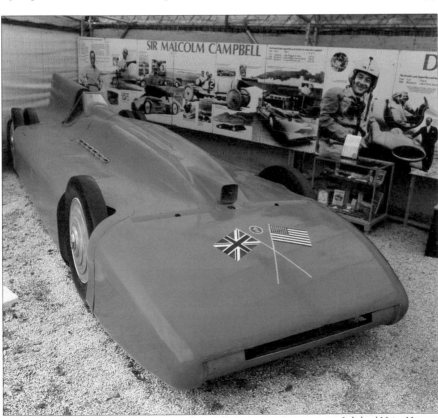

Lakeland Motor Museum.

■ **MUSEUMS & ART GALLERIES**	■ **LEISURE, WILDLIFE & THEME PARKS**
■ **HISTORIC BUILDINGS & GARDENS**	■ **OTHER**

12 HOLKER HALL AND GARDENS

Holker Hall. © Jarrold Publishing.

ADDRESS & TELEPHONE
Cark-in-Cartmel, Grange-over-Sands, LA11 7PL. (01539) 558328.

DIRECTIONS
Follow brown tourism signs from Junction 36 off M6 on A590.

OPENING HOURS
April to October, Sunday to Friday, 10am-6pm (last admission 4.30pm).

DISABLED ACCESS
Yes except to 1st floor of the Hall and Motor Museum and one exhibition.

ACTIVITIES/FACILITIES
Take time to explore 400 years of fascinating history, 125 acres of Deer Park, fabulous award-winning gardens, a wealth of vintage and classic cars and experience live hunting birds of prey. The house is a delightful family home with fine displays of antique furniture and art as well as impressive rooms. The Pleasure Grounds cover 25 acres of formal and woodland gardens with majestic water features and a limestone cascade. Also on offer is a gift shop, cafe, adventure playground and picnic area **Dogs:** Yes in the park but not in the gardens.

13 LAKELAND WILDLIFE OASIS

Lakeland Wildlife Oasis.

ADDRESS & TELEPHONE Hale, Milnthorpe, LA7 7BW. (01539) 563027

DIRECTIONS Situated on the A6, 2.5 miles south of Milnthorpe, 4 miles north of Carnforth.

OPENING HOURS Every day (closed Christmas) 10am-4pm (low season), 10am-5pm (high season).

DISABLED ACCESS Fully accessible.

ACTIVITIES/FACILITIES A unique mix of exotic wildlife and educational 'hands on' exhibits showing the diversity of animal life from microbes to monkeys. Regular animal handling sessions every day. The butterfly house and tropical halls are ideal venues for showery days and the structured exhibitions take you on a fascinating journey through 3,000 million years of evolution and the development of life on earth.
Dogs: Guide dogs only please.

14 HERON CORN MILL & MUSEUM OF PAPERMAKING

ADDRESS & TELEPHONE
Waterhouse Mills, Beetham, Milnthorpe, LA7 7AR. (01539) 563363

DIRECTIONS
Beetham village, 1 mile south of Milnthorpe, 6 miles north of Carnforth.

OPENING HOURS
Easter to September, Tuesday to Sunday, 11am-5pm. Open Bank Holiday Mondays, closed November to February.

DISABLED ACCESS
Mill very limited, possible to part of the Museum with difficulty.

ACTIVITIES/FACILITIES
One of the only fully working lowder corn mills in the area and the only museum of papermaking in the northern region. A unique opportunity to see two of south Lakeland's older industries explained and demonstrated. Occasional demonstrations of hand making of paper. Exhibition in the mill of the last 900 years of milling. Exhibitions in the museum explain the processes of paper making both ancient and modern.
Dogs: On a lead only in the grounds.

15 BREWERY ARTS CENTRE

ADDRESS & TELEPHONE
Highgate, Kendal, LA9 4HE. (01539) 725133

DIRECTIONS
Follow brown tourism signs.

OPENING HOURS
10am-11pm, Monday to Saturday.

DISABLED ACCESS
Yes.

ACTIVITIES/FACILITIES
A large modern art complex comprising a 250 seat theatre/cinema, exhibitions as well as bars, a restaurant and cafe. Entry to the centre is free with ticket prices for events on request.
Dogs: Not in the restaurant.

16 KENDAL NATURAL HISTORY MUSEUM

ADDRESS & TELEPHONE
Station Road, Kendal, LA9 6BT. (01539) 721374.

DIRECTIONS
Follow brown tourism signs from the A6.

OPENING HOURS
Mid Feb to Dec, daily, 10.30am-5pm (closes 4pm in Feb, March, Nov and Dec).

DISABLED ACCESS
Partial access to two floors and toilet.

ACTIVITIES/FACILITIES
One of the oldest museums in the country, housing outstanding displays of archaeology and natural history, both local and global. With many examples of Lakeland flora and fauna, the museum charts developments from prehistoric times through to the 20th century. Other exhibits include local Roman artefacts, Greek pottery and a varied collection of Egyptian relics.
Dogs: Guide dogs only please.

17 ABBOT HALL ART GALLERY

ADDRESS & TELEPHONE Kirkland, Kendal, LA9 5AL. (01539) 722494

DIRECTIONS Follow brown tourism signs from the A591.

OPENING HOURS Daily, April to October, 10.30am-5pm. Nov, Dec, Feb and March 10.30am-4pm.

DISABLED ACCESS Yes (helpers available by appointment).

ACTIVITIES/FACILITIES This impressive Georgian house is one of Britain's finest small galleries containing an extensive art collection. Abbot Hall is highly acclaimed for it's stimulating contemporary exhibition programme, which complements the permanent collection. Light snacks are available in the coffee shop. **Dogs:** Guide dogs by appointment.

18 MUSEUM OF LAKELAND LIFE AND INDUSTRY

ADDRESS & TELEPHONE Abbot Hall, Kirkland, Kendal, LA9 5AL. (01539) 722464

DIRECTIONS Follow brown tourism signs from the A591.

OPENING HOURS Daily, Apr to Oct, 10.30am-5pm. Nov, Dec, Feb & Mar 10.30am-4pm.

DISABLED ACCESS Partial access.

ACTIVITIES/FACILITIES The Museum shows how our Cumbrian ancestors worked, lived and entertained themselves in the changing social climate of the past three hundred years. Our ancestors are long gone, but their belongings live on to tell their story - from the age of the 18th century yeoman farmers, through Georgian and Victorian periods and into living memory. There are changing exhibitions throughout the year as well as a room dedicated to the author of *Swallows and Amazons*, Arthur Ransome.
Dogs: Guide dogs by appointment.

19 THE QUAKER TAPESTRY EXHIBITION CENTRE

ADDRESS & TELEPHONE Friends Meeting House, Stramongate, Kendal, LA9 4BH. (01539) 722975.

DIRECTIONS Park in any car park in central Kendal and enjoy a 10 min stroll by the riverside, or park in the Blackhall Road multi-story. Tapestry centre is on an island between Stramongate and New Road, entrance either side.

OPENING HOURS Easter to October, Mon-Sat, 10am-5pm.

DISABLED ACCESS Step free entrance at Stramongate doors, disabled car parking and toilet facilities, all of the exhibition can be viewed from a wheelchair.

ACTIVITIES/FACILITIES An exhibition that will delight visitors of all ages. Superbly displayed in Kendal's historic Friends Meeting House, over 70 panels of narrative crewel embroidery celebrate the ideas and experience of Quakers since 1652. Beautifully and professionally produced, the exhibition is enhanced by the use of personal headphones and a large screen colour video. Embroidery workshops and courses available.
Dogs: Dogs may be tethered outside, in the garden or car park.

ATTRACTIONS

20 KENDAL CASTLE

ADDRESS & TELEPHONE   Kendal.

DIRECTIONS   The castle is situated on higher ground overlooking the town.

OPENING HOURS   Any reasonable time.

DISABLED ACCESS   No.

ACTIVITIES/FACILITIES   The remains of two towers and parts of the curtain wall and domestic buildings can still be seen of the twelfth century Norman castle, built on high ground overlooking the historic town of Kendal. The castle was the home for four hundred years of the Parr family and the birthplace of the most famous of the dynasty, Catherine Parr, wife to Henry VIII. **FREE ADMISSION.**

Kendal and Kendal Castle. Val Corbett

21 SIZERGH CASTLE

ADDRESS & TELEPHONE

Sizergh, near Kendal, LA8 8AE. (01539) 560070.

DIRECTIONS

3.5 miles south of Kendal, north west of interchange A590/A591.

OPENING HOURS

April to October, Sun to Thurs, 1.30pm-5.30pm. Shop and garden open same days from 12.30pm-5.30pm.

DISABLED ACCESS

Most of garden accessible via mainly gravel paths. Lower Hall and tea-room accessible. Adapted WC. Wheelchair available.

ACTIVITIES/FACILITIES The Strickland family home for more than 750 years; impressive 14th-century pele tower; extended in Tudor times, with some of the finest Elizabethan carved overmantels in the country; good English and French furniture, family portraits; surrounded by gardens including the Trust's largest limestone rock garden; good autumn colour. Tea room in the basement of the pele tower, picnic tables in car park.

Sizergh Castle. Val Corbett

22 LEVENS HALL AND GARDENS

ADDRESS & TELEPHONE

Levens Hall, Kendal, LA8 0PD. (01539) 560321

DIRECTIONS

On the A6, 5 miles south of Kendal (M6 Junction 36). Follow brown tourism signs.

OPENING HOURS

April to September, Sunday to Thursday, 11am-5pm.

DISABLED ACCESS

Yes in the gardens, tearoom and shop. Toilets also.

ACTIVITIES/FACILITIES The Hall is a magnificent Elizabethan mansion built around a 13th century pele tower. It is the family home of the Bagots and contains a collection of Jacobean furniture, fine paintings, the earliest English patchwork and many other beautiful objects. The world-famous Award winning Gardens were laid out in 1694 and create a stunning visual impact. There is also a working steam collection which runs from 2pm-5pm. Home-made lunches and teas are prepared daily in the house kitchens.

ATTRACTIONS

Topiary, Levens Hall. Val Corbett

■ **MUSEUMS & ART GALLERIES**   ■ **LEISURE, WILDLIFE & THEME PARKS**
■ **HISTORIC BUILDINGS & GARDENS**   ■ **OTHER**

23 STOTT PARK BOBBIN MILL

ADDRESS & TELEPHONE Finsthwaite, near Newby Bridge. (01539) 531087

DIRECTIONS Half a mile north of Finsthwaite near Newby Bridge.

OPENING HOURS Easter to October, daily, 10am-6pm (or dusk if earlier in October). Last guided tour 1 hour before closure.

DISABLED ACCESS Wheelchair access to ground floor.

ACTIVITIES/FACILITIES Experience a genuine early 19th century working mill in a lovely woodland setting. View a moving testimony to the industrial revolution by stepping into one of the few surviving and best preserved mills in the country. Take the inclusive 45 minute guided tour and learn the fascinating story of the cotton industry, wooden bobbin manufacturing and the people who worked here. Make time to look around the informative exhibition and enjoy a picnic in lovely surroundings at the southern end of Lake Windermere. Gift shop and souvenir guide available.
Dogs: Yes on a lead.

Stott Park Bobbin Mill. Val Corbett

■ **MUSEUMS & ART GALLERIES**   ■ **LEISURE, WILDLIFE & THEME PARKS**
■ **HISTORIC BUILDINGS & GARDENS**   ■ **OTHER**

24 FELL FOOT PARK & GARDEN

ADDRESS & TELEPHONE
Newby Bridge, Ulverston, LA12 8NN. (01539) 531273

DIRECTIONS
At the extreme southern end of Lake Windermere on eastern shore, entrance from A592.

OPENING HOURS
Park: all year 9am-7pm (or dusk if sooner).
Rowing boat hire: April to Oct. **Tearoom:** April to Oct, 11am-5pm and Nov and Dec 12noon-4pm (weekends only).

DISABLED ACCESS
Accessible but be careful of slopes and unfenced water. Wheelchair and powered buggy vehicle available.

ACTIVITIES/FACILITIES
A 7 hectare National Trust park and garden in the process of being restored to its former Victorian glory, with lakeshore access and magnificent views of the Lakeland fells. Good shows of daffodils and rhododendrons. Boat launching, rowing boats for hire, new children's adventure playground, woodland trail, picnics - ideal for a day's outing. Coffee, light lunches, teas and ice creams in tea room. Picnic sites in park. Admission is free but parking is charged for. **Dogs:** Guide dogs and dogs on leads admitted.

Fell Foot Park. Val Corbett

25 LAKESIDE AQUATARIUM

ADDRESS & TELEPHONE
Lakeside, Newby Bridge, LA12 8AS. (01539) 530153

DIRECTIONS
Follow brown signs (Wind Lake Cruises) from A590.

OPENING HOURS
Daily from 9am except Christmas Day.

DISABLED ACCESS
Yes.

ACTIVITIES/FACILITIES
Opened in May '97, the Aquatarium provides the study of a river from a mountain top origin to Morecombe Bay. Includes the UK's largest collection of freshwater fish as well as a cascading waterfall, living marshland area, a walk over bridge and a walk under tunnel. One of the highlights is a three metre deep display which recreates Lake Windermere itself. Also Aqua Quest, a magnified display providing a hands on experience for children. Gift shop and restaurant.

26 AMAZONIA WORLD OF REPTILES

ADDRESS & TELEPHONE
Windermere Quays Visitor Centre, Glebe Road, Bowness LA23 3HE.
(01539) 448002

DIRECTIONS
Glebe road is located near the steamer piers in Bowness.

OPENING HOURS
Daily except Dec 25th and Jan 1st, Mon-Sat, 9am-6pm.
Sun, 11am-6pm.

DISABLED ACCESS
Yes

ACTIVITIES/FACILITIES
Amazonia has an extensive collection of snakes, lizards, crocodilians, amphibians and insects set amid impressive botanical gardens with beautiful koi and turtle ponds, waterfalls and free nesting tropical birds.

27 THE WORLD OF BEATRIX POTTER

Exhibition model of Peter eating a radish.
Courtesy of World of Beatrix Potter.

ADDRESS & TELEPHONE
The Old Laundry,
Cragbrow, Bowness.
(01539) 488444

DIRECTIONS
Follow brown tourism signs in Bowness and Windermere.

OPENING HOURS
Easter to September, daily, 10am-6.30pm. October to Easter, 10am-4pm (closed Christmas Day).

DISABLED ACCESS
Access and toilets throughout the exhibition, no access to the Tea Room, although snacks can be served to the customer.

ACTIVITIES/FACILITIES
At the World of Beatrix Potter the latest technology is used to tell the story of Beatrix Potter's fascinating life. A video wall and special film (translations in French, German and Japanese) describe how the Tales came to be written and how Beatrix became a pioneering Lakeland farmer and conservationist. Visit Peter Rabbit in his radish patch, call on Mrs Tiggywinkle in the cave and wander past Jeremy Fisher's pond. Here are all the Lakeland tales of Beatrix Potter, brought to life in three dimensions. Also Tearoom and shop.

ATTRACTIONS

28 WINDERMERE LAKE CRUISES

ADDRESS & TELEPHONE   Lakeside, Ulverston, LA12 8AS. (01539) 433046.

DIRECTIONS   Follow brown tourism signs "Lakeside Steamers".

OPENING HOURS   Daily throughout the year during daylight hours. Closed Christmas day.

DISABLED ACCESS   On steamers and larger launches.

ACTIVITIES/FACILITIES   Steamers and launches sail daily throughout the year (except Christmas Day) between Lakeside, Bowness and Ambleside and, in addition to scheduled services, the Company operates private charters, special interest cruises, sightseeing cruises and services to and from the Lakeside & Haverthwaite Steam Railway, the Lake District National Park Visitor Centre at Brockhole, Lakeside Aquatarium and Fell Foot Country Park (National Trust). Cosy welcoming restaurants operate close to the piers and there are coffee shops/licenced bars on the steamers and larger launches, with convenient car/coach parking nearby. All boats have sun decks and covered saloons.

Windermere sightseeing launch 'Miss Lakeland'.

29 WINDERMERE STEAMBOAT MUSEUM

ADDRESS & TELEPHONE   Rayrigg Road, Windermere, LA23 1BN. (01539) 445565.

DIRECTIONS   Follow brown tourism signs on A592 approx. 0.25 miles from the centre of Bowness.

OPENING HOURS   Easter to October, daily, 10am-5pm.

DISABLED ACCESS   The whole site is suitable for wheelchairs and accessible toilets are provided.

ACTIVITIES/FACILITIES   A unique and historic display of steam and motor boats in a lakeside setting. Shop, refreshments, boat trips on the lake available (weather permitting) as well as special events throughout the year.

30 NATIONAL PARK VISITOR CENTRE, BROCKHOLE

ADDRESS & TELEPHONE	Brockhole, Windermere. (01539) 446601
DIRECTIONS	On A591 midway between Windermere and Ambleside.
OPENING HOURS	Easter to October, daily, 10am-5pm.
DISABLED ACCESS	Yes

ACTIVITIES/FACILITIES Beautifully situated on the shores of Windermere, Brockhole provides the ideal introduction to the Lake District. Exhibitions, slide shows, activity trails, varied events programmes, restaurant and tearooms, gardens, lakeshore grounds with regular cruises and an exciting adventure playground. Something for everyone. Admission is free (admission may be charged to Special Events days) but the parking is pay and display.

Brockhole. Val Corbett

31 TOWNEND

ADDRESS & TELEPHONE	Troutbeck, Windermere, LA23 1LB. (01539) 432628
DIRECTIONS	3 miles south east of Ambleside at southern end of village.
OPENING HOURS	April to October, Tues to Fri, Sun and Bank Holiday Mondays, 1pm-5pm (or dusk if earlier).
DISABLED ACCESS	No.

ACTIVITIES/FACILITIES An exceptional relic of Lake District life of past centuries; a 'statesman' (wealthy yeoman) farmer's house, built about 1626, containing carved woodwork, books, papers, furniture and fascinating implements of the past, collected by the Browne family who lived here from that date until 1943. Refreshments available in the village.

Townend, Troutbeck. Val Corbett

32 STAGSHAW GARDEN

ADDRESS & TELEPHONE Ambleside, LA 22 0HE, (01539) 435599

DIRECTIONS Half a mile south of Ambleside on A591.

OPENING HOURS April to June, daily, 10am-6.30pm. July to end Oct: by appointment with National Trust Regional Office, Grasmere, Cumbria, LA22 9QZ (send sae).

DISABLED ACCESS No.

ACTIVITIES/FACILITIES This woodland garden was created by the late Cubby Acland, Regional Agent for the National Trust; fine collection of azaleas and rhododendrons, planted to give good blends of colour under the thinned oaks on the hillside; many trees and shrubs including magnolias, camellias and embothriums. Parking is very limited; visitors may park at Waterhead car park and walk to Stagshaw. No WCs. ✗

Stagshaw Garden. Val Corbett

33 | HAYES GARDEN WORLD

ADDRESS & TELEPHONE
Lake Road, Ambleside, LA22 0DW. (01539) 433434

DIRECTIONS
A short way off the main A591 just south of Ambleside village.

OPENING HOURS
Mon-Sat, 9am-6pm, Sunday, 11am-5pm.

DISABLED ACCESS
Yes except for coffee lounge which is upstairs.

ACTIVITIES/FACILITIES
The perfect all weather attraction from one of the largest and highly renowned garden centres in the country. Its superb landscaped gardens have an impressive display of trees, plants and shrubs and indoors there's an extensive garden shop, plant house and coffee lounge.
FREE ADMISSION. **Dogs:** No access but there is an exercising yards and tethers outside.

34 | GALAVA ROMAN FORT

ADDRESS & TELEPHONE
Near Waterhead, Ambleside.

DIRECTIONS
Park at Waterhead near the Tourist Information Centre. Turn right out of the bottom of the car park and follow the road that leads to Borrans Park; the fort remains are adjacent.

OPENING HOURS
Any reasonable time.

DISABLED ACCESS
No.

ACTIVITIES/FACILITIES
If you are in the Ambleside area, why not seek out the remains of the area's oldest building? The Roman fort of Galava, built as one of a series of fortified structures to protect the vital trade routes through Cumbria, was constructed around AD79 and made use of a strategic position, protected on two sides by water. Although the remains lack the majestic location of Hardknott and impressive structure of the Roman bath house ruins at Ravenglass, Galava has a pleasant situation and is adjacent to the attractive open area of Borrans Park, a waterside park with trees and benches to sit upon and watch the pleasure craft on Lake Windermere. **FREE ADMISSION.**

Galava Roman Fort. Val Corbett

ATTRACTIONS

35 RYDAL MOUNT

Rydal Mount. Val Corbett

ADDRESS & TELEPHONE
Rydal, Ambleside, LA22 9LU. (01539) 433002.

DIRECTIONS
Follow brown tourism signs, 1.5 miles from Ambleside on A591.

OPENING HOURS
March to October, daily, 9.30am-5pm. November to February, 10am-4pm (closed Tuesdays).

DISABLED ACCESS
Limited.

ACTIVITIES/FACILITIES Rydal Mount, in the heart of the Lake District, commands glorious views of Lake Windermere, Rydal Water and the surrounding fells. The house, which now belongs to the descendants of the poet William Wordsworth, retains a lived in family atmosphere and has seen little change since Wordsworth and his family came to live here in 1813. The house contains portraits, personal possessions and first editions of the poet's work and the attic study which he used when he was Poet Laureate can be viewed. The 4 acre garden remains very much as he designed it and consists of rare shrubs and fell-side terraces, including the recently discovered 'Dora's Terrace', lawns, rock pools and an ancient mound.
Dogs: In the garden only.

36 DOVE COTTAGE & THE WORDSWORTH MUSEUM

Dove Cottage, Grasmere. Val Corbett

ADDRESS & TELEPHONE
Dove Cottage, Grasmere LA22 9SH.
(01539) 435544

DIRECTIONS
4 miles north of Ambleside on A591.

OPENING HOURS
Daily, 9.30am-5.30pm. Closed 24-26 Dec and 4 weeks in Jan/Feb.

DISABLED ACCESS
Ground floors of Dove Cottage & Museum fully accessible. Upstairs with help.

ACTIVITIES/FACILITIES Guided tours of Dove Cottage, William Wordsworth's home between 1799 and 1808. The award-winning museum displays the Wordsworth Trust's unique collections of manuscripts, books and paintings and there is a major special exhibition each year. Excellent book and gift shop. Newly refurbished Tea room and restaurant.
Dogs: Guide dogs only please.

37 HILL TOP

ADDRESS & TELEPHONE Near Sawrey, Ambleside, LA22 0LF. (01539) 436269

DIRECTIONS 2 miles south of Hawkshead in hamlet of Near Sawrey, behind the Tower Bank Arms.

OPENING HOURS Easter to October, Sat to Wed & Good Fri 11am-5pm. Last admission 4.30pm.

DISABLED ACCESS Unsuitable for disabled visitors.

ACTIVITIES/FACILITIES Beatrix Potter wrote many Peter Rabbit books in this little 17th Century house, which contains her furniture and china; her 'New Room' where she did much of her work has been restored. The cottage is very small and not suitable for baby backpacks, pushchairs or wheelchairs. Bar lunches and evening bar meals at the Tower Bank Arms (NT owned). Braille Guide. Children's guide to Beatrix Potter available. Parking available 180 metres from attraction. **Dogs:** Guide dogs only please.

38 BEATRIX POTTER GALLERY

ADDRESS & TELEPHONE Main Street, Hawkshead, LA22 0NS. (01539) 436355

DIRECTIONS In the Square.

OPENING HOURS April to October, Sunday to Thursday (closed Friday and Saturday except Good Friday) 10.30am to 4.30pm. NT shop open daily 9.30am to 5.30pm, Easter to Christmas except Thursday and Friday.

DISABLED ACCESS The Gallery is not suitable for wheelchairs.

ACTIVITIES/FACILITIES One of the National Trust's more unusual properties and one that has an interesting link with Beatrix Potter herself. The Gallery, which was once the office of her husband, local solicitor William Heelis, has remained largely unaltered since his day. The gallery houses an annually changing exhibition of a selection of Beatrix Potter's original drawings and illustrations, together with a display telling the story of her life as an author, artist, farmer and determined preserver of her beloved Lake District. **Dogs:** Guide dogs only.

39 HAWKSHEAD GRAMMAR SCHOOL

ADDRESS & TELEPHONE Hawkshead, near Ambleside, LA22 0NT. (01539) 435647

DIRECTIONS Take A593 Ambleside to Coniston road, then to Hawkshead on B5286. Opposite the central car park in Hawkshead, just below the church.

OPENING HOURS Easter to October, Mon-Sat, 10am-5pm (closed 12.30-1.30pm). Sun 1pm-5pm. October - closed at 4.30pm.

DISABLED ACCESS Ground floor only.

ACTIVITIES/FACILITIES The school was founded in 1585 by the Archbishop of York, Edwin Sandys. The ground floor classroom retains many old desks covered in carving done by the boys, including William Wordsworth the poet and his brother John. Upstairs is the headmaster's study and a classroom containing an exhibition relating to the history of the school, the founder and William Wordsworth. The letters, patent of Elizabeth I and the original school seal can also be seen. **Dogs:** Guide dogs only please.

The Old Grammar School, Hawkshead. Val Corbett

40 GRIZEDALE FOREST VISITORS CENTRE

Grizedale Visitor Centre. Val Corbett

ADDRESS & TELEPHONE

Grizedale, Hawkshead, LA22 0QJ. (01229) 373010

DIRECTIONS

South of Hawkshead, west of Lake Windermere.

OPENING HOURS

Visitor centre, tearoom and exhibition throughout the year, daily, 10am-5pm.

DISABLED ACCESS   Yes

ACTIVITIES/FACILITIES

Set deep in the heart of the Grizedale Forest is the superb Grizedale Visitor Centre which includes an exhibition, retail area, tearoom, adventure playground and starting point for superb forest walks (see Mini Walks section). Adjacent is the 'Theatre in the Forest', a 200 seater facility used for concerts, plays, films and lectures (contact (01229) 860291 for details). The Visitor Centre, run by the Forestry Commission, has free admission although payment is charged for parking.

41 STEAM YACHT GONDOLA

ADDRESS & TELEPHONE Coniston Water. (01539) 441288

DIRECTIONS Piers at Coniston, Park-a-Moor at south east end of lake & Brantwood.

OPENING HOURS April to October on a scheduled daily timetable during the season, weather permitting, starting at 11am (except on Saturdays, when sailings start at 12.05pm).

DISABLED ACCESS Not suitable for wheelchairs.

ACTIVITIES/FACILITIES Steam Yacht *Gondola*, first launched in 1859, and now completely renovated by the Trust, provides a steam-powered passenger service, carrying 86 passengers in opulently upholstered and heated saloons. Travel aboard *Gondola* is an experience in its own right, and a superb way to see Coniston's scenery. Parking and WCs at Coniston Pier. NB please note that there is no reduction for Trust members as *Gondola* is an enterprise and not held solely for preservation. **Dogs:** Guide dogs only.

Gondola - *steam launch on Coniston. Val Corbett*

42 CONISTON LAUNCH

ADDRESS & TELEPHONE (Admin only) Castle Buildings, Near Sawrey, Ambleside, LA22 0LF. (01539) 436216.

DIRECTIONS Follow directions to Coniston.

OPENING HOURS April to October, 10.30am-4.30pm (May to Sept until 6pm). November to March, Sundays only, 11.30am-2.30pm.

DISABLED ACCESS Yes if some mobility.

ACTIVITIES/FACILITIES Two traditional timber launches, ML Ruskin and ML Ransome provide a scheduled ferry service for walkers, those visiting John Ruskin's house of Brantwood or anyone who wants a peaceful cruise on Coniston. During the main season, special events include guided cruises such as Campbells on Coniston, Full Lake and Ranger Cruises and Swallows and Amazons.

ATTRACTIONS

43 BRANTWOOD

Brantwood. Val Corbett

ADDRESS & TELEPHONE
Brantwood, Coniston, LA21 8AD. (01539) 441396

DIRECTIONS
3 miles from Coniston village, directly opposite village on other side of Coniston water. Follow brown tourism signs.

OPENING HOURS
Open all year. Mid March to mid November, daily, 11am-5.30pm. Mid November to mid March, Wed to Sunday, 11am-4pm.

DISABLED ACCESS
Ground floor only.

ACTIVITIES/FACILITIES Brantwood is one of the most beautifully situated houses in the Lake District. The home of John Ruskin from 1872 until his death in 1900, Brantwood became an intellectual powerhouse and one of the greatest literary and artistic centres in Europe. Ruskin's drawings and watercolours fill the house and there is a video programme and bookshop. Three miles of nature walks are available in the estate's gardens as well as Ruskin Lace demonstrations every Thursday in the season. Restaurant also.
Dogs: Yes in the grounds but not in the House.

44 HARDKNOTT ROMAN FORT

ADDRESS & TELEPHONE Hardknott Pass.

DIRECTIONS The Hardknott Pass is reached from central Lakeland via the Wrynose Pass. Just after the summit of the Hardknott Pass and before the descent into Eskdale, look for a roadside parking area on the right hand side. The ruins are just a short distance away.

OPENING HOURS Any reasonable time.

DISABLED ACCESS No.

ACTIVITIES/FACILITIES Reached from central Lakeland by arguably the most thrilling and challenging drives in Lakeland, the Wrynose and Hardknott Passes, the remains of the Hardknott Roman Fort cannot fail to impress given their superb location overlooking Eskdale and the sheer scale of enterprise which these ruins represent. Hardknott (known to the Romans as Mediobogdum) must have been a harsh posting for the soldiers in winter; the fort guarding the vital supply route from their port at Ravenglass through central Lakeland to Ambleside. The fort was built in the reign of Adrian between AD118 and 138 and was garrisoned by a cohort of Dalmatian soldiers. The walls surrounded granaries, barracks and a commandants house; the baths with a sequence of three rooms can be seen just outside the main walls. An area of flattened ground to the north east of the fort is believed to have been used as a parade area. **FREE ADMISSION.**

45 ESKDALE HISTORIC CORN MILL

ADDRESS & TELEPHONE   Boot village, Eskdale, CA19 1TG. (01946) 723335.

DIRECTIONS   From central lakes via famous Wrynose and Hardknott Passes. From West coast road A595 via Gosforth. 10 min walk from Dalegarth Station, on the Ravenglass and Eskdale Miniature Railway.

OPENING HOURS   April to September, 11am-5pm, Tues to Sun plus Bank holidays.

DISABLED ACCESS   No.

ACTIVITIES/FACILITIES   Possibly the oldest working mill in England, the original machinery for grinding oats is in full working order and operated daily. Nestling in the foothills of the Scafell range, it's two waterwheels are powered by Whillan Beck as it tumbles down from England's highest mountain. Enjoy a picnic in the mill grounds, surrounded by waterfalls, millponds and magnificent scenery.

46 MUNCASTER CASTLE GARDENS & OWL CENTRE

Muncaster. Val Corbett

ADDRESS & TELEPHONE
Ravenglass, CA18 1RQ.
(01229) 717614

DIRECTIONS
1 mile south of
Ravenglass on the A595.

OPENING HOURS
Gardens & Owl Centre
open all year 11am-5pm.
Castle open mid Mar to
end of Oct 12.30pm-4pm
(last admission) Sun to Fri.

DISABLED ACCESS
Yes.

ACTIVITIES/FACILITIES

An historic castle, extended through the ages and home to the Pennington family since 1208. The castle has many rooms with treasures collected by the family over 700 years. An audio tape tour gives a delightful history of all that is on display. Muncaster is rightfully proud of its 77 acres of woodland and garden with rhododendrons, camellias and azaleas as well as a nature trail and terrace walk. The Owl Centre boasts one of the finest collections of owls in the world ranging from tiny Pygmy Owls to gigantic Eagle Owls. A "meet the birds" opportunity takes place at 2.30pm during the main season. Stables Buttery, gift shops, plant centre and children's play area as well as large picnic areas.   **Dogs:** In gardens on a lead.

47 MUNCASTER MILL

ADDRESS & TELEPHONE   Ravenglass CA18 1ST. (01229) 717232

DIRECTIONS   Just off the A595 north west of Ravenglass.

OPENING HOURS   Easter to Oct, daily, 10am-5pm. Nov to Mar, weekends 11am-4pm.

ATTRACTIONS

DISABLED ACCESS Yes.

ACTIVITIES/FACILITIES A working water powered corn mill with nineteenth century machinery in regular use. Freshly milled stone-ground organic products and souvenirs on sale in the mill. Adjacent to and served by the Ravenglass and Eskdale Miniature Railway. Refreshment/tea room. **Dogs:** To grounds only.

48 RAVENGLASS & ESKDALE RAILWAY

ADDRESS & TELEPHONE Ravenglass, CA18 1SW. (01229) 717171

DIRECTIONS Turn off A595 Barrow-Workington road at Ravenglass, follow brown tourism signs.

OPENING HOURS 8am-5pm daily in the season.

DISABLED ACCESS Yes.

ACTIVITIES/FACILITIES The Ravenglass and Eskdale Railway, or "La'al Ratty" as it is affectionately known, was opened in 1875 to bring iron ore to the Furness Railway. Following financial difficulties through to the 1950's and the conversion of the line to carry granite, the line was finally purchased by a preservation society and converted to a narrow guage of 15 inches. The resultant train journey now travels through beautiful countryside from Ravenglass, calling at Muncaster Mill, Irton Road, The Green and Beckfoot before finally reaching Eskdale. At Ravenglass is a railway museum which houses a wealth of relics, photographs and models and an audio visual show. Bar meals are available at the station tearooms and at the Ratty Arms.

49 WALLS CASTLE

Ravenglass Roman Bath House. Val Corbett

ADDRESS & TELEPHONE
Ravenglass.

DIRECTIONS
Follow brown tourism signs for the 'Roman Bath House' near Ravenglass.

OPENING HOURS
Any reasonable time.

DISABLED ACCESS
Can be seen from the adjacent road.

ACTIVITIES/FACILITIES
Not in fact a castle at all but rather the well preserved walls of the bath house that served the Roman fort of Glannaventa (the fort was unfortunately destroyed in the building of the railway in the nineteenth century). The English Heritage preserved remains have detailed information boards and the twelve foot high walls are the tallest remains of a Roman building in northern England. **FREE ADMISSION.**

50 FLORENCE MINE HERITAGE CENTRE

ADDRESS & TELEPHONE
Egremont, CA22 2NR. (01946) 820683

DIRECTIONS
Follow brown tourism signs from the A595 Egremont bypass.

OPENING HOURS
Easter to October, daily, 10am-4pm. Underground tours on Sat, Sun and Bank Holidays and daily throughout July, August.

DISABLED ACCESS
Access to Heritage Centre.

ACTIVITIES/FACILITIES
Visit the last working iron ore mine in Europe, part of the rich mining tradition of West Cumbria. At the Heritage Centre you can learn about the story of the miners and how they lived and worked, the clothes they wore, the shovels they used and the pipes they smoked. As well as the mining museum, there are geology displays, rocks, fossils and mineral displays and a souvenir and coffee shop. Underground tours start at 10.30am and 1.30pm each Saturday, Sunday and Bank Holidays or during the week by prior appointment. **Dogs:** Access to site but not Heritage Centre Building.

51 EGREMONT CASTLE

ADDRESS & TELEPHONE
Egremont.

DIRECTIONS
The castle overlooks the town.

OPENING HOURS
Daylight hours.

DISABLED ACCESS
No.

ACTIVITIES/FACILITIES
Sandstone ruins of a twelfth century Norman castle situated in a commanding position overlooking the town. Parts of the curtain wall and gatehouse can clearly be seen although much of what was almost certainly a formidable fortress was destroyed in the sixteenth century. **FREE ADMISSION.**

Egremont Castle. Val Corbett

52 THE BEACON

The Beacon, Whitehaven.

ADDRESS & TELEPHONE

West Strand, Whitehaven, CA28 7LY. 01946 592302.

DIRECTIONS

Follow A595 to Whitehaven town centre and harbourside.

OPENING HOURS

Tues to Sun plus all Bank Holidays, (closed Christmas Day).
Easter to Oct 10am-5.30pm.
Nov to Mar 10am-4.30pm.

DISABLED ACCESS

To all areas.

ACTIVITIES/FACILITIES

This award winning visitor attraction tells the story of Whitehaven's social, industrial and maritime heritage. The past, present and future of west Cumbria's Georgian port are told using characters, sounds, graphics and audio visual presentations. Plus interactive Met. Office weather gallery with panoramic views of the historic harbour and town. An annual programme of exhibitions and events in the Harbour Gallery as well as 'Made in Cumbria' souvenirs and gifts available in the Beacon Shop. **Dogs:** Guide dogs only please.

53 WORKINGTON HALL

ADDRESS & TELEPHONE C/O Tourism Section, Allerdale Borough Council, Allerdale House, Workington, CA14 3YT. (01900) 735408

DIRECTIONS Entering Workington on the A66 from Cockermouth, Workington Hall can be found in Curwen Park which is situated on the right. Parking and access to Hall opposite Helena Thompson Museum.

OPENING HOURS Easter to October, Tues-Fri, 10am-1pm & 2pm-5pm. Saturday and Sunday, 2pm-5pm. Bank Holidays, 10am-1pm & 2pm-5pm.

DISABLED ACCESS To ground floor only.

ACTIVITIES/FACILITIES Built up around a Pele Tower dating from the 14th century, this was at one time one of the finest manor houses in the region. This striking ruin, originally owned by the Lords of the Manor of Workington, gave refuge to Mary Queen of Scots in May 1568 and is also home to the ghost of 'Galloping Harry', murdered in 1623. Interpretative plaques give visitors a flavour of the Hall's long and interesting history. The fine cork model of the Hall in it's heyday can be seen at the Helena Thompson Museum. 🐕

54 | HELENA THOMPSON MUSEUM

ADDRESS & TELEPHONE Park End Road, Workington, CA14 4DE. (01900) 62598

DIRECTIONS Enter Workington from Cockermouth on the A66. The museum is opposite Workington Hall.

OPENING HOURS Apr to Oct, Mon-Sat, 10.30am-4pm. Nov to Mar, Mon-Sat, 11am-3pm.

DISABLED ACCESS Not good. Ramped access to ground floor only.

ACTIVITIES/FACILITIES The museum is housed in a fine, listed mid-Georgian building and was bequeathed to the people of Workington in 1940 by local philanthropist Helena Thompson. Displays include pottery, silver, glass, furniture, clothing and jewellery as well as the social and industrial history of Workington and its surrounding area. **FREE ADMISSION.**

55 | MARYPORT AQUARIA

ADDRESS & TELEPHONE South Quay, Maryport, CA15 8AB. (01900) 817760

DIRECTIONS The aquarium is on the South Quay of Maryport Harbour. Follow the signs from the town centre.

OPENING HOURS Daily, 10am-5pm.

DISABLED ACCESS Yes

ACTIVITIES/FACILITIES Discover the amazing underwater world of Cumbria's seas and coasts. The new purpose built Aquaria contains over 30 creative displays. Imagine yourself diving among colourful shoals of fish, see how the crashing waves bring food to the sea life and enjoy a 'hands in' experience in the touch pool. All rounded off with a visit to our sea view cafe and shop.

56 | SENHOUSE ROMAN MUSEUM

ADDRESS & TELEPHONE The Battery, Sea Brows, The Promenade, Maryport, CA10 6JD (01900) 816168

DIRECTIONS Follow brown tourism signs.

OPENING HOURS Apr to Jun, Oct and Bank Holidays, Tues and Thurs to Sun, 10am-5pm. July to Sept, daily, 10am-5pm. Nov to Mar, Fri, Sat & Sun, 10.30am-4pm.

DISABLED ACCESS Yes.

ACTIVITIES/FACILITIES Sculpture and inscriptions from the Roman Fort at Maryport (Aluana) which lies next to the museum. The collection, begun by John Senhouse of Netherall in the 1590's is the oldest in Britain. View the largest collection of Roman altars from a single site in Britain as well as many fine religious sculptures. Reconstruction of the shrine from the fort's headquarters, also interpretative panels describing the fort, the Roman coastal defences and the Senhouse family.

Roman Altar, Senhouse Roman Museum.

ATTRACTIONS

57 MARYPORT MARITIME MUSEUM

ADDRESS & TELEPHONE   1 Senhouse Street, Maryport. CA15 6AB. (01900) 813738

DIRECTIONS   From the A596 in Maryport, turn into Senhouse Street, the Museum is at the bottom of the hill on the left.

OPENING HOURS   Easter to October, Mon-Thurs, 10am-5pm, Fri-Sat, 10am-1pm and 2pm-5pm, Sun, 2pm-5pm. November to Easter, Mon-Sat, 10am-1pm and 2pm-4.30pm.

DISABLED ACCESS   Ground floor only.

ACTIVITIES/FACILITIES   Overlooking the harbour, the museum houses a wealth of objects, pictures, models and paintings that illustrate Maryport's proud maritime tradition. The building, formerly the Queens Head Public House, is built on one of the earliest plots of land developed by Humphrey Senhouse II when the town was built. **FREE ADMISSION.**

58 MARYPORT STEAMSHIPS MUSEUM

ADDRESS & TELEPHONE   Elizabeth Dock, South Quay, Maryport. CA15 8AB. (01900) 815954

DIRECTIONS   By the quay, Maryport.

OPENING HOURS   Every day during the summer, 10am-4pm.

DISABLED ACCESS   No.

ACTIVITIES/FACILITIES   The Steamships Museum includes *The Flying Buzzard* the one time pride of the Clyde Shipping Company's Tug Fleet and now open to visitors who can see how the crew of a the 1950's tug lived and worked as well as visiting the engine room and boilers. The Vic 96 steamship is a fun display for all the family and shows how to tie ship's knots, find out how blocks and tackles increase your muscle power, send a signal, climb into a hammock and see the dramatic story of the *Orion* shipwreck. The Vic 96's engine will be in steam on special days.

59 WORDSWORTH HOUSE

ADDRESS & TELEPHONE   Main Street, Cockermouth, CA13 9RX. (01900) 824805

DIRECTIONS   Follow signs in Cockermouth.

OPENING HOURS   Apr to Oct, weekdays, 11pm-5pm. Also Saturdays July and Aug. Shop same months as house Mon to Sat 10pm-5pm (incl. Sats when house is closed).

DISABLED ACCESS   Unsuitable for wheelchairs.

ACTIVITIES/FACILITIES   The birthplace of William Wordsworth in 1770. This north-country Georgian town house, built in 1745, has seven rooms furnished in 18th-century style, with some personal effects of the poet; also his childhood garden with terraced walk; video display in old stables.

ATTRACTIONS

60 THE PRINTING HOUSE MUSEUM

ADDRESS & TELEPHONE — 102 Main Street, Cockermouth, CA13 9LX. (01900) 824984

DIRECTIONS — On the A66 from Penrith and Keswick, turn right at the Sheep Centre Roundabout and follow directions to Wordsworth House, the Printing House Museum is next door.

OPENING HOURS — Open all year (except Good Friday, Christmas Day and Boxing Day), Mon-Sat, 10am-4pm.

DISABLED ACCESS — Yes.

ACTIVITIES/FACILITIES — The museum is set in an historic sixteenth century building and provides a varied and interesting range of printing presses and equipment brought together from all over Britain. There is an opportunity to gain 'hands on' experience by using the presses displayed to produce cards or keepsakes to remind you of your visit. There is also a shop where you can purchase prints from the museum's archive of historical hand carved printing blocks.

61 THE CUMBERLAND TOY & MODEL MUSEUM

ADDRESS & TELEPHONE — Banks Court, Market Pl, Cockermouth, CA13 9NG. (01900) 827606.

DIRECTIONS — In Market Place, follow brown tourism signs from all public car parks.

OPENING HOURS — February to November, daily, 10am-5pm. Phone for opening times in December and January.

DISABLED ACCESS — Access to ground floor, other three floor difficult due to the steps of the old building.

ACTIVITIES/FACILITIES — Winner of the National Heritage Shoestring Award. The museum exhibits a wide selection of mainly British toys from c1900 to the present. There are many visitor operated displays including tinplate trains, scalextric and lego, etc. Around 3600 square feet of pure nostalgia! Also a family quiz, worksheets based on the National Curriculum and a horrible monster in the water butt. **Dogs:** Guide dogs only.

Scalextric layout, Cumberland Toy and Model Museum.

ATTRACTIONS

62 JENNINGS BREWERY TOUR

ADDRESS & TELEPHONE The Castle Brewery, Cockermouth CA13 9NE. (01900) 823214

DIRECTIONS Near Cockermouth Castle.

OPENING HOURS Tours of the brewery are generally held at 11am and 2pm, Monday to Friday, April to October. During school holidays there is a further tour at 12.30pm and on Sats and Suns at 11am and 2pm.

DISABLED ACCESS Due to many stairways the tour is largely unsuitable for the disabled.

ACTIVITIES/FACILITIES Jennings Brothers have been brewing traditional beers for 160 years and still use today, the same traditional methods that were used by their founder, as long ago as 1828 in the village of Lorton. The 1.5 hour tour takes you around the brewery explaining such intriguing brewery expressions as Hop Back and Mash Tun. Sorry, no children under the age of twelve can be taken on the tour.

63 LAKELAND SHEEP & WOOL CENTRE

ADDRESS & TELEPHONE Egremont Road, Cockermouth, CA13 0QX. (01900) 822673

DIRECTIONS At the junction of the A66 and A5086 near Cockermouth.

OPENING HOURS Daily, 9am-6pm.

DISABLED ACCESS Yes.

ACTIVITIES/FACILITIES Come inside and meet 19 breeds of live sheep. Witness a sheep being shorn, a one man and his dog demonstration, all in one exciting show. Sheep shows mid February to mid November, 10.30am, 12 noon, 2pm and 3.30pm. A shop stocks quality woollens and gifts, refreshments available all day. Admission charge to sheep show, museum/shop/restaurant free admission. **Dogs:** Guide dogs only please.

64 WYTHOP WATERMILL

ADDRESS & TELEPHONE Wythop Mill, Embleton, Cockermouth, CA13 9YP. (01768) 776394

DIRECTIONS 0.5 miles from A66, follow brown tourism signs.

OPENING HOURS Easter to October 10.30am-5.30pm. Closed Mondays.

DISABLED ACCESS To Restaurant & toilets, partial access to Museum.

ACTIVITIES/FACILITIES Set in the beautiful hamlet of Wythop Mill, this fascinating and unique museum displays vintage woodworking tools and machinery powered by an overshot waterwheel. Victorian kitchen, wheel-wright and blacksmiths displays as well as a local history exhibition of Wythop showing aspects of village life over the last 2,000 years.

MUSEUMS & ART GALLERIES — LEISURE, WILDLIFE & THEME PARKS
HISTORIC BUILDINGS & GARDENS — OTHER

65 WHINLATTER VISITOR CENTRE

ADDRESS & TELEPHONE Braithwaite, Keswick, CA12 5TW. (01768) 778469

DIRECTIONS Well signed on the B5292 Whinlatter Pass between Cockermouth and Keswick.

OPENING HOURS Daily from 10am.

DISABLED ACCESS Access to Visitor Centre and one forest trail.

ACTIVITIES/FACILITIES Situated in England's only mountain forest, Whinlatter Visitor Centre offers an interesting insight into the life of a working forest through the use of films, computers, models and audio-visual techniques. With 14 miles of forest roads open to cyclists and miles of woodland paths open for walking and orienteering, Whinlatter also offers superb outdoor leisure activities as well as a tea room and much to interest children. Free admission though there is a charge for parking.

Whinlatter Visitor Centre. Val Corbett

66 MIREHOUSE HISTORIC HOUSE & GARDENS

ADDRESS & TELEPHONE Mirehouse, Keswick, CA12 4QE. (01768) 772287.

DIRECTIONS On the A591 3.5 miles north of Keswick, signed (blue/white signs) from A66/A591 roundabout.

OPENING HOURS Easter to October. Gardens and tea room daily 10am-5.30pm. House open Sundays, Wednesdays (also Fridays in August) 2pm-4.30pm (last entry). At any time by appointment for groups.

DISABLED ACCESS Yes.

ACTIVITIES/FACILITIES A small scale historic house where the owners enjoy being very much involved with looking after their visitors. The varied and sheltered gardens provide four woodland adventure playgrounds and are uncommercialised and peaceful with lakeside walks through woods and parkland. The house has an unusually wide range of literary and artistic connections and items collected by the Spedding family over 300 years. **Dogs:** Only if on a lead.

67 TROTTERS & FRIENDS ANIMAL FARM

Trotters and Friends Animal Farm.

ADDRESS & TELEPHONE
Coalbeck Farm,
Bassenthwaite Lake,
Keswick. (01768) 776239

DIRECTIONS
Follow brown tourism
signs on the A591 or A66.

OPENING HOURS
April to November, daily,
10am-5.30pm. November
to March, Sat and Sun,
11am-4.30pm.

DISABLED ACCESS
Yes

ACTIVITIES/FACILITIES

Set in 25 acres of grazing land, paddocks and barns are more than 500 animals on show including rare breeds and more traditional farm animals. Plenty of opportunity to "touch and feel" as well as a reptile house, birds of prey centre, daily animal presentations, Fantasy Land, pony and tractor rides, Tearoom and gift shop and picnic areas. 🐕

68 CASTLERIGG STONE CIRCLE

ADDRESS & TELEPHONE Near Keswick.

DIRECTIONS Follow brown tourism signs near Keswick.

OPENING HOURS Any reasonable time.

DISABLED ACCESS No.

ACTIVITIES/FACILITIES Lakeland's best known and most easily accessible stone circle, set in an impressive mountain setting near Keswick. Castlerigg is Neolithic in origin and contains 38 stones in a circle with a further 10 in a rectangle; its position between the summits of Helvellyn and Skiddaw, two of Lakeland's four peaks above 3000 feet, has led some to believe its location is as a result of powerful 'lay lines' although most scholars agree it was some sort of important meeting place with possible religious or ceremonial uses.
FREE ADMISSION. 🐕

Castlerigg Stone Circle. Val Corbett

ADDRESS & TELEPHONE

Keswick Launch Company Ltd., 29 Manor Park, Keswick, Cumbria, CA12 4AB. (01768) 772263.

DIRECTIONS

Follow the brown tourism signs from A66.

OPENING HOURS

Open all year from 9am. Finish times depend on time of year.

DISABLED ACCESS

Yes.

ACTIVITIES/FACILITIES

Launches leave regularly (every half hour during summer) for a 50 min cruise around the lake. There are various landing stages around the lake to enable people to drop off, possibly for a walk, and pick up the boat at a later time. Guided evening cruises take place each evening from mid May until mid September and include a glass of wine or a soft drink. Rowing boat hire available all year. Motor boat hire available Easter to October. **Dogs:** Yes all areas, no charge for transport on launch.

Keswick Launch, Derwentwater. Val Corbett

ATTRACTIONS

70 KESWICK MUSEUM & ART GALLERY

ADDRESS & TELEPHONE Station Road, Keswick, CA12 4NF. (01768) 773263.

DIRECTIONS Follow signs for leisure pool in Keswick.

OPENING HOURS Easter to October, daily, 10am-4pm including Bank Holidays.

DISABLED ACCESS Ramped front access, fully accessible to wheelchairs.

ACTIVITIES/FACILITIES A Victorian Museum, full of character, with local and natural history displays, curios and curiosities including a stone xylophone, 500 year old mummified cat and a important collection of original lake poet manuscripts. A unique scale model of the Lake District, made in 1834, sets the background for a fine collection of rocks and minerals.
Dogs: Guide dogs only please.

71 CUMBERLAND PENCIL MUSEUM

ADDRESS & TELEPHONE Southey Works, Keswick, CA12 5NG. (01768) 773626

DIRECTIONS Follow brown tourism signs from A66 and A591.

OPENING HOURS Open all year (except 25/26 Dec & 1 Jan) 9.30am-4pm (last admission).

DISABLED ACCESS Yes.

ACTIVITIES/FACILITIES Through words, pictures and lovingly restored machinery, the Rexel Cumberland Pencil Museum takes you through the pencil's fascinating history, from the discovery of Borrowdale graphite to present day manufacture, and also describes the various stages of pencil production. A replica of Seathwaite Graphite Mine is on display, also machinery displays, video shows of pencil making and artistic techniques, children's drawing area and competition, brass rubbings and a gift shop.
Dogs: Guide dogs only please.

72 CARS OF THE STARS MOTOR MUSEUM

ADDRESS & TELEPHONE Standish Street, Town Centre, Keswick, CA12 5LS. (01768) 772090

DIRECTIONS From the Town Square walk through Pack Horse Court.

OPENING HOURS Easter to New Year & February Half Term, daily, 10am-5pm. Weekends only in December.

DISABLED ACCESS Good in all areas.

ACTIVITIES/FACILITIES Features vehicles from TV and films, including Chitty Chitty Bang Bang, the Batmobile, Back to the Future Delorean, The Munsters Koach, Kitt, Herbie plus many famous vehicles, not to be missed. Also film set displays and vehicles from Mad Max, Postman Pat, The Saint and many more.

■ MUSEUMS & ART GALLERIES	■ LEISURE, WILDLIFE & THEME PARKS
■ HISTORIC BUILDINGS & GARDENS	■ OTHER

73 THE BOWDER STONE

Bowder Stone. Val Corbett

ADDRESS & TELEPHONE
Borrowdale.

DIRECTIONS
Head south on the B5289 from Keswick. A National Trust car park is signed from the road.

OPENING HOURS
Daylight hours.

DISABLED ACCESS
Possible but should only be considered with sufficient help as the path has a slight incline.

ACTIVITIES/FACILITIES
Reached after a ten minute walk from the car park is the 2,000 ton Bowder Stone, a glacial erratic or giant lump of rock deposited by a glacier thousands of years ago. The rock is situated in lovely countryside and is so big that a series of large wooden steps have been created to allow access to the top. Admission is free but there is a charge for parking.

74 ULLSWATER SAIL & MOTOR YACHTS

Ullswater Cruises. Val Corbett

ADDRESS & TELEPHONE
Ullswater Navigation & Transit Company Ltd., 13 Maude Street, Kendal. LA9 4QD.
(01539) 721626, or Pier House, Glenridding (01768) 482229.

DIRECTIONS
Ullswater.

OPENING HOURS
Full Service at Easter, Whitsun and from mid May until the end of Sept.

DISABLED ACCESS
Yes but best to pre book so crew can be prepared.

ACTIVITIES/FACILITIES
M.Y. Raven and *M.Y. Lady of the Lake* are two 19th century steamers now converted to oil cruising on Ullswater, one of the most beautiful of the lakes in the Lake District National Park, it's 9 mile length running from Glenridding in the heart of the mountains to Pooley Bridge where the River Eamont flows out of the lake. In the full season there are three scheduled services daily between the three stopping off points of Glenridding, Howtown and Pooley Bridge. There are five shorter one hour cruises between Glenridding and Howtown. **Dogs:** Well behaved dogs on leads only please.

ATTRACTIONS

75 DALEMAIN HISTORIC HOUSE & GARDEN

Dalemain.

ADDRESS & TELEPHONE
Penrith, Cumbria, CA11 0HB. (01768) 486450

DIRECTIONS
On the A592 between the A66 and Ullswater (brown tourism signs).

OPENING HOURS
Easter to September, Sundays to Thursdays 11.15am-5pm.

DISABLED ACCESS   Free admission to wheelchair disabled. Access to ground floor and garden. Toilets.

ACTIVITIES/FACILITIES   A historic house full of surprises, not least that the Georgian facade actually fronts an Elizabethan house! The houses remains occupied by the same family who have lived here for more than 300 years. Dalemain has its fair share of grand public rooms, including the breathtaking Chinese Room, with its original hand-painted wallpaper, furniture and fittings. In the public rooms there are many examples of fine furniture and portraits. Walks in the grounds passing Dacre Castle. The gardens have many rare plants and a collection of over 100 old-fashioned roses as well as a 85 foot high Abies cephalnonica planted in 1685. There is also a licensed restaurant, gift shop and agricultural museums.
Dogs: No dogs allowed beyond the car park please.

76 PENRITH CASTLE

Penrith Castle. Val Corbett

ADDRESS & TELEPHONE
Penrith.

DIRECTIONS
Follow the A592 to Penrith from the M6 intersection with the A66. Castle Park will be found on the right hand side, opposite the railway station.

OPENING HOURS
Daylight hours.

DISABLED ACCESS   Limited.

ACTIVITIES/FACILITIES   The striking red sandstone remains of the 'Castle of the Kings' is freely available to visit, situated in the pleasant surroundings of Castle Park on the southern edge of Penrith near the railway station. The castle's deep moat, crossed via a wooden footbridge to allow access to the English Heritage maintained ruins, gives a real impression of the task that would have faced medieval besiegers. William Strickland, Bishop of Carlisle, built the first castle on the site at the end of the fourteenth century, primarily as a defence to the frequent and devastating Scottish raids. The castle was enlarged after passing into the possession of the Neville family and was occupied for a time by Richard III before he became King in 1483. The remains that can be seen today largely date from this time.
FREE ADMISSION.

77 MAYBURGH HENGE AND KING ARTHUR'S ROUND TABLE

ADDRESS & TELEPHONE Near Penrith.

DIRECTIONS Follow brown signs from the A6 just south of Penrith. King Arthur's Round Table is at the intersection of the A6 and B5320, Mayburgh Henge is about 400 yards away on the B5320 next to the M6. In both cases, there is no designated car park so park on the side of the road.

OPENING HOURS Any reasonable time.

DISABLED ACCESS No.

ACTIVITIES/FACILITIES Two antiquities dating from between 2,000 and 1,000 years before the birth of Christ and easily visited together as they are only a short distance apart. **MAYBURGH HENGE** is a massive prehistoric monument measuring nearly 400 feet across. There is a single entrance through a huge circular bank which is made all the more significant when you realise that the whole mound was constructed using rocks taken from the nearby river. A single standing stone remains in the interior though there were once eight. Its exact reason for existence is unknown though its importance must have been substantial given the effort required to create it.

KING ARTHUR'S ROUND TABLE is something of a misnomer as it has nothing to do with the legend of Camelot and its knights. Like Mayburgh Henge, the earthwork is believed to be around 4,000 years old and consists of a wide ditch enclosing a flat area. Similarly believed to have been a prehistoric meeting place, the earthwork is more impressive when one considers the effort required to construct it given that its builders would only have had antlers as tools as well as a life expectancy of maybe twenty or twenty five years.

FREE ADMISSION.

Mayburgh Henge. Val Corbett.

■ **MUSEUMS & ART GALLERIES**   ■ **LEISURE, WILDLIFE & THEME PARKS**
■ **HISTORIC BUILDINGS & GARDENS**   ■ **OTHER**

ATTRACTIONS

78 PENRITH MUSEUM

Penrith Museum. Val Corbett.

ADDRESS & TELEPHONE

Robinson's School, Middlegate, Penrith CA11 7PT. (01768) 867466

DIRECTIONS

Follow signs for museum and tourist information centre, building located near town hall.

OPENING HOURS June - Sept, Mon-Sat, 10am-5pm, Sun 1pm-5pm. Oct - May, Mon-Sat, 10am-5pm.

DISABLED ACCESS To ground floor only.

ACTIVITIES/FACILITIES A recently refurbished museum covering the local history, geology and archaeology of the Penrith area. Exhibits include some Roman pottery from the Roman fort near Plumpton and 'cup and rong' stones from Maughanby. A temporary exhibition gallery features regularly changing exhibitions of local interest. **FREE ADMISSION.**

79 BROUGHAM CASTLE

ADDRESS & TELEPHONE Penrith. (01768) 862488

DIRECTIONS 1.5 miles south-east of Penrith on minor road off A66.

OPENING HOURS Easter to October, daily, 10am-6pm (or dusk if earlier in October).

DISABLED ACCESS Wheelchair access (except keep).

ACTIVITIES/FACILITIES Wander through the impressive ruins of a 13th century fortress. Admire its lovely location on the gentle banks of the River Eamont. Discover the intriguing story of its charismatic one-time owner Lady Anne Clifford. Climb the castle's keep to take in lovely views of the surrounding area and enjoy an exhibition containing important Roman tombstones from the nearby fort. Brougham Castle is a delightful historic site and also makes a perfect place to enjoy a family picnic. **Dogs:** Well behaved dogs on a lead please.

Brougham Castle. Val Corbett.

80 LOWTHER LEISURE & WILDLIFE PARK

Trip to Lowther Park. Val Corbett

ADDRESS & TELEPHONE
Hackthorpe, Penrith, CA10 2HG.
(01931) 712523.

DIRECTIONS
6 miles south of Penrith on the A6,
follow the brown tourism signs.

OPENING HOURS
10am-6pm in season. Easter holidays,
April weekends and then May to
August.

DISABLED ACCESS Yes.

ACTIVITIES/FACILITIES Set in 150
acres of beautiful parkland and regarded
as the Lake District's premier all day
attraction. Superb attractions including
an hour long circus show in the big top,
wildlife area, scenic miniature railway,
imaginative adventure play areas,
boating lake and sporting activities
ensure there is something for everyone. The average stay is around 5 hours.

81 LAKELAND BIRD OF PREY CENTRE

ADDRESS & TELEPHONE Lowther near Penrith, CA10 2HH. (01931) 712746

DIRECTIONS Follow brown tourism signs, from the A6 near Shap.

OPENING HOURS Daily March to October. Flying demonstrations at 12 noon, 2pm
and 4pm daily.

DISABLED ACCESS Yes.

ACTIVITIES/FACILITIES Situated in the walled garden of Lowther Castle surrounded by
unspoilt parkland, visitors are able to see a variety of birds of prey at close quarters
including eagles, hawks, falcons and owls. Sample traditional country food and look
around the arts and crafts in the Tea Shop or Tea Garden.

82 SHAP ABBEY

ADDRESS & TELEPHONE Shap.

DIRECTIONS 1.5 miles west of Shap village on the bank of the River Lowther.

OPENING HOURS Any reasonable time.

DISABLED ACCESS No.

ACTIVITIES/FACILITIES The English Heritage maintained remains of an abbey established

ATTRACTIONS

here in 1199, the last to be founded in England and interestingly, the last to have been dissolved by Henry VIII in 1540. Most of the buildings are thirteenth century in origin though the striking west tower is early sixteenth century. A short path leads over fields from the abbey to a small sixteenth century chapel in the care of the National Trust (key held in village-see notice on chapel door). **FREE ADMISSION.**

Shap Abbey. Val Corbett

83 APPLEBY CASTLE AND CONSERVATION CENTRE

ADDRESS & TELEPHONE Appleby Castle, Appleby, CA16 6XH. (01768) 351402

DIRECTIONS Follow tourism signs on A66 from Penrith.

OPENING HOURS April to October, daily, 10am-5pm (closes 4pm in October).

DISABLED ACCESS Access Limited due to nature of attraction.

ACTIVITIES/FACILITIES Set in 27 acres of beautifully laid out riverside grounds, the Castle provides an excellent setting for rare breeds of farm animals and a large collection of birds and waterfowl. The spectacular Norman Keep and Great Hall of the house are open to the public. Facilities include an exhibition of 'Made in Cumbria' Crafts, gift shop, Courtyard Tea Rooms, picnic areas and children's adventure play area. Special events, vintage car rallies and historical re-enactments throughout the season. **Dogs:** Permitted in grounds on a lead.

84 WETHERIGGS COUNTRY POTTERY

Wetheriggs Pottery. Val Corbett

ADDRESS & TELEPHONE Clifton Dykes, near Penrith, CA10 2DH. (01768) 892733

DIRECTIONS Take the A6 south of Penrith through Eamont Bridge. Turn left towards Cliburn/Clifton Dykes and follow road for approx.1.5 miles.

OPENING HOURS Daily, 10am-5.30pm (closed during Xmas holidays). Tea-room open 10am-5pm, daily.

DISABLED ACCESS Yes with ramps and toilets.

ACTIVITIES/FACILITIES Many new attractions including a pottery shop, country store and a collectibles shop. The Fantasy Gallery, a new 'Have a Go' studio, where you can throw your own pot or paint your own Piggin Pig, Pocket Dragon, Flippin Frog, Cheeky Monkey or Newt figurine. Also Play areas, Tea-room, Museum and nature walk and rare breeds of pigs. Watch the potters at work on the exclusive Wetheriggs earthenware and terracotta gardenware, produced using original Victorian designs dating back to 1855. **FREE ADMISSION.**

85 HIGHGATE FARM & ANIMAL TRAIL

ADDRESS & TELEPHONE Highgate Farm, Morland, Penrith, CA10 3BB. (01931) 714347

DIRECTIONS Follow brown tourism signs from A66 and A6.

OPENING HOURS Easter to Sept, daily 10.30am-5.30pm. Oct daily, 11am-3pm.

DISABLED ACCESS Yes.

ACTIVITIES/FACILITIES Farm park with plenty of opportunity to meet lots of new animal friends. Collect freshly laid eggs, feed the pet lambs, enjoy story time told by granny Annie, falconry display, sheep races, pigs suppertime, ferret racing, ducklings picnic, an animal trail, pets corner, have your photo taken with Frankie the Llama, a pony ride and country quizzes for all the family.
Adventure play barn and indoor picnic area for wet weather as well as children's play area, cafe and shop.

86 ACORN BANK GARDEN & WATERMILL

Acorn Bank. Val Corbett

ADDRESS & TELEPHONE
Temple Sowerby, near Penrith, CA10 1SP. (01768) 361893

DIRECTIONS
Just north of Temple Sowerby, 6 miles east of Penrith on A66.

OPENING HOURS
Easter to Oct, daily, 10am-5.30pm (last admission 5pm). Shop open as garden (except Oct when weekends only).

DISABLED ACCESS
Wheelchair accessible and available.

ACTIVITIES/FACILITIES
The north of England's largest collection of culinary and medicinal plants surrounded by a 1 hectare garden protected by fine oaks under which grow a vast display of daffodils. Inside the walls are two orchards with fruit trees; surrounding the orchards are mixed borders with shrubs, herbaceous plants and roses. A circular woodland walk runs beside the Crowdundle Beck; the recently restored watermill is now open to visitors.
Dogs: Yes in wild garden and woodland areas but must be left tethered prior to entering walled gardens.

87 LONG MEG & HER DAUGHTERS

Long Meg and her Daughters. Val Corbett

ADDRESS & TELEPHONE
Near Little Salkeld, north east of Penrith.

DIRECTIONS From the junction of the A6 and A66 south of Penrith, follow the A686 (signed Alston). After 4.5 miles, in the centre of Langwathby, turn left and follow signs for the village of Little Salkeld from where the antiquity is signed.

OPENING HOURS Any reasonable time.

DISABLED ACCESS Adjacent to the road.

ACTIVITIES/FACILITIES Some distance from the National Park, in fact nearer to the Pennines than to the Lake District, is the stone circle of Long Meg and her Daughters, Wordsworth's 'noble relick', well worth seeking out if you have an interest in antiquities and wish to enjoy some stunning scenery with few people around. It is quite simply one of the finest stone circles in the north of England.

The circle has a diameter of around 350 feet making it one of the biggest in the country. Fifty nine stones, of different sizes, geology and position make up the 'daughters' while Long Meg herself, just a few yards away, is an exceptional megalith some eighteen feet high and weighing about 17 tons. As with all stone circles, the exact reason for the circle's construction is unknown though it is generally agreed that the stones were erected between 2000 and 4000 BC and was likely to have been used as a meeting place or for some form of religious activity. Certainly there is something lonely and mysterious about the place, local legend has it that when the stones were last 'tampered' with, in the eighteenth century a farmer attempted to remove some of them, there followed a storm unlike anyone could previously remember and they have since been left in place for visitors to experience. **FREE ADMISSION.**

88 HUTTON-IN-THE-FOREST

ADDRESS & TELEPHONE Penrith, CA11 9TH. (01768) 484449

DIRECTIONS From M6, Junction 41, 3 miles on B5305 to Wigton, 6 miles from Penrith.

OPENING HOURS **House:** Easter then May to September, Thurs, Fri and Sun, 1pm-4pm (last entry) as well as Bank Holidays and Weds in August. Tearoom open 12.30pm-4.30pm (on the same days). **Grounds:** 11am-5pm daily (closed Sat).

DISABLED ACCESS Poor due to gravel paths and some steps in garden. House: only 3 accessible rooms on the ground floor.

ACTIVITIES/FACILITIES The house is based on a 14th century Pele Tower with substantial additions in the 17th, 18th and 19th centuries. The house has been in the same family since 1605 and contains fine collections of furniture, ceramics, tapestry and portraits. The grounds encompass a walled garden dating from the 1730's with an ever expanding herbaceous collection, as well as trained fruit and old roses, terraces with 19th century topiary, woodland walk with many specimen trees identifiable from leaflet, a 17th century Dovecote, stream and cascade. Also picnic areas. **Dogs:** On leads permitted in grounds.

89 PRIEST'S MILL

ADDRESS & TELEPHONE Priest's Mill, Caldbeck. (01697) 478369

DIRECTIONS Easily found near the church in the tiny village of Caldbeck.

OPENING HOURS Mar-Oct, Tues-Sun, 11am-5pm. Mons, gift shop & cafe 11am-4pm. Nov-Feb, weekends and at other times (ring prior).

DISABLED ACCESS Yes, and toilets.

ACTIVITIES/FACILITIES Priest's Mill is housed in an eighteenth century stone grinding cornmill which was restored in 1986 and the fourteen foot diameter waterwheel now restored to working order. The complex houses a large restaurant overlooking the river, interesting shops including a countryside card and gift shop, antiques, pine furniture, second hand books and a goldsmith.

FREE ADMISSION. **Dogs:** Yes, except cafe.

90 CARLISLE CASTLE

ADDRESS & TELEPHONE Carlisle. (01228) 591922

DIRECTIONS In the centre of Carlisle.

OPENING HOURS Easter to Oct, daily, 9.30am-6pm (or dusk if earlier in Oct). Nov to Mar, daily, 10am-4pm (closed 24-26 Dec).

DISABLED ACCESS Access for visitors in wheelchairs (except interiors). Toilets.

ACTIVITIES/FACILITIES Visit the great medieval fortress that has watched over the city of Carlisle for over nine centuries. Discover a thrilling and bloody past and enjoy panoramic views that take in the city and the hills of the Lake District and southern Scotland. Today visitors can explore fascinating and ancient chambers, stairways and dungeons and find the legendary 'licking stones'. Here, parched Jacobite prisoners found enough moisture to stay alive, only to be brutally executed on Gallows Hill. Uncover a fascinating history through lively exhibitions, offering an insight into William Rufus, Mary Queen of Scots and Bonnie Prince Charlie. Take a guided tour of the castle and watch children make the most of their visit with an Activity Sheet. There is an interesting gift shop where you can browse through a range of souvenirs with a medieval theme. **Dogs:** Yes to castle but not to Border Regiment Museum.

Carlisle Castle. Val Corbett

ATTRACTIONS

91 CARLISLE CATHEDRAL

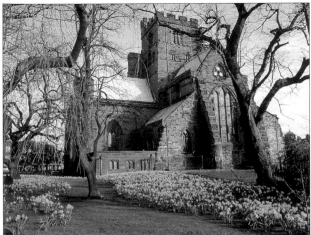

Carlisle Cathedral. Val Corbett

ADDRESS & TELEPHONE

Carlisle. (01228) 35169

DIRECTIONS

Carlisle city centre, car parks nearby. Railway station 10 mins walk.

OPENING HOURS

Mon-Sat, 7.30am-6.15pm. Sun 7.30am-5pm. Bank Holidays, 10am-6.15pm.

DISABLED ACCESS

Yes.

ACTIVITIES/FACILITIES

Founded in 1122, the Cathedral's glories include the East Window, the Brougham Triptych - a magnificent 16th century carved Flemish altarpiece and fine painted panels depicting the lives of saints. The fifteenth century choir stalls are notable examples of medieval carving. Treasury exhibition. Gift shop and restaurant.
FREE ADMISSION.

92 BORDER & KING'S OWN ROYAL BORDER REGIMENTAL MUSEUM

ADDRESS & TELEPHONE Queen Mary's Tower, The Castle, Carlisle, CA3 8UR. (01228) 32774

DIRECTIONS On the north side of the City centre, 10 minutes from the railway station. Adjacent car-park on Devonshire walk on the west side of the Castle.

OPENING HOURS April to Sept, 9.30am-6pm, Mon-Sat, Sunday 10am-6pm. October 9.30am to dusk. Nov to March, 10am-4pm.

DISABLED ACCESS To ground floor of museum only.

ACTIVITIES/FACILITIES Located within the Inner Ward of Carlisle Castle, the museum relates the history of Cumbria's County Infantry Regiment, the Border Regiment and its successor The King's Own Royal Border Regiment, and local Militia, Volunteer and Territorial Army units from 1702 to the present day. Displays comprise of uniforms, weapons, equipment, medals (including four VCs), silver, pictures, memorabilia, dioramas, video presentations and anti-tank guns. Outside is a 25-Pounder Field gun of 1940 and a Ferret Scout Car. Preserved within the Castle's walls are the barrack and other military buildings dating from the nineteenth century. The museum has its own shop with many souvenirs and publications. Admission to the museum is included in the entry charge to the castle.
Dogs: Guide dogs only please.

MUSEUMS & ART GALLERIES   **LEISURE, WILDLIFE & THEME PARKS**
HISTORIC BUILDINGS & GARDENS   **OTHER**

93 TULLIE HOUSE MUSEUM & ART GALLERY

Tullie House, Carlisle.

ADDRESS & TELEPHONE Castle Street, Carlisle, CA3 8TP. 01228 34781

DIRECTIONS Follow brown tourism signs from the M6 motorway exits into the city. Tullie House is opposite Carlisle Castle.

OPENING HOURS Every day (except Christmas), Mon-Sat, 10am-5pm. Sun 12am-5pm.

DISABLED ACCESS Comprehensive.

ACTIVITIES/FACILITIES Journey back in time to the Roman occupation and uncover the mysteries of Hadrian's Wall. Travel through the Dark Ages and grind corn as the Celts did, experience the highs and lows of England's Civil War, voyage through the Debatable Lands - home of the Border Reivers, marauding family gangs whose terrifying family feuds left many a Border widow *bereaved*.....Visit the Middle Ages and return by the Edwardian railway carriage. There is also a gift shop and restaurant. The art gallery is the best equipped in the north of England featuring work by artists from tomorrow's hall of fame. Early Bird Offer: arrive before 11am and gain admission to the museum for half price. **Dogs:** Guide dogs only please.

94 FOUR SEASONS FARM EXPERIENCE

ADDRESS & TELEPHONE Sceugh Mire, Southwaite, Carlisle, CA4 0LS. (01697) 473753

DIRECTIONS A6 between High Hesket & Low Mesket, south of Carlisle (follow brown tourism signs).

OPENING HOURS Good Friday to mid September, daily, 10am-5pm.

DISABLED ACCESS Yes

ACTIVITIES/FACILITIES The perfect day out in the country for all the family. Four Seasons is based on a working farm and there is plenty to see, touch and feed including deer, pigs, Clydesdale horses, donkeys, rabbits, goats and Highland Cattle. Make your own bread and butter in the traditional way or explore the woods on the 'Woodland Quest'. Discover the ponds with their ducks, geese and swans as you walk around the farm. Enjoy the adventure playground, or a picnic in the grounds, food and drink is available from the souvenir shop.

95 SOUTH TYNEDALE RAILWAY PRESERVATION SOCIETY

ADDRESS & TELEPHONE Railway Station, Alston, Cumbria, CA9 3JB. (01434) 382828

DIRECTIONS Look for brown tourism signs of the A686 Hexham road, north of Alston town centre.

OPENING HOURS Easter to December, timetable varies greatly - please enquire.

DISABLED ACCESS A carriage with access for wheelchair users is available - advance booking is recommended.

ACTIVITIES/FACILITIES England's highest narrow gauge railway. Preserved steam and diesel locomotives from Britain and overseas run between Alston Station (875 feet above sea level) and Gilderdale, following part of the route of the old Haltwhistle - Alston branch line along the South Tyne valley, in the Eden District of Cumbria. All around is the attractive scenery of the North Pennines, an Area of Outstanding Natural Beauty. A Railway shop and Tourist Information Office is available. Free parking and picnic area.

96 TALKIN TARN COUNTRY PARK

ADDRESS & TELEPHONE Brampton. CA8 1HN (01697) 73129

DIRECTIONS Follow signs near Brampton.

OPENING HOURS Easter to Sept, daily. Weekends in winter.

DISABLED ACCESS Yes

ACTIVITIES/FACILITIES 183 acres of unspoilt and beautiful countryside in the foothills of the Pennines on the B6413 to Castle Carrock. Facilities include nature trails, picnic areas, children's play area and tearoom. **FREE ADMISSION.**

Talkin Tarn Country Park. Val Corbett

97 LANERCOST PRIORY

ADDRESS & TELEPHONE Lanercost, Brampton. (01697) 73030

DIRECTIONS Off minor road south of Lanercost, 2 miles north-east of Brampton.

OPENING HOURS Easter to October, daily, 10am-6pm (or dusk if earlier in October).

DISABLED ACCESS Unfortunately lots of small steps but if you can manage the first step into quad. then there would be no charge whilst friends looked around. Disabled access to church.

ACTIVITIES/FACILITIES Close to Hadrian's Wall, experience this 12th century Augustinian priory. See the fine family tombs in the priory church and view replicas of Roman altars found nearby. Picnic at the priory's beautiful location between the River Irthing and Hadrian's Wall.

GOLF IN CUMBRIA

APPLEBY GOLF CLUB

Address & Tel. No. Brackenber Moor, Appleby, CA16 6LP. (01768) 351432

Directions 2 miles south east of the town to the north of the A66.

Details The course provides panoramic views of the north Pennines and Lakeland fells and has the distinction of forming a circle around the Moor. Long par 4s and no par 5s make sure nobody goes to Appleby and finds it an easy course but every one comes back to play it again. Club House, golf shop and resident professional. Casual visitors are always welcome but due to its popularity visitors should phone in advance.

BARROW GOLF CLUB

Address & Tel. No. Rakesmoor Lane, Barrow-in-Furness LA14 4QB. (01229) 825444/832121

Directions Approx. 3 miles from Barrow, turn left off A590, Bank Lane (opposite Kimberly Clarke).

Details 6137 yards Par 69 Men, 73 Ladies. No parties at weekends unless booked in advance, Facilities include catering, bar, showers and snooker. Visitors welcome, contact the professional for times of play (Mr J McLead 01229 832121). Ladies day Friday, standard golf dress applies. Handicap certificates required.

BECKSIDE GOLF CLUB

Address & Tel. No. Ellerbeck Farm, Crook, near Kendal LA8 8LE.

Directions From roundabout at north end of Kendal bypass A591, take B5284. After 2 miles, at Crook, fork left for Underbarrow. Clearly signed golf course. Ellerbeck Farm is at the bottom of hill 400 yards on the right. Golf course car park is 0.5 mile beyond farm at first road junction.

Details 9 hole Par 64, 4430 yards scenic Lakeland golf course. Handicap not required. Visitors very welcome, usual dress code. Club hire available.

BRAMPTON GOLF CLUB

Address & Tel. No. Talkin Tarn, Brampton, CA8 1HN. (01228) 401996 or (01697) 72000

Directions The course is situated 1.5 miles from Brampton on the B6413 Brampton to Castle Carrock road.

Details Rolling fell countryside 18 hole course with excellent panoramic views (Par 72, 6407 yards off competition tees, 6258 yards off forward tees). Practice facilities; games room with snooker, pool and Sky TV. Catering available every day during play season & most days during winter months. Visitors welcome but prior booking recommended.

CARLISLE GOLF CLUB

Address & Tel. No. Aglionby, Carlisle, CA4 8AG. (01228) 513029

Directions 0.25 miles east of M6 Junction 43. Take A69 signed to Hexham, golf club entrance clearly signed.

Details Parkland course of 6,200 yards. Open Championship qualifying course. Handicap certificates required. Visitors welcome except Saturday. Full Restaurant and Bar Facilities available.

COCKERMOUTH GOLF CLUB

Address & Tel. No. The Clubhouse, Embleton, Cockermouth, CA13 9SG

Directions Exit A66 at junction signed for Embleton. Proceed for 150 yards, cross old main road, up 1 in 3 hill.

Details 18 hole course offering magnificent views of the Lakeland hills and Solway Firth. Yardage Men 5496 Par 69, Ladies 4843 yards Par 70. Visitors welcome. Bar snacks available.

DISTINGTON GOLF COURSE & DRIVING RANGE

Address & Tel. No. Charity Lane, High Harrington, Workington. (01946) 833688

Directions From the A595 Lilyhall to Distington road, take the B road at traffic lights signed High Harrington. After 400 metres turn left signed Lowla, entrance to the course and range 400m on the left.

Details 16 bay all weather driving range- E.G.T.F. Teaching Centre and professional Tuition. 9 hole pay and play golf course, Par 34 2450 yds. Flat and easy to walk. Open daily 9am to dusk. Juniors must play with an adult.

DUNNERHOLME GOLF CLUB

Address & Tel. No. Duddon Road, Askam-in-Furness LA16 7AW. (01229) 462675

Directions Turn left over the railway crossing at Askam, from Dalton on the A595.

Details 10 holes, 18 tees Links course with water hazards on 4 holes. 6154 yards Par 72 or 5074 yards Par 71.

EDEN GOLF CLUB

Address & Tel. No. Crosby on Eden, Carlisle, CA6 4RA. (01228) 573003

Directions 5 miles from Junction 44 of the M6, then on the A689 to Lower Crosby and golf course.

Details Parkland course with many water hazards and well guarded greens. Par 72. White tees (Men) 6368 yards. Red tees (Ladies) 5535 yards. Restaurant offering bar/dining facilities from 10am. Full practice facilities and floodlit driving range. Visitors welcome - advise to book in advance.

GRANGE FELL GOLF CLUB

Address & Tel. No.   Fell Road, Grange-over-Sands, LA11 6HB. (01539) 532536

Directions   Exit Junction 36 from M6. A590 towards Barrow then follow signs to Grange. Go through town and the course is on the road from Grange to Cartmel.

Details   Hillside course with panoramic views of Morecombe Bay and the Lake District mountains. 9 holes, yardage for 18 holes Men 5287, Ladies 4716. Visitors welcome. Tuesday is Ladies day. Closed most Sundays for competitions, no catering.

GRANGE-OVER-SANDS GOLF CLUB

Address & Tel. No.   Meathop Road, Grange-over-Sands, LA11 6QX. (01539) 533180

Directions   Leave the A6 at Levens Bridge and take the A590. At the roundabout take first left signed to Grange. Course on the left on the outskirts of Grange.

Details   A flat parkland course with water features and plantations giving added interest. Mens course 5958 yards Par 70, Ladies course Par 71 5080 yards. Visitors welcome, book prior to visit. Golf Professional in attendance, clubhouse and bar open daily. Catering available except on Tuesdays. Visiting parties by arrangement. Handicap certificate required.

KENDAL GOLF CLUB

Address & Tel. No.   The Heights, Kendal, LA9 4PQ. (01539) 733708 (am) or (01539) 723499 (prof. shop).

Directions   On the A6 1 mile west of Kendal Town Hall.

Details   Parkland course situated partly in the Lake District National Park overlooking the historic market town of Kendal. Handicap Certificate required. Visitors welcome especially mid-week. Full clubhouse facilities including catering (Monday's by prior arrangement). Current course ydg: Men 5534 Par 66, Ladies 4905 Par 70. New course: Men 5825 Par 70, Ladies 5250 Par 71.

KENDAL GOLF DRIVING RANGE

Address & Tel. No.   Oxendale Road, Kendal LA9 7HG. (01539) 733933

Directions   Situated on the B6254, just off the A65, close to Oxenholme Station.

Details   10 large covered floodlit bays. Open Sat and Sun 10am-6pm. Mon, Wed to Fri 10am-9pm (closed Tues). Open every Bank Holiday except Christmas Day. Club hire available. Shower, locker and changing facilities, Accessories and gift tokens on sale.

KESWICK GOLF CLUB

Address & Tel. No.   Threlkeld Hall, Threlkeld, Keswick CA12 4S. (01768) 779010.

Directions   4 miles east of Keswick on south side of A66.

Details   White 6225 yards Par 72, Yellow 5940 yards Par 70, Ladies 5384 yards Par 74. Refreshments and full club facilities available. Visitors welcome but must book tee, up to 7 days in advance.

MARYPORT GOLF CLUB

Address & Tel. No.   Bankend, Maryport, CA15 6PA .

Directions   Turn off the A596 Maryport to Carlisle Road onto the B5300 Maryport to Silloth Road. 1.5-2 miles after turnoff, turn left to clubhouse and course.

Details   9 holes links course and 9 holes parkland, Men's yardage 5883 Par 70, Ladies 5322 Par 71. Bar open from 11am, catering except Mondays, visitors welcome, handicaps not essential but preferable.

SEASCALE GOLF CLUB

Address & Tel. No.   Seascale, CA20 1QL. (01946) 728202

Directions   2 miles off the A595 at Gosforth, on the B5344.

Details   18 hole links course; 6416 yards off white tees; 6103 yards off yellow tees; 5743 yards for ladies. Catering available from 11am to 10pm. Parties by arrangement. Full bar facilities. Visitors welcome.

SEDBERGH GOLF CLUB

Address & Tel. No.   Catholes-Abbot Holme, Sedbergh, LA10 5SS. (01539) 621551

Details   Gently undulating grassland course in superbly scenic location in the Yorkshire Dales National Park. 9 holes, 5588 yards white Par 70, 5271 yards yellow Par 70, 4967 yards LGU Red Par 72. Licensed bar, catering, shop, club and trolley hire available. Visitors are welcome and are required to bring handicap certificate or evidence of golf club membership.

SILLOTH ON SOLWAY GOLF CLUB

Address & Tel. No.   Silloth, Carlisle, CA5 4BL. (01697) 331304

Directions   From south: M6 Junction 41, B5305 to Wigton, B5302 to Silloth. From north: M6 Jnc 43, A69 Carlisle, A595/596 to Wigton, B5302 to Silloth.

Details   Panoramic views over the Solway Firth to Scotland as well as to Skiddaw and the Lakeland Hills. Seaside Championship Links Golf Course, 6614 yards Par 72. Practice facilities.

WORKINGTON GOLF CLUB

Address & Tel. No.   Branthwaite Road, Workington. CA14 4SS.

Directions   After leaving Cockermouth follow Whitehaven road. At major roundabout turn right and drive for half a mile to reach the course.

Details   18 hole wooded scenic course, Men's yardage: 6056, Par 72, Ladies 5400, Par 72. Handicap preferred. Refreshments, locker rooms, showers, Professional shop, Ladies day Tuesday 9.45am to 11.15am & 4.45pm to 5.15pm. Visitors are welcome but it is advisable to ring in summer.

RIDING IN CUMBRIA

The following riding establishments have been issued with a licence by the individual District Councils:

CARLISLE CITY COUNCIL
Covering the far north of Cumbria

PENNINE TRAIL RIDING CENTRE
Tindale, Brampton.

BAILEY MILL TREKKING CENTRE
Bailey, Newcastleton. (01697) 748617

NAWORTH RIDING CENTRE
Lanercost, Brampton.

EDEN DISTRICT COUNCIL
Covering western Cumbria including Penrith and Appleby

ROCKHOUSE RIDING CENTRE
Alston. (01434) 382800

ALSTON & KILHOPE RIDING CENTRE
Cowshill, Wear Dale. (01388) 537600

GREYHORSE RIDING STABLES
Brough. (01768) 341651

HARDHILLS RIDING STABLES
Brough, North Stainmore. (01768) 341624

HILLSIDE HOUSE
Newby, Penrith. (01931) 714370

ROOKIN HOUSE FARM
Troutbeck, Penrith. (01768) 483561

SOCKBRIDGE TREKKING CENTRE
Sockbridge, Penrith. (01768) 863468

PARKFOOT TREKKING CENTRE
Pooley Bridge, Penrith. (01768) 486696

SIDE FARM TREKKING CENTRE
Patterdale, Penrith. (01768) 482337

ALLERDALE DISTRICT COUNCIL
Covering the north western coast, Maryport, Workington, Cockermouth and Keswick

ALLONBY RIDING SCHOOL
Allonby, Maryport. (01900) 881273

ARMATHWAITE HALL EQUESTRIAN CENTRE
Bassenthwaite, Keswick. (01768) 776551

LANE HEAD STABLES DEANSCALES
Cockermouth.

SNITTLEGARTH FARM
Ireby, Carlisle. (01697) 371973

CALVERT TRUST
Old Windebrowe, Keswick. (01768) 774395

SOLWAY HOLIDAY VILLAGE RIDING CENTRE
Silloth, Carlisle. (01697) 331236

SILLOTH RIDING CENTRE
West Silloth, Carlisle.

SETMABANNING RIDING SCHOOL
Threlkeld, Keswick. (01768) 779229

SOUTH LAKELAND DISTRICT COUNCIL
South Cumbria including Windermere, Kendal and Sedbergh

WYNLESS BECK STABLES
Ambleside Rd, Windermere (01539) 443811

HALL MORE FARM
Hale, Milnthorpe. (01539) 562375

LARKRIGG
Natland, Kendal.

HOLMESCALES RIDING CENTRE
Old Hutton, Kendal. (01539) 729388

HIPSHOW RIDING STABLES
Patton, Kendal.

SPOONHALL TREKKING CENTRE
Coniston (01539) 441391

BIGLAND HALL RIDING SCHOOL
Haverthwaite, Ulverston. (01539) 531728

BIRKBY COTTAGE RIDING
Cartmel, Grange-over-Sands.

LAKELAND TREKKING CENTRE
Flookburgh, Grange-over-Sands. (01539) 558131

CROOK BARN STABLES
Torver, Coniston. (01539) 441088

TARNSIDE FARM
Crosthwaite, Kendal.

RYDAL FARM
Rydal, Ambleside.

LOW HAYGARTH
Cautley, Sedbergh.

WITHERSLACK HALL FARM
Witherslack, Grange-over-Sands. (01539) 55244

COPELAND BOROUGH COUNCIL

Covering the south western part of Cumbria including Whitehaven

LOW COCKHOW
Kinniside, Cleator.

BRIDLEMOUNT TREKKING CENTRE
Haverigg, Millom.

SPOUT HOUSE STABLES
Whitehaven.

IRTON HALL
Irton, Holmrook. (01946) 726040

BARROW-IN-FURNESS COUNCIL

Covering the Barrow-in-Furness Peninsula

SEAVIEW RIDING SCHOOL
Biggar Village, Walney Island. (01229) 474251

Horse riding on Loughrigg Terrace. Val Corbett.

LEISURE CENTRES

COPELAND SWIMMING POOL

Address & Tel.	Cleator Moor Road, Hensingham, Whitehaven, (01946) 695021.
Directions	On the B5295 south east of Whitehaven town centre.
Opening Hours	Open all year on a daily basis. It is advisable to ring and confirm public swimming times.
Disabled Access	Yes.
Activities/Facilities	Main swimming pool and teaching pool with comfortable spectator area. Free car parking.
Dogs	Guide dogs only please.

LEISURE LINKS COCKERMOUTH

Address & Tel.	Castlegate Drive, Cockermouth, CA13 0HD. (01900) 823596
Directions	Half a mile within the 30 mph limit on old A66 Cockermouth to Keswick road.
Opening Hours	8am-10pm, Mon to Fri. 9am-5pm Sat, Sun and Bank Holidays.
Disabled Access	Yes though no hoist for pool.
Activities/Facilities	25 metre 4 lane swimming pool as well as sauna, solarium, table tennis, climbing wall, fitness suite, creche, sports hall, keep fit/circuit training, aerobics, badminton, 5-a-side football, bouncy castle and soft play.
Dogs	No.

LEISURE LINKS WORKINGTON

Address & Tel.	Newlands Lane South, Moorclose Estate, Workington, CA14 3LL.
Directions	Follow A66 into Workington, then follow road signs to the Leisure Centre.
Opening Hours	Monday to Friday, 10am-10pm, Sat and Sun, 10am-4pm, Bank Hols, 10am-6pm.
Disabled Access	Yes at centre and pools.
Activities/Facilities	Swimming pools, squash, badminton, table tennis, cricket, bowls, aerobics, step, circuit training, fitness suite, tumble time sessions, football coaching, karate, judo and gymnastics.
Dogs	No.

KENDAL LEISURE CENTRE

Address & Tel.	Burton Road, Kendal, Cumbria, LA9 7HX. (01539) 729702 *Theatre*, (01539) 729777 *Sports*, 01539 729511 *Admin*.
Directions	On the south side of Kendal (A65 brown tourism signs).
Opening Hours	All year, daily, including most Bank Holidays, 7.45am-11pm.
Disabled Access	Yes. Good facilities throughout.
Activities/Facilities	Large multi-purpose sports hall, theatre/concert provision, two swimming pools, outdoor hard play area, sauna and solarium suite, fitness room, glass backed squash courts, licensed bar and cafeteria. Large car park.
Dogs	Guide dogs only.

KESWICK LEISURE POOL

Address & Tel.	Station Road, Keswick, CA12 4NE. (01768) 772760
Directions	Follow brown tourism signs from A66.
Opening Hours	Public Swim times: Winter, Wed-Fri 12 noon-5pm, Sat & Sun 10am-5pm. Holidays, Mon-Fri 11am-6pm, Sat & Sun 10am-6pm. High summer Mon-Friday 11am-8pm, Sat & Sun 10am-6pm.
Disabled Access	Yes.
Activities/Facilities	Public swimming pool with wave machine, superslide and seating area. Food and drinks available.
Dogs	No.

THE PARK LEISURE CENTRE

Address & Tel.	Greengate Street, Barrow-in-Furness, LA13 9DT. (01229) 871146
Directions	Take A590 into Barrow (Abbey Road) and turn left at Whitehouse Hotel into Park Road. After 500 yards turn into Greengate Street (first right).
Opening Hours	The centre is usually open between 7.30am-9.30pm week days and 9am-6pm at weekends. It is advisable to ring to confirm public swimming times.
Disabled Access	Yes, with lift to upper floor and toilets.
Activities/Facilities	Leisure pool with wave machines, water cannons and slide as well as climbing wall, fitness suite, badminton, short tennis and all weather sports pitch.
Dogs	No.

THE POOLS SWIMMING AND HEALTH CENTRE

Address & Tel.	James Street, Carlisle, (01228) 22105
Directions	Follow directions to Town Centre from where the pool is 2 minutes walk.
Opening Hours	Daily all year. Please ring to confirm public swimming times.
Disabled Access	Yes.
Activities/Facilities	3 swimming pools (33m, 20m and 10m) including a water slide. Gym, sunbeds, sauna, massage, beauty therapy and refreshments available.
Dogs	No.

TROUTBECK BRIDGE SWIMMING POOL

Address & Tel.	Troutbeck Bridge, Windermere, LA23 1HP. (01539) 443243
Directions	On the A591 Windermere to Keswick road, 3 miles from Ambleside. Follow signs for Lake School.
Opening Hours	It is advisable to ring and confirm public swimming sessions as availability depends on school holidays and the like.
Disabled Access	Yes.
Activities/Facilities	25 metre heated indoor pool with free car park. Sauna/steam room, sunbeds and cafeteria.
Dogs	No.

WHITEHAVEN SPORTS CENTRE

Address & Tel.	Flatt Walks, Whitehaven, CA28 7RJ. (01946) 695666
Directions	In the centre of the town.
Opening Hours	Open daily all year.
Disabled Access	Accessible but no ramp to entrance.
Activities/Facilities	Five-a-side pitches, squash courts, badminton courts, fitness suite, soft play area, table tennis, solarium, creche, steam room, climbing wall and fully licensed bar.
Dogs	Guide dogs only please.

Lynne and Emma, MDN.

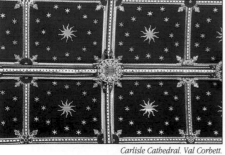

Carlisle Cathedral. Val Corbett.

Grizedale Forest. Val Corbett.

'Cathedral of Unknown Desires', Geurt Van Dijk.
Grizedale Forest. Val Corbett.

Loughrigg Tarn. Val Corbett.

Howtown, Ullswater. Val Corbett.

Stock Ghyll, Ambleside. Val Corbett.

Skiddaw, Keswick and Derwentwater. Val Corbett.

The perfect gift for a friend, relative or even yourself

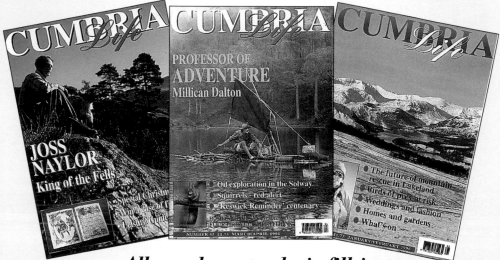

All you have to do is fill in the coupon to subscribe to

CUMBRIA *Life*

If the subscription is a gift we provide an attractive gift card in which we can include a message from you. The cost of 6 issues is £10.50 (postfree).
Overseas details: Europe £18.55 • Canada & America £24.50
• Australia £26.75. Surface mail rates on application.

I would like to subscribe to Cumbria Life ❏ *for myself* ❏ *for a friend*

Details: (self)
Mr/Mrs/Miss/Ms/Other:..........................
Address: ....
....
....
Postcode: ....

Details: (friend)
Mr/Mrs/Miss/Ms/Other:..........................
Address: ....
....
....
Postcode: ....

Payment Details:
Send your order to Cumbria Life (freepost), 16-20 Lowther Street, Carlisle. CA3 8BR
Please make cheque payable to: AGT Ltd, or debit my Access ❏ Visa ❏ Expiry date: ....
Card No.. Signature: (I am over 18)...

Ullswater. Val Corbett.

Above Ullswater. Val Corbett.

Borrans Park, Ambleside. Val Corbett.

255

Kirkstone. Val Corbett.